TREASON BY WORDS

MISCHEEFES
MYSTERIE:
OR,
Treasons Master-peece,
The Powder-plot.

Inuented by hellish Malice, preuented by heauenly
Mercy : truely related.

And from the Latine of the learned and reuerend Doctour
HERRING *translated, and very much dilated.*

By IOHN VICARS.

The gallant *Eagle,* soaring vp on high :
Beares in his beake, *Treasons* discouery.
MOVNT, noble EAGLE, with thy happy prey,
And thy rich *Prize* to th' *King* with speed conuay.

LONDON,
Printed by E. GRIFFIN, dwelling in the Little Olde
Bayly neere the signe of the Kings head. 1617.

TREASON BY WORDS

Literature, Law, and Rebellion
in Shakespeare's England

REBECCA LEMON

CORNELL UNIVERSITY PRESS

ITHACA AND LONDON

Frontispiece: Title page to *Mischeefes Mysterie* (1617), by John Vicars. This item is reproduced by permission of The Huntington Library, San Marino, California.

Cornell University Press gratefully acknowledges receipt of a grant from the University of Southern California, which aided in the publication of this book.

First published 2006 by Cornell University Press

Printed in the United States of America

Library of Congress Cataloging-in-Publication Data

Lemon, Rebecca, 1968–
    Treason by words : literature, law, and rebellion in Shakespeare's England / Rebecca Lemon.
        p.   cm.
    Includes bibliographical references and index.
    ISBN-13: 978-0-8014-4428-9 (cloth : alk. paper)
    ISBN-10: 0-8014-4428-4 (cloth : alk. paper)
    1. English drama—Early modern and Elizabethan, 1500–1600—History and criticism.   2. English drama—17th century—History and criticism.   3. Treason in literature.   4. Literature and state—Great Britain—History—16th century.   5. Literature and state—Great Britain—History—17th century.   6. Great Britain—History—Elizabeth, 1558–1603.   7. Gunpowder Plot, 1605.   I. Title.
    PR658.T77L46 2006
    822'.309358—dc22

                                              2005032277

Cornell University Press strives to use environmentally responsible suppliers and materials to the fullest extent possible in the publishing of its books. Such materials include vegetable-based, low-VOC inks and acid-free papers that are recycled, totally chlorine-free, or partly composed of nonwood fibers. For further information, visit our website at www.cornellpress.cornell.edu.

Cloth printing   10 9 8 7 6 5 4 3 2 1

Contents

Acknowledgments

While my lasting fascination with betrayal could suggest to some readers a lack of faith in my fellow humans, I have in fact been very lucky in my friendships. Several friends at the University of Southern California (USC) read sections of the book and offered invaluable commentary, including Judith Jackson Fossett, Heather James, Natania Meeker, David Román, Hilary Schor, and Bruce Smith. I am especially grateful to Heather and Bruce for reviewing significant portions of the manuscript and offering generous feedback. Heather read several drafts of the chapters and, thanks to her comments, I was able to reshape, at just the right time, the first half of the book.

The Huntington Library has served as my research home, and I am very grateful to director Roy Ritchie and the library staff, including Steven Tabor, Mary Robertson, Sue Hodson, Romaine Ahlstrom, Susi Krasnoo, and others. I particularly appreciated my time at the library as a Huntington Mellon fellow during the summer of 2004, and the efforts of the staff to aid my research during this period. Among the Huntington's readers, Cyndia Susan Clegg, David Colclough, Karen Cunningham, Paul Hammer, Constance Jordan, Steven Pincus, and Kevin Sharpe were especially valuable interlocutors or readers of my work. I am grateful to have had Karen's engagement with my work, particularly given her own expertise in the area of treason law and literature. Cyndia generously shared her work with me, and read mine, and, in the process, saved me from confusion around dates in the *State Papers*.

This book was completed during a year at the Stanford Humanities

Center, one of the best writing environments I have ever experienced. John Bender, Marilynn Desmond, Jeff Dolvan, Jared Farmer, Denise Gigante, Lorna Hutson, Vicki Kahn, Stephen Orgel, and David Riggs offered friendship and critical insight on the book. Stephen was an especially warm and generous host, both to me and to my silly dog, Clio. I am happy to record my debt, during this year, to the American Council of Learned Societies Mellon Fellowship for its support of the book. For their encouragement through the fellowship process, I am deeply indebted to David Loewenstein, Kevin Sharpe, and Susanne Wofford. Thanks also to dean Beth Meyerowitz and my department chair, Joe Boone, for helping to accommodate my time as I finished the manuscript.

I presented chapters of this book to audiences at the University of Chicago, Oxford University, and the Renaissance literature seminar at the Huntington Library, and I am grateful to Steve Pincus, David Norbrook, and Cyndia Susan Clegg, respectively, for inviting me to present my work in these venues, and to the audiences there for feedback. Steve offered a particularly valuable reading of chapters 6 and 7 and, as a result, helped me tighten the argument of the book as a whole. Audiences at the annual meetings of the Modern Language Association (MLA), the Renaissance Society of America (RSA), and the Shakespeare Association of America (SAA) helped me sharpen my argument and, although I won't name all the helpful questioners, I want to record special thanks to Alistair Bellany, David Como, Karen Cunningham, Cynthia Herrup, Jean Howard, Heather James, Constance Jordan, Stephen Mullaney, Richelle Munkhoff, Cristine Varholy, and Paul Yachnin for their responses to my work; to Peter Herman for organizing an SAA panel; and to David Loewenstein for organizing an MLA panel. Finally, I am extremely grateful to both Susanne Wofford and David Loewenstein for their long-term engagements, at various MLA and SAA meetings, with this book. Susanne's faith in the project from its inception at the University of Wisconsin–Madison helped encourage me along an unfamiliar academic road, and I feel very lucky to be in her debt.

I am happy to acknowledge Bernhard Kendler and the anonymous readers for Cornell University Press for their insightful and much appreciated commentary. A portion of chapter 2 appeared as "The Guilty Verdict in 'The Crown v. John Hayward,'" in *SEL: Studies in English Literature, 1500–1900* 41.1 (winter 2001): 209–32, and a portion of chapter

4 as "Scaffolds of Treason in *Macbeth,*" in *Theatre Journal* 54.1 (March 2002): 25–43. I am indebted to the anonymous readers at both journals. I am also thankful to USC for a Zumberge Individual Research Grant to consult manuscript material in the British Library, and to graduate students Erika Wright, Lucia Hodgson, Judy de Tar, and David Tomkins for research and editing assistance.

On a personal level, my family, including Heidi Lemon, Kristin Lemon, Richard Lemon, and Arthur Okner, supported my puzzling academic obsession without question and, in the final stages of the book, proved to me just how much I can rely on them to help. Dearest friend and traveling companion Nic Bilham provided me not only with a London home during my research summers but also an annual vacation to Devon, where his family continues to beat me at table tennis and board games, much to my chagrin. Emma Mason has offered a decade of inimitable friendship; she has also kept me up to date on British food, music, and television—without her, I would no doubt be confined to my sofa, watching reality TV and eating potato chips out of the bag. Bob Darcy—cherished friend and intellectual ally—followed the project from the very first stages to the end. Were this a book on happiness in friendship, rather than on treason, I would most certainly dedicate it to him.

TREASON BY WORDS

CHAPTER ONE

Sovereignty, Treason Law, and the Political Imagination in Early Modern England

The discovery of the treasonous Gunpowder Plot depended on a letter. An anonymous note, delivered at night to William Parker, Lord Monteagle, attempted to warn him away from the Parliament building: its cellar was stocked with gunpowder ready to be ignited once the king and his councilors entered on November 5, 1605. Monteagle, however, could not decipher the letter, nor could the secretary of state Robert Cecil, the earl of Salisbury. Only King James, as the story goes, could discover the treasonous event it foretold:

> After the reading of it, the king made a pause, and then reading it again, said, that there seemed somewhat in it extraordinary, and what was by no means to be neglected. The Earl replied, That it seemed to him to be written by a Fool or a Madman for who else could be guilty of saying, *The danger is past as soon as you have burn'd the Letter?* For what Danger could there be in that, which the burning of the Letter would put an end to? But the king, considering the smartness of the stile and withal what was said before, That they should receive a terrible Blow, and yet should not see who hurt them, did conclude, as he was walking and musing in the Gallery, that the Danger must be sudden, like the blowing up by gunpowder.[1]

In an act of careful reading, James uncovers the most sensational treason plot in English history.

This familiar story has raised a host of questions for Jacobean prosecutors and later scholars.[2] Who wrote the note? Is the story of its delivery to Lord Monteagle real or fabricated? Perhaps Monteagle composed the letter himself to demonstrate his loyalty to the state, in question owing to his Catholic faith and his participation in the earl of Essex's 1601 rebellion four years earlier. Yet, even if the anonymous delivery proves true, what about the king's riddle solving: was his act of fortuitous reading genuine or stage-managed? Lord Monteagle and the earl of Salisbury may have merely indulged James's well-known pride in his own powers of detection. The interpretive conundrums surrounding the document resonate with its central riddle; like its message, its author and manner of delivery are obscure.

Arguably these questions about the letter have little to do with the treasonous event itself. The crime is king killing, not letter writing. Barrels of gunpowder, armed men, violent action—these are the materials of treason. Invoking the charge of treason, the state claims to discover the intruder in its midst, the "dangerous familiar" uncovered by Frances Dolan's crucial work on domestic crime, be it in the form of a Catholic recusant, a crown-seeking nobleman, or a foreign agent.[3] Yet early modern England saw no cases of successful treason between the wars of the Roses and 1649, belying the commonplace that treason is a crime with the death of the king at its center. Certainly treason in the restrictive sense of king killing exists. The murders of Edward II (1309) and Richard II (1399) in England, and those of Henry III (1589) and Henry IV (1610) in France, justify the fear of treason during the early modern period. In the Elizabethan and early Jacobean state, however, the crime never manifests itself in the killing of a king. Treason does not reside in a core of violent action that can be uncovered through state or scholarly investigations. Instead, subjects and monarchs report on and narrate the crime not as it materialized but as it might have been. In a variety of textual forms, early modern society replays, again and again, the horror that might have happened, simultaneously imagining it and exorcising it through these narrative creations.[4] We can only understand, as early modern subjects did, treason by words.

What happens to our notion of the crime and the event itself when we approach it not as violent action but as a verbal phenomenon? This book takes up this question and investigates the discursiveness of treason. This notion of discursive treason is theorized by the 1534 Tudor statute on "treason by words" from which I draw my title. According to the statute, quoted more fully below, subjects who "by express writing or words" claim that the king "should be heretic, schismatic, tyrant, infidel, or usurper of the crown" will be condemned as traitors.[5] This statute posits the eventfulness of speech, condemning certain types of language as treason out of a fear that they both prompt and constitute violent action.[6] Treason, I contend, is thus doubly linguistic. It is an event created in the texts circulating after a plot, evinced in the Monteagle letter and the variety of other texts on the Gunpowder Plot. The crime is also, as the treason by words statute insists, a form of speech that anticipates, or functions as, violence to the monarch. To understand treason by words requires that we hold these two related but distinct manifestations of discursive treason together.

Moving away from popular conceptions of treason as a demonic crime undertaken against the state, then, this book's focus on treason by words allows us to view the crime not as an action but as a political and legal construction. The category of treason relies, I argue, on other equally potent terms of political philosophy: "sovereignty," "allegiance," "conscience," and "law." Like these terms, "treason" requires continous redefinition and interpretation; it is not a self-evident charge. To reduce treason to violent spectacle evacuates it of the varied interpretive work that helps to produce it.[7] First, as the recent studies of John Barrell and Karen Cunningham demonstrate, treason trials themselves are interpretive events where judges and juries strive to discover the "imagination" or intention of the traitor.[8] Second, as this book explores, early modern treasonous events are textual phenomena. Monteagle's anonymous letter functions as one of the languages of treason that produces the Gunpowder Plot. It is, as the state lawyer Sir Edward Coke claimed in his prosecution of the plotters, "the means" through which we know of the plot. "Considering the admirable discovery of this treason," he writes, "the means was by a dark and doubtful letter."[9] The letter exposes the plotters and the gunpowder, but it also, even more fundamentally, stands in for the event itself. The woodcut on this book's frontispiece—the image of an eagle delivering Monteagle's letter to Cecil and James—testifies to the letter's role as a signifier of both the event and its providential discovery. Like the subsequent stories of the treason, the letter disseminates information about the plot that never happened; it shapes it in the imagination rather than represents it based on eyewitness accounts.

Focusing on treason as a textual phenomenon resituates imaginative fiction as a key site for conceiving of and negotiating with the treasonous event. While treason emerges out of the expected trial transcripts, scaffold speeches, and political polemic, as we shall see, contemporary conceptions of the crime appear equally in classical translations, domestic prose histories, and stage plays. Such imaginative texts compete with state propaganda on the crime, because both sets of texts offer dramatic, topical depictions of treason. Furthermore, this dramatic competition is ideologically freighted. Rather than accept the official language on the traitor as a monster discovered by the state, imaginative texts frequently implicate the state itself in the production of treason, exposing how it expands the legal boundaries of the crime to assert its own authority. Understanding early modern treason involves not only representing attempted but forestalled criminal activity, then, but also acknowledging the political work of treason law itself.[10] Aware of how sovereign prerogative expands through exaggerated claims of crisis and treason in post-Reformation England, the writers explored in this book prove critical of state innovations in the name of security even as they profess loyalty to the state itself and condemn traitorous action.

Laying bare the political and cultural work accomplished for the state through the weapon of the treason charge itself, writers, including William Shakespeare, Ben Jonson, John Hayward, and John Donne, foreground treason as a legal and conceptual category rather than as a merely incendiary event. Imaginative texts connect treason to issues of law, sovereignty, and allegiance, at times resonating with polemic addressing the criminal crisis. Yet such texts nevertheless help to foster freer and less ideologically rigid responses to this emergency. Following Victoria Kahn, we can say that "it is theatrical or aesthetic form which allows for action that is not merely a repetition of the historically given."[11] In other words, through the imagination, as expressed in dramatic or narrative form, writers free themselves from the dialectic—between treason and tyranny—that frequently defines historical responses to the crime. A dynamic interplay thus emerged between the state's definition of treason and the competing representations propounded by its subjects, who actively explored rival theories of law and government, turning to classical and continental models in order to voice challenges to the monarch's increasing articulations of absolute sovereignty. In a culture which lacked the discourses of pluralism and toleration that emerge later in the seventeenth century, the articulation of such diverse ideologies produced increasingly fractured conceptions of the crime of treason and, as a result, supported an emerging conception of subjects' rights, based in rights of liberty, law, and conscience.

Even as the charge of treason operated as the state's legal solution to the opposition of recusant Catholics and unruly aristocrats, then, this apparent solution stimulated the formation of public debates on precisely those rights suspended in a time of treasonous crisis. Rather than capitulate to the state's definition of a crisis, subjects questioned the alleged seriousness of the threat that occasioned innovative legislation and multiple executions. Consequently crises of treason in the early modern period were really crises of sovereignty, not simply because the monarch suffered a violent threat but more frequently because the monarch's response raised questions about the rights and prerogatives of sovereignty itself. "Treason and guilty men," as Jonson skeptically puts it after the Gunpowder Plot, "are made in states / Too oft to dignify the magistrates."[12]

Tudor Treason Law

Henry VIII's innovative 1534 statute on treason by words reshaped definitions of the crime for the next hundred years. It did so with its innovative claim that treason is based in language. While earlier treason law condemned violence to the monarch's body, the 1534 statute regulated speaking as a treasonous attack on his or her dignity as well. Such an expansion in statute law from action to words, from body to dignity, dramatically altered the scope of the crime.[13]

Prior to Henry's law, a 1352 statute passed by Edward III served as the standard definition of treason (and continues to serve today as the backbone of English treason legislation). Unlike the Henrician policy, this 1352 statute focuses mainly on action, claiming that an attempt to kill the king or his representatives is treason but to attack him in words is not. The statute catalogues violence to the king's body, condemning plots on his life or on the lives of his representatives while in office:

> When a man doth compass or imagine the death of our lord the king, of our lady his Queen, or of their eldest son and heir . . . or if a man slays the chancellor, treasurer, or the King's justices . . . in their places and attending to their offices: And it is to be understood, that in the cases above rehearsed, it ought to be judged treason which extends to our lord the king and his royal majesty.[14]

This definition of treason as a violent attack on the king extends to more tangential but nonetheless physical assaults such as making war, counterfeiting, and rape. In the latter two cases, the traitor attempts to destroy authentic reproductions of the king, whether in the form of legal tender or a legitimate heir. Thus violating "the king's consort," or "the king's eldest daughter being as yet unmarried," or bringing "false money into this realm, counterfeit to the money of England," is treason.[15]

Notably, the 1352 treason law does not condemn attempts to depose or wound the king. Instead, as John Bellamy's seminal work on treason history argues, the law offers "a decidedly narrow interpretation to treason. Seriously diminished were the king's chances of obtaining forfeitures, and on the face of it royal power suffered a decline."[16] In policing primarily violent action, the 1352 act restricted the scope of the treason charge. Such a limited definition protected subjects from prosecution-hungry judges and monarchs. In fact, in future years, subjects occasionally invoked the statute's language in their own defense.[17] Sir Nicholas Throckmorton took the judges to task during his indictment for treason in 1554, when he claimed that, according to the 1352 statute then in force, evidence of guilt must lie in action. He asks his examiners, "Where doth appear the open deed of any compassing or imagining the Queen's death?" As he repeats, "Where doth appear in me an open deed, whereunto the Treason is specially referred?"[18] In the absence of evidence of an "open deed," Throckmorton suggests, the state cannot prosecute him regardless of its suspicions.

While the 1352 act attempted to restrict the definition of treason, the inclusion of the word "imagine" gave the statute an interpretive flexibility perhaps unintended at the time of its passage. King Edward III passed the 1352 statute, as Bellamy argues, in an effort to restrict treason law. Accordingly, the use of the term "imagine" initially functioned as a synonym for compass, meaning to plot or plan ("when a man doth compass or imagine the death of our lord"). Over time, however, judges took advantage of this flexible term in order to expand the law's application.[19] They did so by creating the category of "constructive treason" by which judges redefine or "construct" the crime to include spoken words as evidence.[20] The state's attorney prosecuted the duke of Norfolk and his servant under the 1352 statute, for example, by declaring their "open deed" as their "declaration of the mind."[21] He elaborates in saying, "letters, tokens, speeches, messages, and such like," all declarations of mind, "be overt-facts" required by the act. This association of mind with action appears in the shaky defense launched by Norfolk's servant Robert Hickford: "I know the law hath not intent to the conscience, or intent of man; but is to judge only of the mind, according to the appearing of outward facts."[22] Ceding that the law can judge the mind as a form of action and that words function as "outward facts," Hickford here upholds the constructive applications of the 1352 statute that will lead to his execution.[23]

This category of constructive treason has attracted the attention of a handful of literary scholars who explore the appearance of the term "imagination" in the context of treason. Karen Cunningham's *Imaginary Betrayals* explores how in sixteenth-century England, because of the legal application of "imagination" as intention, the "history of treason trials is also a history of competing notions of subjectivity."[24] The three treason trials she studies—Katherine Howard in 1542, and Mary, queen of Scotland and the Babington plotters in 1586—expose each of the defendants as "a fearsome border-dweller" (20) who challenges notions of sexual, social, and national fidelity in ways that resonate with imaginative staging by playwrights. Imagining treason, as Cunningham argues, signifies imagining or redefining the realm with its competing allegiances and loyalties.

Even if the state initially translated "imagine" as "intend," then, the very flexibility of the term "imagination" defies such interpretive limitations. John Barrell makes precisely this point in his study of treason in England between 1793 and 1796: "'imagine' meaning 'intend' could be confused," he writes, "with this 'weak' or 'familiar' sense of the word, 'picture in the mind,' which made it possible for the legal meaning of the word to become confused . . . with the [literary] connotations."[25] Barrell explores tangled definitions of imagination in the context of Romantic redefinitions of the word, arguing that the treason trials of 1793–96 evince a political struggle over the term "imagination" at the precise moment when Burke, Wordsworth, and Coleridge were introducing new conceptions of the word into the language. This political struggle led to the passage of the Treasonable Practices Act of 1794, which expanded treason beyond "imagining the king's death" to imagining the death of the crown and constitution.

Even before the Treasonable Practices Act studied by Barrell, the state realized the limitations of "imagining the king's death" in the 1352 statute.[26] In establishing the constitutional changes brought about by the Reformation, Henry VIII and his advisers found that the 1352 act lacked the direct condemnation of speech and writing needed by the Tudor state in the aftermath of its break with Rome. Their solution was the 1534 Treason Act:

> If any person or persons, after the first day of February next coming, do maliciously wish, will or desire by words or writing, or by craft imagine, invent, practice or attempt any bodily harm to be done or committed to the King's most royal person, the Queen's or their heirs apparent, or to deprive them or any of them of the dignity, title or name of their royal estates, or slanderously and maliciously publish and pronounce, by express writing or words, that the King our sovereign lord should be heretic, schismatic, tyrant, infidel or usurper of the crown, . . . then every such person and persons so offending in any premises after the said first day of February, their aiders, counsellors, consenters and abettors, being thereof lawfully convict[ed] according to the laws and customs of this realm, shall be adjudged traitors; and that every such offense in any premises that shall be committed or done after the said first day of February, shall be reputed, accepted and adjudged high treason.[27]

This act proved a legal milestone, advancing the definition of treason by openly regulating speech. The notion of treason by words had precedents in common law and constructive treason rulings, but nevertheless this 1534 statute proved innovative and threatening.[28] As Bellamy records it, Robert Fisher, the brother of the condemned Bishop Fisher, complained in February 1535 that "speaking is made high treason which was never heard of before."[29]

Indeed, Henry's son, Edward VI, immediately abolished the statute on taking office. The preamble to Edward's 1547 law, in which Lord Protector Somerset reinstated the 1352 treason statute, acknowledges the ferocity of Henry's act:

> Almighty God with his help and man's policy hath always been content and pleased to have stayed that sharper laws as a harder bridle should be made to stay those men and facts that might else be occasion, cause and authors of further inconvenience; the which thing caused the prince of most famous memory King Henry the Eighth . . . to make and enact certain laws and statutes which might seem and appear to men of exterior realms and many of the King's Majesty's subjects very strait, sore, extreme and terrible. . . . But as in tempest or winter one course and garment is convenient, in calm or warm weather a more liberal race or

lighter garment both may and ought to be followed and used, so we have seen divers strait and sore laws made in one Parliament, the time so requiring, in a more calm and quiet reign of another prince by like authority and Parliament repealed and taken away.[30]

Here, the phrase "harder bridle" invokes a spectacle not only of taming subjects but also of silencing them, restraining their behavior through controlling their mouths. Even as this repeal acknowledges the violence of the earlier law, however, it attempts to naturalize the ferocity by casting it as the effect of a tempestuous season. This metaphoric language obfuscates the relationship between state, subjects, and law. While the preamble argues that unruly subjects, like untamed horses and wild weather, require "harder" measures, these same metaphors equally could locate the tempest of winter as a product not of unruly subjects but of a tyrannical government. Using coercive measures to institute change, Henry VIII produced the very tempest that Edward VI now calms. Even as the preamble attempts to elide natural change and government innovation, it also evokes an alternate reading of the repealed treason by words legislation: it is not a necessary, seasonal response to unrest but instead a "very strait, sore, extreme and terrible" measure condemned at home and abroad. In fact, the "cruel and bloody laws of Henry VIII" were so condemned: as Throckmorton termed them in his trial, they were "Draco's laws, which were written in blood."[31]

Despite Somerset's repeal of the law as unnecessary in the "calm and quiet reign" of Edward, the charge reappeared. Elizabeth reinstated this "harder bridle" almost immediately on taking office after the reign of Mary I, a move that goes against the usual monarchical practice of repealing unpopular laws early in one's reign. Building on the language of Henry's 1534 act, a 1571 Elizabethan act expanded the form and type of words considered treason: it will now be treason if a subject "shall by writing, printing, preaching, speech, express words or sayings, maliciously, advisedly and directly publish, set forth, and affirm that the Queen our said sovereign lady Queen Elizabeth is an heretic, schismatic, tyrant, infidel or an usurper of the crown."[32] While Henry condemned "words or writing," Elizabeth now specified a greater variety of forms in her category of treasonous words, a category that remained until 1628.[33] This shift from Henry's language to Elizabeth's, from the more general "writing" to the more specific "writing, printing, preaching, speech," signals a proliferation rather than a diminishing of treasonous speech acts. Writing, printing, speaking, and preaching all offer occasions, Elizabeth suggests, for treasonous dissent. With increased precision, the state names and condemns these multiple avenues of political expression.

Treason and Words

A history of subjects prosecuted under the treason-by-words law has yet to be undertaken. Scholars such as John Bellamy, G. R. Elton, Lacey Baldwin Smith, Samuel Rezneck, and Isobel Thornley have initiated this work, but significant room remains for a comprehensive study of how and when the state applied this law.[34] Such a history might range from the emergence of the charge in fifteenth-century common law rulings to its role as a major statutory plank in administering the Reformation. Yet a history of treason by words would be difficult to write. The state continued to prosecute subjects under the less controversial 1352 legislation if at all possible. As a result, charges of treason by words appear patchy and episodic rather than coherent and programmatic. For example, only sixty-three people were executed for speaking treasonous words between 1532 and 1540, a significant number but one that belies the "general air of a reign of terror" associated with the treason-by-words charge, as G. R. Elton notes.[35] Furthermore, in nearly thirty cases from this period, either the state failed to gain an indictment or a trial jury refused to convict; an accused subject was three times more likely to have his or her case dismissed than to be executed. Such numbers suggest a hesitation on the part of judges and juries to convict subjects for treason by words without regard for evidence or due process. Instead, the charge helped to bolster existing treason laws. Sir Edward Neville, Sir Geoffrey Pole, Henry Lord Montacute, and the Marquis of Exeter were prosecuted under both the 1352 and 1534 statutes, for example.[36] This combination strengthened the state's case, suggesting the use of treason by words as a supplementary rather than a primary charge, a point made by Bellamy in his study of Tudor treason law.

Rather than focus specifically on the legislative history of the treason-by-words statute, then, this book concentrates on the deeper conceptual linkage of treason and texts articulated in the charge. I analyze this linkage through a study of the two most sensational treasons in Shakespeare's England: first, the treason of the earl of Essex, arrested initially for his behavior in Ireland in 1600, and then for his London uprising in 1601; and, second, the infamous Gunpowder Plot of 1605. I choose these events because, in addition to their notoriety, they share an unusual but highly revealing textuality. Not only did Shakespeare and Jonson write plays that have been connected to each event, but other writers, including lawyers such as Edward Coke and Francis Bacon, as well as pamphleteers, dramatists, and historians such as Samuel Daniel and John Hayward, wrote about these two incidents of treason. More than the Northern Rebellion, more than the Babington Plot, these events generated a textual explosion that included not only trial transcripts, witness reports, scaffold speeches, and political pamphlets but also translations, prose histories, plays, and poems associated with the incidents.

The texts surrounding these two events do not conform merely to a propagandistic celebration of the demise of treason, although the pamphlets and trial transcripts frequently make such a move. Instead, the literary texts engage with the event more subtly, at times helping to articulate its ideological stakes for the rebels as well as the state. These texts offer, even in the midst of the state's propaganda campaigns surrounding these treasons, alternative conceptions of the crime. The engagement of such literary texts in these particular political events, unlike polemical propaganda and oppositional dissent, relies on the imagination, on characterization, and on theatrical staging in order to effect its contribution. In representing treason, these texts negotiate with the crime: they variously stage its perpetrators and prosecutors, at times questioning the crime's definition. In doing so, they mediate conceptions of the treasonous event itself and address fundamental political questions, such as the relation of law to sovereignty, and of obedience to resistance. Such interrogations occur less at the level of pragmatic engagement since the texts I examine often imagine treason independently of personalities and the stark contrasts of polemic and propaganda. Rather, these literary texts theorize the crime; they stage hypothetical outcomes and arguments, imaginatively producing them as a means of testing out the policies and political beliefs articulated by the writers' contemporaries. This is one of the points made compellingly in Constance Jordan's study of Shakespeare's romances—whose rulers offer "hypothetical renderings" of contemporary debates on absolutist rule.[37] Such renderings of contemporary debates in the moment of treasonous crises shift readers from stock responses toward an examination of the representational issues at stake in the tangle of sovereignty, treason, and law that characterizes a state of emergency.

Treasonous events are thus textual events. Understanding the Essex Rebellion requires grappling with contemporary narratives on the event, but it equally involves study of the literature associated with the earl of Essex and his allies in the years prior to their rebellion. Savile's and Grenewey's translations of Tacitus (1591 and 1598, respectively), John Hayward's Tacitean history *Henry IV* (1599), and Shakespeare's *Richard II* (ca. 1595), all texts associated with Essex, engage with multiple conceptions of treason based in civil, common, and classical theories of the crime. As a result, treason appears variously as a legitimate response to tyranny, as a source of political chaos, or as ungodly rebellion. In their texts associated with Essex, Savile, Grenewey, Hayward, and Shakespeare, are not univocal in their approaches to representing treason even as they share an interest in understanding the crime as a legal and conceptual category more than as a sensational, violent event.

The Gunpowder Plot evinces a similar interplay between text and event as the state's definition of treason contends with competing conceptions of the crime propounded by its subjects. Attempting to assert royal authority over Catholic recusants immediately after the failed plot, King James instead provoked paper warfare on the issues of tyranny and subjects' rights. Discussing treason after the plot necessarily included debates about sovereignty, allegiance, and the rule of law. Treason is not simply an act of demonic violence but a political and legal charge deployed advantageously by monarchs. Shakespeare's *Macbeth* (1606), for example, represents various models of rulership in a manner that undercuts Jacobean pretensions to divine right monarchy in the aftermath of the Gunpowder treason. John Donne and Ben Jonson participate in this post-plot paper warfare as well, producing their most polemical works, *Pseudo-Martyr* and *Catiline*. These two former Catholics, each moderate Protestants in 1611 when publishing their texts, address the issues posed by the Jacobean oath of allegiance. In the process, they defend both the Catholic right of conscience and the right of law against James's increasing exercise of prerogative.

I have structured this book around the Essex Rebellion and the

Gunpowder Plot, then, because in their proliferation of textual materials, these events expose the interplay of state, recusant, and imaginative writings on a specific crime. It is this interplay that challenges the simple but all-too-inviting understanding of treason as merely violent opposition to the state. Instead, through an approach to these two events, we can see precisely how the Elizabethan and Jacobean states attempted to capitalize on treason only to provoke textual warfare. Such warfare countered not only state conceptions of the crime of treason itself but also the more contentious, related conception of sovereignty. This tangled relation of treason and sovereignty occurs because, as Lisa Steffen argues in *Defining a British State,* treason is a crime that is always associated with the expansion and contraction of prerogative—it is a central plank in the articulation of sovereign power. Even as the treason charge may help to protect the commonwealth from its enemies, it can equally bolster a king's tyrannical designs: by suspending or altering the definition of treason, monarchs can prosecute increasing numbers of subjects for newly criminalized activity, eliminating political enemies and gaining their estates in the process.[38]

In an effort to secure its political power, the state uses the case of a treasonous rebellion to circulate, on the one hand, a textual variety of propaganda, scaffold speeches, and statutes. Such materials suggest an attempt on the part of the state to digest, narrate, and understand the event since, to follow Pierre Nora's claim, "the succession of events defines a society's surface."[39] On the other hand, the state's overzealous attempt to control traitorous or seemingly traitorous populations precipitates the production of oppositional textual readings even from loyal subjects. These texts put in play—most obviously through depicting past moments in British or classical history—other conceptions of sovereignty, other methods of governance.

This book, in its focus on the textually rich Essex Rebellion and Gunpowder Plot, pairs two events that are never studied together. Indeed, each appears to represent an opposite manifestation of the crime: Protestant versus Catholic, aristocrat versus gentry, court versus margin, Elizabethan versus Jacobean. The first event, the Essex Rebellion, has been deemed quasi-feudal and aristocratic.[40] Like other traitorous nobles before him, the earl contested the exercise of royal authority over his estate and affairs, although notably, unlike Norfolk or Howard, he was a Protestant loyalist employed by the state rather than a Catholic accused of plotting with foreign rulers.[41] The Gunpowder Plot, by contrast, represents the culmination of an opposite and much more prevalent strain of treason in early modern England. Emerging out of the same recusant frustrations that fueled the Northern Rebellion, the Babington Plot, and the other conspiracies surrounding Mary of Scotland, the Gunpowder Plot was a Catholic attempt to secure religious toleration (or domination) and political influence.[42] Unlike Essex, whose power struggle with Elizabeth concerned his personal fortunes and sway at court, Guy Fawkes, Robert Catesby, and others were on the political and religious margins, hoping through an act of desperation to secure England for Catholicism. Further, if Essex appeared to threaten the queen herself, the plotters attacked not simply the monarch's body but the entire state.

Despite the apparently opposite concerns of each rebellion, a number of Catholics participated in both the Essex Rebellion and the Gunpowder Plot, a point rarely noted. This fact seems counterintuitive, since Essex is frequently cast as a Protestant hawk at court and not a supporter of recusants. Not only did he advocate military engagements against Catholics abroad, but he was associated with the discovery of multiple Catholic plots in the 1590s, most famously the Lopez Plot.[43] Yet Essex moved from being the nobleman responsible for discovering Catholic treason to associating in 1601 with various recusants who participated in his rebellion. Such a shift is partially explained by Paul Hammer's analysis: although Essex remained staunchly anti-Spanish, this hawkishness should not be mistaken for broad anti-Catholicism. Indeed, at the same time that Essex pursued treasonous Catholic threats to Elizabeth, he supported the position of anti-Spanish Catholics.[44] After the failure of the Spanish Armada against England and the death of Mary of Scotland, a greater portion of Catholics began to express loyalty to England in the face of threats of foreign invasion. Hammer describes this phenomenon as "a broader mental shift away from simple anti-Catholicism towards inclusive nationalism and anti-Spanish sentiment, which had been pioneered by Huguenot thinkers and began to take hold in England after the defeat of the Armada in 1588."[45] Hence, despite the earl's Protestant agenda abroad, domestically he supported a mixed group of followers, including Catholic recusants.

The failure of the Essex Rebellion, however, left the earl's Catholic allies out in the cold. The presence of Catholic gentry in the patronage network of a Protestant earl yields, after 1601, to the stark alienation of such figures as Thomas Percy and Robert Winter, who began to participate opportunistically in more radical Catholic plots. Having enjoyed the earl's support in the years before his rising, these recusants now found themselves devoid of any influence at court, a situation that continued after the accession of King James when perhaps these men had hoped to find a more sympathetic ruler. With their continuing alienation came the last, most notorious gasp of Catholic treason in England: the Gunpowder Plot. This event testifies to the continuing difficulties for Catholics in England, many of whom found the path of moderation to be unacceptably precarious. Hopeful that James might prove tolerant or that the war with Spain would lead to Catholic triumph over England, Catholics instead found themselves confronted after 1603 with both renewed recusancy legislation and a Jacobean peace with Spain. The Gunpowder Plot speaks to the lingering existence of radical Catholic hope in a change of state and religion, and thus resonates with the multiple examples of sixteenth-century Catholic treason.

After the Gunpowder Plot, however, the state's anti-Catholic legislation was greeted by a population more sophisticated in their responses to such opportunistic measures. No longer could the monarch make political hay out of treason without experiencing dissent even from more mainstream subjects, in addition to the familiar radical voices. In contrast to the aftermath of the Northern Rebellion or the Babington Plot, after 1605 numbers of Protestant subjects, perhaps following the lead established earlier by Essex himself, distinguished between papist traitors and loyal English subjects of the Catholic faith. As a result, such subjects protested James's innovative policies, joining European Catholic voices to do so. Examining the Essex Rebellion and Gunpowder Plot side by side opens up these otherwise obscured connections, and thus reveals the increasing growth of moderate Protestant and Catholic subjects loyal to the state but critical of its policies on treason. Now, a population familiar with conspiracies and increasingly secure in its Reformed Church became less willing to stomach the state's sensationalism or expansion of prerogative through its response to treason. Instead, many of Elizabeth's and James's subjects took a more knowing attitude toward divisive politics and began to exercise their political muscle through their textual responses to state policy, responses ranging from polemic to plays.

Treason, Moderation, and Public Debate

This project focuses on a period when, as J. P. Sommerville writes, "Elizabethan clerics were expressing nakedly absolutist ideas" and writers composed in the shadow of increasing state power.[46] Nevertheless, the repressive effects of emerging absolutism on writers can be overemphasized, as Cyndia Susan Clegg's work on Elizabethan censorship practices helps to demonstrate: the infamous Bishop's Ban of 1599 arose, she argues, out of local politics, not the systematic condemnation of writers.[47] This book turns from censorship to the other half of the repression equation, namely, treason law. The late Elizabethan and early Jacobean states did indeed employ weapons of treason law and prosecution in an authoritarian attempt to silence opposition. But such attempts were hardly successful. Even as the monarch strove to assert his or her sovereign power in the fight against treason, the writers examined in this book offered dissenting responses that were at once moderate and oppositional.

While Jean Bodin's *Six Livres de la République* and Niccolò Machiavelli's *Prince* helped to influence English royalists in the 1590s, other theories of state also circulated in England in this period: through Tacitus's classical history and Machiavelli's *Discorsi*, subjects learned of Republican theories of government; through the re-publication of texts by Thomas Smith and John Fortescue, they read about the English tradition of constitutional or mixed rather than absolute monarchy.[48] Further, such alternate theories of government could be presented onstage to diverse audiences. Subjects who might not read Tacitus or Machiavelli could see the staging of Republican Rome through *Coriolanus*, *Catiline*, and *Julius Caesar*, just as subjects uninformed on questions of treason, sovereignty, and law in English history could see the staging of the various governments of Edward II, Richard II, or Richard III.[49] Through these dramatic stagings, subjects engaged with theories of rule that resonated with the variety of continental political theory and English legal texts circulating among elite audiences.[50]

While the appearance of absolutist rhetoric is not simply a sign that England experienced monarchical tyranny, then, nor was this a period, as Glenn Burgess posits, of broad consensus on the nature of kingship.[51] Instead, the state's application of absolutist rhetoric in the context of treason generated dissent from moderate subjects reluctant to endorse expansive theories of sovereignty, even as they condemned treason. Such activism of subjects on the topics of sovereignty and treason between 1590 and 1610 was not, however, entirely new. Radical theorists ranging from monarchomachs to Puritans certainly had attacked the Elizabethan regime throughout the queen's reign, as Peter Lake's work impressively demonstrates. They had voiced their support for resistance theory, Catholic supremacy, or godly policies, despite the monarch's attempt to regulate words. Notable textual resistance of writers like William Allen, Robert Persons, and Edmund Campion challenged the allegedly tyrannical recusant policies of the English state.[52] Throughout the 1580s Campion and his followers frustrated state efforts to control their searing polemics, since, as Lake reveals, even the jails themselves came to function "as centres of religious debate and conflict."[53] Despite traffic to and from prison in the form of both people and texts, the debates of incarcerated subjects had only a limited claim on broader cultural authority outside the radical Catholic community. Such dissident writers contrast with, yet to a degree anticipate, the writers analyzed in this book, who equally address issues of obedience, tyranny, and treason but from a position of greater cultural legitimacy.

Between the most outspoken royalists and the radical monarchomachs, this book examines the more moderate, less polemical writers who engage, even from a position of allegiance to the monarch, in a sustained dialogue with threatening state policies. Such moderate figures appear not only in authors such as Donne and Hayward, who represent a form of loyal opposition to crown sovereignty, but also in literary characters: Shakespeare's York and Malcolm, like Jonson's Cicero, strive to uphold the state during a period of crisis, and, in doing so, chart a perilous and uncomfortable path between necessity and law. What happens, in a time of political crisis, to the middle ground occupied by characters of compromise or reconciliation? The space allowed to moderation shrinks with treasonous trauma, and, as a result, the figures who attempt to occupy a middle ground find themselves under increasing scrutiny: dismissed, condemned, exiled, or arrested, the political moderates face accusations from the Left and Right, from resisters and royalists, as their plots frequently turn tragic.

In depicting or claiming a position of moderation, the authors in this project do not profess a single political platform or slogan. As a result, looking at the role of moderate or indefinable literary writers in staging these treasonous events for a wider audience moves us beyond reductionist categorizations of royalist and subversive, conservative and oppositional. While the oppositions between Catholics, Protestants, and Puritans, between monarchomachs and royalists, were crucial to the structure of the early modern political landscape, defining the political field by its extremes flattens the quality of political debate and reduces both the ingenuity and flexibility of the literary text in relation to such debate.

While the literary text proves flexible in its polemical engagements, this is not to say that it has no political effect. The very act of staging multiple definitions of treason within a play has the effect of weakening the state's unilateral position on the crime. The state's definition of treason thus contended with the imaginative representations of the crime by its subjects, who depicted alternate theories of treason and sovereignty through the precedent of classical and continental models. The literary fictions examined here, each associated with contemporary treasonous events, offer creative representations familiar to but distinct from political polemic. Not pressed to take sides, to offer solutions, to solve crises, imaginative texts instead work at the intersection of policy and philosophy, history and literature. In doing so, they construct and mediate the treasonous event even as they imagine the state beyond such a crisis.

Embedded in my analysis of the textual communities forged out of treason is a larger argument about the political culture of the turn of the seventeenth century: the readers and writers charted in this book, as they articulate the rights of law, of conscience, and of the crown, help to produce the phenomenon of the "early modern public sphere." This sphere is what Jürgen Habermas deems, in the eighteenth century, "a debate over the general rules governing relations" conducted through "people's public use of their reason."[54] In invoking Habermas's famous model in relation to early modern literary and political culture, I produce two claims. My first contention, following the work of scholars such as Peter Lake, Nigel Smith, and David Norbrook, is that the model of the public sphere can be applied earlier than Habermas suggests, in order to illustrate the diverse political culture of the turn of the seventeenth century.[55] In its early modern manifestation, this sphere lacks the characteristics of the "bourgeois" economy central to Habermas's formulation, as Steven Pincus has recently argued.[56] Writings associated with both the Essex circle and the Gunpowder Plot nevertheless unfailingly function, even in propagandistic pamphlets, as discussions of government ("the rules governing relations") and pose questions about the monarch's relation to law and prerogative. The "public use of reason" in these debates appears to confirm Habermas's model, since these readers and writers engaged in actively shaping discourses on political theory and rights in early modern England.[57]

In the case of the Essexians, even as Essex served as a prominent noble member of the Elizabethan regime, his allies included soldiers and recusants, as well as a socially various set of scholars including Henry Savile, Henry Cuffe, Richard Grenewey, John Hayward, and Francis Bacon. Their interests in comparing models of rulership indicates a sophisticated engagement with issues of political theory in a manner characterizing a public sphere of debate that is, at least initially, independent of monarchical control. Similarly, the reading and writing communities that emerged out of the Gunpowder Plot offer a story of origins in the creation of the early modern public sphere. If the story began with the discovery of the plot by James and his set of courtiers, this initial audience of monarchical readers and writers supporting James soon became a more politically varied one, as writers took up the issues of treason and sovereignty from absolutist and oppositional perspectives. The post–Gunpowder Plot debates demonstrate how incidents of treasonous exchange create a public out of a space of private communication: the public practice of interpreting treason forges a reading and speaking community that upholds rights of law and conscience.

In supporting scholarly work on the early modern public sphere, this book offers a second, related claim, one that challenges Habermas's model: the public sphere is not determined by rational discourse alone; instead, it is propelled by the interpretive struggle surrounding the allegedly irrational language and actions of the traitor. In other words, treasonous activities require interpretation, a center point of the present book which takes seriously the perspective offered in Katharine Eisaman Maus's work on English criminal trials. Such trials are "an arena in which urgent questions of interpretation—questions with implications for a wide variety of social and intellectual practices—had to be addressed in practical terms before a large and curious audience."[58] In dramatic cases of treason, this struggle to interpret itself produces the phenomenon of the early modern public sphere. By stressing the role of treasonous language in producing the public sphere, this book critiques Habermas's model for excluding non-rational forms of communication. The same point is made by Joan B. Landes, who argues that the Habermasian public sphere, "identified with truth, objectivity and reason," labels certain abilities and interests as "improper subjects for public debate," dismissing them as nonrational or self-interested.[59] Whereas Landes's article concentrates on the gendered nature of such nonrational topics, this book examines how political irrationality in the crime of treason, rather than prove to be an "improper" subject for public debate, provokes the rational debate that characterizes the public sphere. The writers examined in this book, including Shakespeare, Hayward, Jonson, and Donne, represent this process of interpreting treason by dramatizing the multiple definitions of the crime within their texts. In response to these various definitions of the crime, characters in *Richard II, Henry IV, Macbeth,* and *Catiline* debate the nature of treason publicly, be it on the Welsh coast, on the battlefield, or in the Roman Senate. Such debates on treason expose the characters' variant political affiliations, from royalist to rebellious, thereby demonstrating the interconnection of treason with theories of rulership. These writers thus allow their readers to witness the process of interpreting, recognizing, and challenging treason that produces public debate on the "rules governing relations."

If the characteristics of the public sphere are debate, exchange, and communication about the rules governing relations, in early modern England a strong deterrent against this sphere was emerging in the form of treason and censorship legislation. Yet debate began to flourish precisely at the time when the state expanded its treason laws to include words as well as acts. Such debate was fueled in part because the state built a communicative crisis into its most potent instrument of repression. By making treason itself a matter of words, the very charge that should have silenced debate now required interpretation. In what context are words such as "heretic," "tyrant," and "infidel" treasonous? Under what conditions do subjects level such charges against their monarch? In its formulation of treason by words, the law rehearsed those oppositional voices and interpretive challenges to monarchical sovereignty. The Elizabethan legislation precipitated, and indeed presupposed, the existence of a public opposition fueled by political and religious principles rather than by violent actions. As a result, the state embedded in the crime itself the very existence of verbal dissent that characterizes the public sphere. It is my theory, then, that this public sphere as it emerged in early modern England cannot be separated from the crime of treason, a crime that provoked the reading, writing and play-going public who debated principles of law and sovereignty.

This book develops in two parts. The first analyzes the writing associated with the earl of Essex in the years before his 1600 and 1601 treason trials, foregrounding shifts in the interpretation of treason by scholars, courts, and subjects. Chapter 2 centers around the case of John Hayward, condemned by the crown for his 1599 history of Henry IV. Teasing out the legal and military interests linking Hayward and the earl of Essex, I reassess *Henry IV* as a loyalist text nevertheless condemned retrospectively, after the earl's alleged treason in Ireland in 1600. Further representations of Richard II, in texts such as Robert Persons's *A Conference about the Next Succession to the Crown of England* (1594) and Shakespeare's *Richard II* (1595–96), both explored in chapter 3, help to illuminate how depictions of the king serve as cyphers for competing conceptions of sovereignty, treason, and obedience. Shakespeare's play fully engages this tangle of treason and sovereignty by offering two kings who are at once traitors and monarchs: while Richard's tyranny constitutes a form of treason to the state, Henry's bold treason is articulated through his claims to law. Shakespeare's resulting portrait pushes beyond the opposition of law-based and divine-right rulership, evident in Hayward, to demonstrate the cost of political chaos for moderate subjects who become, in their attempts to navigate through a dangerous political landscape of tyranny and treason, merely slavish fools.

These political debates around treason, marking the years before the Essex Rebellion, continue up to and beyond the 1605 Gunpowder Plot, to which the book turns in its second half. The discovery of the plot, in prompting royal triumphalism and an expansion of recusant legislation, provoked debate as much as celebration. Thus Shakespeare's *Macbeth*, explored in chapter 4, proves a play more complicated in its responses to the treason than its status as the "royal play," coined by Henry Paul, allows. The play undermines the rhetoric of divine right kingship through its representation of Malcolm, while staging multiple forms of sovereignty familiar from Essexian political philosophy. Debates on kingship equally mark the controversy surrounding James's 1606 oath of allegiance, the subject of chapters 5 and 6. This oath policy, prompting international critique and domestic debate, caused Donne and Jonson to produce their most polemical works. Donne's *Pseudo-Martyr,* the subject of chapter 5, defends the Jacobean subject's right of conscience against James's increasingly invasive policies on recusancy. Similarly, as chapter 6 explores, Jonson's *Catiline* questions the dangerous application of emergency power in the fight against treason. By demonstrating how conscience and law are infringed in a time of crisis, both Donne and Jonson, along with Shakespeare and Hayward, expose the parasitic relationship of sovereignty to treason, as the state capitalizes on the threat of treason to justify its own expansion at the expense of the emerging rights of subjects.

CHAPTER TWO

The Treason of Hayward's Henry IV

Conveyed to the Tower in 1600 for writing an allegedly seditious history of Richard II, four years later the writer and lawyer John Hayward found employment as a history tutor to King James's son. He wrote about one of his conversations with Prince Henry, noting how he cautioned the prince against history writing; he told him that

> men might safely write of others in maner of a tale, but in maner of a History, safely they could not: because, albeit they should write of men long since dead, and whose posteritie is cleane worne out; yet some alive, finding themselves foule in those vices, which they see observed, reproved, and condemned in others; their guiltinesse maketh them apt to conceive, that whatsoever the words are, the finger pointeth onely at them.[1]

Hayward here warns the prince of the dangers of writing political history in which guilty readers might too easily believe that "the finger pointeth onely at them." His own fortunes confirm his advice. In 1599 he published a prose history covering the last years of King Richard II's reign and the first year of King Henry IV's under the rather misleading title *The First Part of the Life and Raigne of King Henrie IIII*. While the earl of Essex's rebellion offers the most famous coupling of a seditious activity and a representation of "King Henry the Fourth, and of the killing of Richard the Second," Hayward's *Henry IV* attracted the crown's attention even before the 1601 rebellion.[2] The history's topic, its immense popularity (as the printer claimed, "no book ever sold better"), and its dedication to the earl of Essex led the crown to suspect Hayward of treason.[3] With the text confiscated and burned after its second publication in May 1599, the crown then interrogated the printer, the licensor, and the author himself the following year, in July 1600. Held in the Tower, Hayward remained there for the rest of Elizabeth's reign.

This sensational publication history of *Henry IV* has determined readings of the text ever since. As a result, studies of Hayward's Elizabethan prose history rarely acknowledge his fortunes as a royalist writer under James, instead focusing on the author's alleged sedition in *Henry IV*.[4] Hayward's detention and interrogation exemplifies, for example, Elizabethan methods of "public surveillance," exposing the dangers that faced writers such as Shakespeare who produced historical fiction in an atmosphere of "despotism."[5] Yet the suspicions of the Elizabethan regime may have been warranted, as several scholars argue.[6] In producing a politic history on the sensitive topic of Richard II's deposition, Hayward betrayed his arguably seditious motives: his case shows "evidence of treasonous ambitions," as Arthur Kinney argues; Leeds Barroll likewise notes that the history was "topical, current, scandalous and suppressed," and John Guy writes that, since the subject matter was the overthrow of Richard II, the text's "implications were obvious."[7] This argument on Hayward's topicality is even more convincing if we posit his *Henry IV* as the text performed the night before the earl of Essex's 1601 rebellion, as Blair Worden does. He writes not only that "Hayward's 1399 is 1599 in thin disguise" but also that "the play performed at the instigation of Essex's followers in February 1601 was the dramatization of Hayward's book that had been applauded by the earl in 1599."[8] The earl, Worden speculates, had attended this alleged dramatization from the time of the book's first publication in 1599.

The potential use of Hayward's text in fomenting rebellion does not, however, verify the author's guilt. "He had no treasonable purpose," as Worden writes (24). Instead, as several scholars have argued, Hayward's *Henry IV* appeared seditious to the crown because of its association with the earl of Essex. F. J. Levy argues that "had Hayward not dedicated his book to Essex, all might still have gone well"; concurring, Cyndia Susan Clegg writes that the censorship of *Henry IV* resulted from "the singular affairs of Essex, Whitgift, and the Irish campaign."[9] According to these recent studies, the history itself was "innocuous" and constituted only a "minor breach of decorum."[10] It was the series of disastrous political events surrounding Essex that caused the prose history to attract the crown's attention.

This chapter necessarily reopens the case against Hayward in order to assess anew the seditious nature of his text. In investigating Hayward, we look beyond the crown's judgment, resituating the author within a complex set of professional and intellectual relationships. We also examine his text, which is almost universally overlooked in favor of the politics surrounding it.[11] Doing so helps reveal that, although the crown was the most powerful reader of *Henry IV*, it was certainly not the only interpreter. Even at the most sensational moment of *Henry IV*'s publication history, the text invited readings that stood independently from the state's censorious response. As this chapter demonstrates through the case of Hayward, however, the state reduces, in a moment of crisis, a proliferation of interpretations on a particular text or historical moment to a unilateral reading. Positing a constricted theory about the causal relation between treason and reading, the threatened state insists that reading about deposition and murder spurs thoughts of king killing, and thus texts on treason signal seditious desires.

The state's constricted theory ironically proves not preventative but productive. By and through its suspicious reading, the state produces the very treason it fears. In other words, it is this tyrannical attempt to limit interpretive possibility, to fix the meaning of a text, that itself precipitates treason. And it does so for two reasons. First, in enforcing its unilateral reading, the state performs the very tyranny that traitors claim to oppose, giving an apparent legitimacy to their cause. Second, the state's interpretive tyranny alienates readers who may have engaged in various ways with a now treasonous text. In narrowing the interpretive possibilities of a text, and insisting on its treasonous content, Elizabeth's administration discovers treason where there might have been merely dissent or even loyal obedience. Specifically, the case of Hayward and Essex exposes how unthreatening texts, when labeled seditious, convert their readers into rebels. Counter-intuitively, then, the state's suspicions help to produce the very events it claims merely to interpret.

To understand the Hayward case requires reopening the state's argument as rehearsed in the *State Papers,* and reviewing the position of the examiners Sir Edward Coke and Lord Chief Justice Popham. To account for the state's suspicions more fully, I examine Hayward's text in relation to contemporary pamphlets voicing theories of resistance to Elizabeth's monarchy. Unexamined in Hayward scholarship, the resonance between *Henry IV* and the pamphlet material may have provoked the state's suspicions. In representing the political theory of contemporary radicals, however, Hayward did not espouse their beliefs, as the state charges. Instead, he offered one side of a current debate on sovereignty; the other half comes later in the text. This chapter traces the source of Hayward's fascination with such variant political models to two sources: his Tacitism and his professional training in the civil law. Pairing a speech on resistance theory with one on absolute monarchy, he reproduced contemporary sovereignty debates in a manner typical of both his Tacitism and his civilian (i.e., civil law) training. Examining Hayward in terms of his professional context as a civil lawyer also illuminates his arguably royalist sympathies, a political affiliation generally ignored by critics of *Henry IV*.[12] Rather than supporting sedition, he instead held an interest in legal questions that dangerously intersected with, but should not be mistaken for, radical political theories. It is this legal engagement of *Henry IV*, rather than the author's radical politics that contributed to the false perception of his text as seditious.

The Crown versus John Hayward

Hayward opens *Henry IV* with a forceful defense of history writing. In the preface he argues that the historian is the most praiseworthy of writers. By describing "what events have followed what counsailes, [historians] have set foorth unto us not onely precepts, but lively patterns, both for private directions and for affayres of state, whereby in shorte time young men may be instructed, and ould men more fullie furnished with experience then the longest age of man can affoorde" (62).[13] Addressing the fortunes of both "mighty states" and "famous men," Hayward combines the chronicle history of Holinshed with the biographical history of Plutarch. His history comes to life through examples or "patterns" rather than through abstract "precepts." Using "lively patterns" to teach readers, Hayward echoes Sir Philip Sidney's Horatian argument in *Defence of Poesy* that one should teach and delight through literature. As Hayward soon discovered, however, the crown took umbrage with his practice when he rendered the deposition of Richard II in "lively patterns." To use the words of Sir Edward Coke in his interrogation of Hayward, the selection of "a story 200 years old" and the precise "choice of that story only" aroused royal suspicion, particularly given the belief that Hayward compared Richard II's reign with Elizabeth's own.[14]

The state twice called Hayward before its examiners, first in June 1600 and then again in January 1601. They challenged his method of writing history, arguing that he masked his interest in spurring rebellion with his claim to represent history through, as he claims in his preface, "not onely precepts, but lively patterns." Hayward defended his practice as conventional, insisting that "it is a liberty used by all good writers of history to invent reasons and speeches" and that he follows "after the example of the best historians."[15] To the state, however, Hayward employed "lively patterns" to invent seditious arguments supporting deposition of the monarch. As Chief Justice Popham's interrogation notes for Hayward, drawn up in February 1600, read, "What moved him to maintain . . . that it might be lawful for the subject to depose the king?"[16] Since these invented speeches exhibit the imaginative and rhetorical power typical of theater, the author added dramatic effect to an already sensational tale.

The state built their case against him on the provocative invented speech of the archbishop of Canterbury. Here Canterbury convinces Henry Bolingbroke, duke of Hereford, to seek the crown because, he insists, deposition of a weak king is legal and honorable. During their interrogation of Hayward in 1601, the state's examiners "demanded the reason why he set forth the orations of the Bishop of Canterbury and the Earl of Derby, seeing they tend to things most unlawfull, [Hayward] sayeth that there can be nothing done be it never so ill or unlawfull but must have a shadow, and every counsel must be according to the action."[17] Hayward's statement that "every counsel must be according to the action" recalls his use of the term "counsailes" in his preface to *Henry IV*, quoted above: the historian describes "what events have followed what counsailes" as part of his or her "lively patterns." "Counsailes" here refers to the advice that precedes a historical action; that is, "counsailes" are the cause and "events" are the effect. This preface helps to decipher his testimony that "every counsel must be according to the action." In other words, Hayward is asserting in his testimony that, in writing history, he represents the "counsel" that must have led to a historical event. While he has no record of the actual conversations that preceded events, he claims that his job lies in reconstructing this "counsel." He has no motive in inventing speeches any more than the sun has a prejudice in casting shadows: in representing events "ill or unlawfull," his history must represent, or "shadow" forth, historical action. Hayward depicts the archbishop's speech not because he agrees with it but because he recognizes the likelihood of its articulation.

Disregarding Hayward's defenses, the examiners suspected his support for Canterbury's sentiments, suspicions apparently borne out by the publication history of *Henry IV*. First, Hayward's title appeared to misrepresent the subject matter, purporting to cover the life of Henry IV while actually focusing on the last years of the reign of Richard.[18] Second, both the licenser Samuel Harsnett and the printer John Wolfe claimed to Attorney General Edward Coke in July 1600 that Hayward submitted his text without the offending dedication to the earl of Essex. The book, Wolfe claims in his examination, had "no epistle dedicatory nor to the reader" when first brought to him.[19] Harsnett also notes how, when he received the book, "it was hedlesse without epistle, preface or dedication at all which moved me to thinke it was a meer rhetorical exornation of a part of our Englishe history to shewe the foyle of the Author his witt."[20] Harsnett attempts to defend himself through the opposition of sedition to "rhetorical exornation," and treason to mere "witt." Yet, in doing so, he denies the state's coupling of treason and words: wit and rhetoric are precisely the stuff of treason. Harsnett nevertheless concedes, in the process of defending himself, the incendiary potential of the dedication to Essex. Had he seen it, he reassures his examiners, "I protest I shold never have allowed the rest of the Pamphlett."[21] Not surprisingly, Harsnett vigorously defends his decision to license the history by claiming that Hayward hid from him the radical associations of the text.

These seemingly furtive publication details and the prefatory matter of *Henry IV* validated the state's suspicion about the text on two levels. First, the apparent suppression of the Essex dedication, combined with the text's popularity, seemed to confirm both Hayward's and the earl's treasonous motives. The state's notes, listing "evidence in support of treason against the earl of Essex," charge the earl with "permitting underhand that treasonable book of Henry IV to be printed and published; it being plainly deciphered, not only by the matter, and by the epistle itself, for what end and for whose behalf it was made, but also the earl himself being so often present at the playing thereof, and with great applause giving countenance and liking to the same."[22] This abstract, while baffling critics by entangling a printed book with a dramatic performance, appears to cement the case against both Essex and Hayward. Regardless of the book's content and methods of argumentation, its treason is "plainly deciphered" through association with the guilty earl, just as the earl's "great applause" of the text verifies his sedition. The state's circular suspicions serve to condemn both Hayward and the earl through mutual association.

If the publication details seem to confirm Hayward's guilt, so, too, does "the matter," as the state suggests above. Scholarly attention has focused primarily on the publication history of *Henry IV* at the expense of the text's arguments, but, as even a brief examination of Canterbury's speech reveals, his argument in favor of deposition mirrors the rhetoric of contemporary resistance theory pamphlets written against the Elizabethan monarchy. Although the state does not explicitly note this parallel, the examiner focuses on the central argument of Canterbury's speech, one that is clearly indebted to resistance theories as the following discussion helps to demonstrate. While the precise correspondence of Hayward's text and the resistance theory helps to account for the state's alarm, I will also argue that this similarity illuminates Hayward's broader intellectual debts in *Henry IV*. He complements his interest in radical theory with his equal investment in royalist arguments later in the text. Balancing variant political theory, Hayward's academic approach to history led him to articulate arguments that, out of context, appeared seditious. Yet in context, Hayward's style of argumentation confirms what any reader of Tacitus would recognize: the losing argument, namely the resistance theory of Canterbury, comes first, while the later royalist polemic holds the position of victory, coming second.

Canterbury's speech lies in an inflammatory scene absent from Shakespeare's rendition of events in his *Richard II*. Initiating the rebellion against Richard, several English nobles travel to France to meet with Henry Bolingbroke. Once in Paris, Canterbury secures a private conference with Bolingbroke and persuades him to assume leadership of the endangered English state. The archbishop begins: "We are sent unto you (right high and noble prince) from the chief lords and states of our land, not to seeke revenge against our king upon private injury and displeasure, nor upon a desperate discontentment to set the state on fire, nor to procure the ambitious advancement of any perticular person, but to open unto you the deformities and decais of our broken estate, and to desire your aide, in staying the ruinous downfall of the same" (113). Canterbury's speech serves as a rhetorical set piece in constructing a successful revolution. Dismissing private justifications for rebellion, he instead asserts his own loyalty to the state. Out of an apparently noble desire to protect his country, he turns to Bolingbroke as a means of "staying the ruinous downfall" of England. Canterbury implies that he and his supporters are far from rebellious: they merely seek to protect the threatened state. In a rhetorical inversion, the bishop complains that the supporters of Richard are themselves the rebels, forwarding the "deformities and decais of our broken estate" (113).

Convinced by Canterbury, Bolingbroke agrees to seek the English crown out of loyalty to the faltering state. He then questions the soldiers who have flocked to support him, asking their motives for leaving the lawful King Richard to support a challenger; he tells them, "your name is in suspence, whether to be tearmed rebels or subjects, until you have made manifest that your allegiance was bound rather to the state of the realme then the person of the prince" (121–22). Like Canterbury, Bolingbroke demonstrates the power of revolutionary rhetoric, a passage that suggests, against Harsnett's construction above, how mere "rhetorical exornation" proves the stuff of treason. Ostensibly questioning the motives of his followers, he teaches them how to justify their rebellion: these men will appear to be loyal subjects rather than traitors if they "manifest that [their] allegiance was bound to the state." He supplies these men with his own argument for deposition, since, like the soldiers, he claims to protect the state by replacing an incompetent leader.

The issue of loyalty at stake in the speeches of Canterbury and Bolingbroke mirrors the central argument of the resistance theory pamphlets circulated among Hayward's contemporaries—such pamphlets justify resistance once a king has abandoned his duty—and this similarity may have fueled the state's suspicion that "the finger pointeth only at them." Between 1584 and 1596, the years preceding Hayward's history, theories of resistance offered increasingly sophisticated explanations for opposing a monarch. Protestant resisters such as George Buchanan, John Ponet, and the anonymous author of *Vindiciae, contra*

Tyrannos had articulated such theories earlier in the sixteenth century, but, in the 1590s, these theories were adapted by Catholic resistance writers who criticized Elizabeth and voiced conventional support for the pope's religious authority.[23] Significantly, like earlier Protestant resistance writers, these authors also believed in popular opposition to the king, a theory that consisted of two parts: first, the authority of kings derives from popular consent, not God; second, the coronation oath represents a contract between the king and his people which, when broken, could result in his lawful deposition. These arguments, offered by Cardinal William Allen in *A True, Sincere and Modest Defence of English Catholics,* are echoed in fellow pamphleteer Robert Persons's work, both writers pivotal to the development of resistance theories under Elizabeth.

Persons, like Allen, emphasized the contractual nature of the coronation oath, writing in *A Conference about the Next Succession to the Crown of England* (1594) that the king has a "power delegate, or power commissioned from the commonwealth."[24] If the prince breaks the law, or otherwise fails to uphold his office, then he no longer rules legitimately. As Persons claims,

> by authority also you have heard it proved, of al law-makers, Philosophers, Lawyers, Divines, and Governours of common wealthes, who have set downe in their statutes and ordonances that kings shal sweare and protest at their entrance to government, that they wil observe and perform the conditions their [*sic*] promised, and otherwise to have no interest in that dignity, and soveraintie. (2:62)

On taking the coronation oath, the sovereign promises to rule according to the "conditions" of the office; failing to do so, the king loses his "dignity, and soveraintie." Challenging the absolute authority of the monarch, Persons marshals his legal arguments, based in "statutes and ordonances," to detail the limitations of monarchy and the king's duties to his subjects.[25]

Persons, in addition to providing arguments founded on the coronation oath, offers a historical analysis of Richard II's deposition by Henry IV in relation to issues of law and tyranny. Dedicated to Essex, published under a false imprint and under the pseudonym "Doleman," *A Conference* defends the deposition of Richard II in the context of a resistance tract on succession. Richard's tyrannical reign, he argues, threatens civil society. Sovereignty, or "al kingly authority," Persons writes, "is given [to kings] only by the commonwealth, and that with this expresse condition, that they shal governe according to law and equity ... which end being taken away or perverted, the king becometh a tyrant" (2:61). In his attempt to exercise absolute sovereignty Richard, in particular, distorts the law of treason into a tyrannical tool to use against his noble subjects. Expanding the law through wicked statutes, Persons's Richard then prosecutes his nobles with "fayned" treason: the king "had made many wicked statutes as wel against the church and state Ecclesiastical, as also to intangle the realme and nobility with fayned crymes of treason against his regaltie, as then he termed them" (2:59). Notably the term "wickedness," commonly applied to traitors, here designates the king's laws; the "fayning" often associated with treasonous deception, refers in this context to corrupt arrests and prosecutions. Persons thus turns the rhetoric of treason on its head by employing the very language reserved for criminals to designate the king and his corrupt laws.

Persons then shifts his argument to consider the contrasting rule of Henry IV. While Richard breaks his contractual obligation to the commonwealth, Persons argues, Henry upholds the law. According to his analysis, Richard and Henry represent opposite models of government: one tyrannical, illegal, and therefore illegitimate, and the other law-based, accountable, and therefore sanctioned by God and Parliament. Persons strongly supports the claims of the Lancastrians in the civil war, a position that has implied consequences for the unsettled Elizabethan succession. The Lancastrians were more effective, and hence (Persons contends) more legitimate kings. This argument shifts the issue of succession away from bloodline toward another standard for legitimacy, based in the efficacy of one's rule. Richard and Henry effectively serve as symbolic shorthand for opposing theories of state circulating in England in the 1590s: the divine right of kings, propounded by Elizabethan clerics, and mixed monarchy, based in a long legal tradition theorized by writers such as Bracton, Smith, and Fortescue. These two traditions might not always be opposed—medieval theorists such as Bracton articulated notions of sacred kingship exercised under the law. But in the 1590s the attributes of divine right sovereignty, including obedience and nonresistance, began to challenge customary mixed monarchy. Polemicists such as Persons only widened this divide by differentiating the two models entirely.

Encountering opposition from other pamphleteers throughout the 1590s, Persons responded vigorously, continuing to present arguments in favor of resistance. In "A Temperate Ward-Word, to the turbulent and seditious Wach-word of Sir Francis Hastinges, Knight," for example, he chronicles historical and religious precedents for deposing kings, writing that "many kingdoms were disposed of and princes deposed by mortal children of men, and the same also allowed by God himself." Specifically targeting his opponent, Francis Hastinges, he adds, "and in our kingdom of England since it was a monarchie . . . he shall finde very many examples of mutations in the like manner . . . which yet he must approve for good and lawful."[26] Here Persons marshalls the authority of both God and law in support of deposition. Furthermore, he turns to English history itself for precedent. Adducing examples of deposition from English history, Persons defends the depositions of Edward II and Richard II much as Canterbury does in Hayward's text.

Arguing that Richard is a bad king and that his subjects owe their loyalty to the state and not to the crown, Hayward's Canterbury voices the central arguments of the contemporary Catholic writers who challenge Elizabeth.[27] Indeed, this parallel of Canterbury and Persons may signal Hayward's conscious construction of the archbishop as a symbol of Catholic treason. Rather than inviting the reader to sympathize with Canterbury, Hayward could have expected that his 1599 audience would condemn the character's seditious, and familiarly Catholic, rhetoric. Nevertheless, Canterbury's speech, in accurately echoing resistance theory rhetoric, alarmed the crown. For his interrogation of Hayward, Lord Chief Justice Popham's notes of February 1600 ask, "What moved him to set down . . . that the subjects were bound for their obedience to the State and not to the person of the King?"[28] The question focuses on Canterbury's argument as if it were Hayward's own, highlighting the loyalty debate at the heart of both resistance theory and Canterbury's persuasive speech. Inventing treasonous arguments, Hayward was "moved," Coke implies, by his own seditious desires. In Hayward's *Henry IV*, Canterbury's speech not only mirrors the rhetoric of treasonous discourses; it also provokes the rebellion against Richard. Hayward thus uses the success of the historical rebellion to prophesy the overthrow of Elizabeth, or so Coke suspected. In his notes for the case from July 11, 1600, Coke wrote that Hayward "selecteth a story 200 year old, and publisheth it this last year, intending the application of it to this time."[29]

Applying his tale "to this time," Hayward's innovative form of "political history" appeared to invite an allegorical reading of Richard's reign in terms of contemporary events and rulers, a point elaborated by subsequent critics of Hayward's text. As Leonard F. Dean argues, for example, Hayward's history reveals his "desire to make his examples applicable to the current political situation," particularly the intrigues of Essex.[30] The characters of Richard and Bolingbroke could be read as allegorical representations of Elizabeth and Essex, with Richard's defeat in Ireland doubling for Elizabeth's own failed Irish policy. With the earl's return from his disastrous and potentially seditious campaign in Ireland, where he repeatedly disregarded the queen's orders, the tangling of Hayward, Essex, and Irish history became all the more suspect and the state accused Hayward of sedition. The author thus became the unfortunate victim of a retrospective reading in which the earl's 1600 fortunes were read back onto the lawyer's 1599 history.

This relationship between waning political fortunes and the queen's suspicious reading is highlighted by the entirely opposite fate of Persons's *Conference*. This much more incendiary text, discussed above, also had been dedicated to Essex. But this dedication was treated not as evidence of sedition but as an embarrassment. In 1594, when the text was published, Essex was at the height of his power at court, and in close association with the queen; as a result, the dedication to Essex could be dismissed and had no apparent negative effect on his reputation or standing. Indeed, Hammer stresses Elizabeth's solicitude for his standing at court: "In November 1595, when Elizabeth was anxious publicly to vindicate Essex after the embarrassment of his receiving the dedication of a treasonous book on the succession, she pointedly relied on him alone to answer foreign correspondence on her behalf."[31]

By 1600, however, Essex's fall spurred, or indeed produced, the state's suspicion of Hayward. As noted above, the potentially inflammatory content of *Henry IV*, together with its difficult publication history, led to the charge that Hayward radically challenged the Elizabethan monarchy. The state's examiners focused their attention solely on selected, provocative speeches in *Henry IV*, not only to build their case against Hayward's history writing but, more crucially, to snare Essex on charges of treason. Robert Cecil's exhaustive notes for the interrogations of Hayward, Harsnett, Wolfe, and others suggest his efforts to expose treasonous behavior in the earl even as Essex had, in the June 1600 York House proceedings, been cleared of the charge, a point that Cyndia Susan Clegg carefully establishes.[32] The complex political associations of Hayward and his 1599 history defy, however, the narrow scope of these investigations. The next section evaluates Hayward in light of evidence either ignored by, or unavailable to, the crown's interrogators, Cecil, Coke, and Popham. This additional evidence, drawn from Hayward's professional life and his later writings, challenges the state's selective focus on Canterbury's speech and the dedication to Essex, thereby undermining the foundation of the state's case against Hayward. Broadening the scope of the investigation, the argument presented here reexamines Hayward's political interests while exonerating him of the charge of treason.

Hayward's Defense

While the state's suspicion arose from the allegedly provocative parallels between Hayward's history and contemporary politics, the timing of the book's publication undermines the theory of Hayward's sedition. In fact, his history *predated* Essex's revolutionary activity. Published in February 1599, the first edition of Hayward's text appeared a month before Essex's departure to Ireland. Commanding the most expensive military expedition ever sent to Ireland, clearly Essex enjoyed enough royal favor to win the commission; otherwise his appointment to the post would have been foolhardy. In writing the epistle to Essex, then, Hayward dedicated his book to a man who appeared at the time to be a valued public servant of the state, not a rebel. In 1599 Essex was, as Hayward writes in his offending preface, "great indeed, both in present judgment and in expectation of future time, in whom once blind fortune can seem now to have regained her sight, since she moves to heap with honors a man distinguished in all virtues" (61). At its moment of composition and printing in 1599, this preface articulated the widely shared support for Essex as he embarked on his Irish expedition, leading the queen's troops against the rebel Tyrone. Hayward's phrase "expectation of future time" indicates his hope that Essex will triumph against the Irish, just as he had done in former military endeavors for the state. Further, in his examination before

Coke, the printer John Wolfe claims that, when Hayward brought him the text without a dedication or preface, he suggested Essex as a potential dedicatee: Essex was "a martial man, and was for to go unto Ireland, and the book treated of Irish causes."[33] The dedication to Essex may have seemed all the more appropriate to the author given his position as the Chancellor of the University of Cambridge, where Hayward received his B.A. and his civil law training.

In dedicating *Henry IV* to Essex as a "martial man" serving the Elizabethan state, Hayward and Wolfe followed a conventional practice: military texts and Tacitean histories were especially associated with the earl during the 1590s, when he commanded state expeditions abroad and fostered a circle of scholars at home. Alberico Gentili, the Regis professor of civil law at Oxford, dedicated all three commentaries on his *De Jure Belli* (1588 and 1589) to his patron, the earl. Gentili writes of Essex: "Distinguished in the knowledge of arms and war, most eminent as well in letters and arts of peace, in the affairs of the kingdom, most wise."[34] Here, his description resonates with Hayward's later offending dedication, with its praise of Essex as "great indeed." Essex was also friend and patron to Sir Roger Williams, who dedicated his 1590 *A Briefe discourse of warre* to the earl from "a Soldier that hath but small skill in writing or inditing." Williams begs Essex to "command my life."[35] In addition to the laudatory dedication, Williams narrates, in the body of his text, some of Essex's military successes such as his expedition with Norris to Lisbon (9).[36] George Chapman's dedication to his 1598 translation of *The Iliad* also highlights Essex as a war hero, "Most true Achilles (whom by sacred prophecie Homere did but prefigure in his admirable object)," and defends his translation on the grounds that Homer may provide military knowledge to the earl: "Nor can it be reputed an unworthy incitement, to propose the true image of all vertues and humaine governement (even in the hart of this tumultuous season) to your other serious affaires: especially since it contaynes the true portraite of ancient stratagems and disciplines of war."[37] Chapman imagines the earl to be interested in "true . . . humaine governement" and interprets his militarism in this light: Essex fights in a "tumultuous season" to uphold virtue and order, serving as an Achilles to defend his nation.

Along with Gentili, Williams, and Chapman, Shakespeare also praises Essex as a "conquering Caesar" in 1599. In order imaginatively to evoke King Henry's popular reception in London after his military triumph abroad, the Chorus to act 5 of *Henry V* references the expected reception of Essex upon his return from Ireland:

Were now the General of our gracious Empress—
as in good time he may—from Ireland coming,
Bringing rebellion broachèd on his sword,
How many would the peaceful city quit
To welcome him! Much more, and much more cause,
Did they this Harry.

(5.0.30–35)

This image of Essex with "rebellion broachèd on his sword" would be incendiary if, in 1599, the earl were seen as a traitor to the crown. Instead Shakespeare, like Hayward, writes with the expectation of his success in Ireland and his continued royal favor. Of course, Shakespeare's reference to Essex is far from transparently jingoistic; it instead, Katharine Eisaman Maus writes, "registers both the patriotic excitement generated by the prospect of a military venture in foreign parts and the dread of war in a notoriously difficult environment."[38] The juxtaposition of the "peaceful city" and Essex's rebellious sword drives home this dread of war. Furthermore, the earl's military career demonstrates what Stephen Orgel calls, in another context, "the ambiguities of chivalry."[39] As is well known, for example, Essex distributed money and honors among his soldiers more liberally than Elizabeth would, rewarding his loyal soldiers with knighthoods and dividing the spoils of war among them. This behavior, while ostensibly serving the queen, had threatening ideological implications. As Richard McCoy cogently notes, in establishing his reputation Essex was confronted with "one of the most volatile contradictions of Elizabethan politics: the conflict between aristocratic honor and ambition and the demands of obedience and duty to the monarch."[40] Even given the fractious politics surrounding the earl's patronage and popularity, however, his reputation in 1599 was such that writers, including both Shakespeare and Hayward, merely followed convention in highlighting his widely recognized service to the crown: as with the dedications and prefaces by the earl's Oxford friends, Shakespeare's *Henry V* helps confirm Essex's status as an Elizabethan military hero, a "General of our gracious Empress."

The earl's connection to military histories further appears with a series of 1590s translations of Tacitus.[41] First, Essex was patron of Sir Henry Savile, an Oxford scholar and (with the earl's help) eventual provost of Eton who produced the first English translation of Tacitus in 1591.[42] Essex also served as the dedicatee of Richard Grenewey's 1598 translation, *The Annales of Cornelius Tacitus,* where Grenewey writes of the virtues of history in offering "an image of mans present estate, a true and lively pattern of things to come."[43] Grenewey's phrase "lively pattern" is adopted directly by Hayward himself in the dedication to *Henry IV* where he describes history, as noted above, as "lively patterns, both for private directions and for affayres of state" (62). A preface to Savile's 1598 second edition of Tacitus fully elaborates this utility of Tacitus as a source of private and public "direction." This preface, written by Essex himself, notes how "there is no treasure so much enriches the minde of man as learning; there is no learning so proper for the direction of the life of man as Historie; there is no historie . . . so well worth the reading as Tacitus."[44]

If contemporary scholars, like the Elizabethan state itself, question the precise utility of history's "lively patterns" for Essex, Savile's translation helps reinforce the portrait of a loyalist earl turning to history for his military education.[45] An often overlooked appendix to Savile's translation of the *Histories* provides an anatomy of Tacitus along such military lines. This sixteen-page addition, entitled "A View of Certaine Militari Matters, for the better understanding of the ancient Roman stories," asserts military knowledge as the heart of Tacitus's contribution for contemporary readers: in order to follow the history of the empire, one must know the organization and methods of its army.[46] In the same spirit as Williams's text and Chapman's dedication, Savile's appendix on military matters offers history as a guide for the earl's already established military career. Furthermore, in dedicating his translation to Queen Elizabeth, Savile announces not only the loyalist interests shaping his translation but also his awareness of the queen's interest in Tacitus: "The cause that I published [this translation] under your Majesties name and protection (beside the testification of my bounden duetie) was the great account your Highnesse most worthily holdeth this Historie in."[47] While the occasion surely dictates the tone and part of the content of Savile's address, nevertheless he writes, beyond occasion-driven rhetoric, as one who is convinced of the queen's familiarity with and affection for Tacitus. She holds Tacitus, as he goes on to claim, in "great account" and, indeed, her writings frequently adopt the dense, epigrammatic Tacitean prose style.[48]

Tacitus, at least as presented both by Savile in his dedication to Elizabeth and by Essex in the 1598 preface, offers a useful model for diplomatic education. In a letter to Robert Naunton, discussed by Paul E. J. Hammer, Essex spells out this utility: "rules and patternes of pollecy are aswell learned out of olde Greeke and Romayne storyes as out of states which are at thys daye." Essex, Hammer writes, "worked hard at extracting guidance for his future actions from both kinds of sources," Greek and Roman, Homeric and Tacitean.[49] Further evidence for Essex's interest in comparative models of sovereignty and governance, at stake in his reading of Tacitus, appears in his advice to his cousin, the earl of Rutland, as he begins his travels. Essex tells him,

> above all things I would have you understand the manner of government of the place where you are. Where the sovereignty is, in one as in a monarchy, in a few, or in the people: or if it be mixed, to which of these forms it most inclines. Next what ministers of State and subalternate governors as counsaile and magistrate. Thirdly, by what laws or customes it is governed. And lastly, what is the position of justice in peace and their discipline in war.[50]

Essex's anatomy of government, ranging from magistrates to laws to the military, fills the translations of Tacitus, which not only offered support for resisting tyranny and upholding the liberties of subjects but also contained military wisdom and advice on leadership. Savile echoes these sentiments in his own letter of advice to Rutland, writing of the necessity for instruction: "above all other books be conversant in histories, for they will best instruct you in matters moral, politicke, and military, by which and in which you must ripen and settle your judgment."[51]

In 1599, at the time of the *Henry IV*'s initial publication, then, Essex was a highly appropriate choice of dedicatee, given his association with Tacitean and military history in the prior years. Celebrating Essex as a military hero in the text's dedication, Hayward also offers the earl the same Tacitean "lively patterns" as Grenewey had done the year before.[52] These lively patterns are not simply reminiscent of the techniques of the Elizabethan translators of Tacitus; in fact, they are drawn directly in their language. As Lisa Richardson has helped to demonstrate, a significant portion of *Henry IV* comes directly from Savile's translation of the *Histories*.[53] Hayward's history does not merely evoke but literally builds upon the 1590s editions of Tacitus produced by the earl's Oxford allies. By incorporating such large sections of classical history, Hayward was, as J. J. Manning writes in his edition of *Henry IV*, "the first after Savile's 1591 translation of Tacitus to develop in English the implications of Tacitean historiography on a British topic" (36). Hayward himself acknowledges these classical and domestic debts in the "Epistle Apologeticall" to his second edition. Referring to the allegations of sedition that were brought against his text, he writes that he has "purposely passed over many imputations, as some secrete sences, which the deepe searchers of our time have rather framed then found, partly upon the science of myne owne conscience, and partly seeing no reason wherefore they should be more applied to this book, then to the originall authors out of which it hath been gathered" (65). Why should his text attract more suspicion, he asks, than the "originall authors" he has "gathered"? He defends his text by suggesting that it is merely the copy of another's original.

Hayward as Civilian

Beyond Hayward's Tacitism, the most potent evidence challenging the state's case concerns Hayward's association with civil law. His professional allegiance is universally ignored in analyses that place *Henry IV* next to Shakespeare's *Richard II* as an exemplary site of Elizabethan censorship. While his training and practice as a civil lawyer has been overlooked, his method of history writing exhibits a clear debt to this civilian training. Reexamining Hayward within the context of this broad professional movement, at once royalist and yet threatening to the crown, disabuses readers of the notion that *Henry IV* served as a straightforward political polemic. Instead, the 1599 text raised sensitive political questions in the form of historical debates, the very manner in which civilians were trained. In particular, civilians were taught to question the nature of sovereignty in order to determine its prerogatives. They followed the lead of continental political theorists, among them French absolutist thinkers such as Jean Bodin who had been grappling with questions of sovereignty throughout the sixteenth century.[54] Still, English debates had only begun to define the parameters of monarchical power. English civil lawyers in the 1590s freshly inter-rogated political issues that had occupied classical and continental thinkers before them, debating questions such as a monarch's relation to the law and the duty of a subject to the crown. Indeed, the civil law as contained in Justinian's *Digest* "encouraged its readers to inquire into the nature of sovereignty, to ask where it was located in the state, and to determine exactly the relationship of the king to the law," as Brian P. Levack notes in his studies of civil lawyers in England.[55] Not only did these lawyers raise potent questions about English monarchy but also, because civil lawyers were trained in foreign source texts, they debated definitions of sovereignty that diverged from domestic mod-els. In questioning the nature of sovereignty, then, the civil lawyers commonly juxtaposed alternate theories or practices gathered from domestic, continental, and classical precedent.

Hayward used the style of argumentation typical of civil law in de-picting the debate over deposition in *Henry IV*. Rather than promote resistance theory or allegorically represent the earl of Essex, he pro-duced instead a form of domestic history that employed civilian ar-guments on sovereignty. His history significantly dramatized these sovereignty debates, marshaling the rhetorical power of the invented speech to create a form of history that proved highly popular once in print. Bringing his historical characters to life, he modeled political de-bate, not seditious behavior, through his "lively patterns." His text sets the arguments of absolutist and resistance theorists next to each other, reproducing two strains of contemporary thinking on the place of the monarch in relation to her subjects and the law. Unlike resistance or absolutist theory, however, which both take an extreme position in such arguments, Hayward's own text refrained from explicit judg-ment. Instead, he participated in the conventional professional prac-tice of weighing the various definitions of sovereignty, studying rather than advocating them.

Placing the archbishop of Canterbury's speech within the broader narrative of *Henry IV*, Canterbury's set piece appears as only part of a polemic debating the nature of sovereignty. While the archbishop pre-sents one side of the debate on deposition, the history also contains the companion set piece, spoken by the bishop of Carlisle, arguing against rebellion. When Bolingbroke and his supporters are poised to take the throne from Richard, Carlisle enters to voice his passionate defense of the monarch. His extended speech contrasts English monarchy to the governments of foreign lands, where resistance is often justified. In England, Carlisle argues, the prince is the sovereign majesty and therefore beyond the reproach of his subjects. Kings "have their rule and authority immedyatly from God," and "no power within theyr dominion is superior to theirs" (145). The archbishop forcefully claims of Richard, "although for his vices he bee unprofitable to the subjectes, yea hurtfull, yea intollerable: yet can they [his subjects] lawfully neyther harme his person nor hazard his power, whether by judgement, or els by force. For neyther one nor all magistrates have any authority over the prince, from whome all authority is derived. . . . As for force, what subjecte can attempt, or assist, or counsaile, or conceale violence against hys prince, and not incurre the high and heynous crime of treason?" (143–44). Insisting on the authority of the king over his subjects and the law, Carlisle argues that even if Richard were a tyrant his subjects would be forbidden to rise up against him, for subjects have a legal obligation to obey their ruler: "can they lawfully neither harme his person nor hazard his power."

Pushing his argument to encompass even the "intollerable" monarch, he vehemently condemns resistance either by "force" or "judgement." Further, he argues for the sovereign power of the anointed king, claiming that kings "have their rule and authority immedyatly from God, which if they abuse, they are not to bee adjudged by theyr subjects, for no power within theyr dominion is superior to theirs" (145). While Bolingbroke's party attempts to ground their rebellion in the king's position under the law, Carlisle hollows out such claims, saying "neyther one nor all magistrates have any authority over the prince." Despite Bolingbroke's earlier attempt to avoid the charge of traitor by emphasizing his loyalty to the state over the crown, Carlisle now charges him with treason.

Carlisle's speech expresses a theory of sovereignty that closely follows Jean Bodin's 1576 *Six livres de la république*. Bodin's understanding of sovereignty countered Huguenot theories of resistance by arguing that no subject has the right to resist a legitimate sovereign, even if the sovereign were a tyrant. In lines that could serve as an exact source for Carlisle's speech, Bodin writes that it is illegal for "any subject individually, or all of them in general, to make an attempt on the honor or the life of the monarch, either by way of force or by way of law, even if he has committed all the misdeeds, impieties, and cruelties that one could mention."[56] Subjects may not resist their sovereign, regardless of the "cruelty" of his or her reign. Bodin further argues that the sovereign alone makes the law, since, just as Carlisle claims in his speech, "no power within theyr dominion is superior to theirs." Bodin's belief in unlimited sovereignty circulated widely at Cambridge, where Hayward received his B.A. in 1581. Writing in 1579, during Hayward's tenure, Gabriel Harvey remarked of Cambridge, "You can not stepp into a schollers study but (ten to one) you shall lightly finde open either Bodin de Republica or Le Royes Exposition uppon Aristotles Politics."[57] This widespread popularity of Bodin among students helps to verify Hayward's familiarity with his absolutist arguments.

Just as Canterbury's support for deposition reveals a debt to resistance theories, so, too, does Carlisle's defense of Richard echo Bodin's monarchism. Balancing oppositional and royalist arguments, *Henry IV* offers its readers a study in contemporary sovereignty theory. Hayward himself insisted on the pairing of these speeches, indicating his methodological debt to his profession when he defended his history before the crown. In his examination he concedes to the Lord Keeper that "the stories mentioned in the archbishop's oration, tending to prove that deposers of kings and princes have had good success, were not taken out of any other chronicle, but inserted by himself; afterwards in the history the Bishop of Carlisle confutes the same."[58] Hayward conveys that the speeches of Canterbury and Carlisle function as two sides of a debate. If Canterbury, in his speech, is "tending to prove" deposition, Carlisle "confutes" him in a manner typical of legal disputes. The balancing of these arguments does not indicate Hayward's implicit support for Canterbury's radical argument. In fact, comparing the two speeches, the author appears to weight the argument toward Carlisle: while Hayward cannot alter the historical triumph of Bolingbroke's party, he nevertheless orders the speeches to give greater weight to the second (in the style of Tacitus). Further, he develops Carlisle's argument over several pages, making his speech twice as long as Canterbury's. Carlisle's attack on his opponent's earlier argument potently refutes the resistance theory so offensive to Elizabeth's ministers, as Hayward himself indicates in his testimony: his word "confutes" implies the total confusion or confounding of the opposition.

The shared political affiliation of civil lawyers also challenges the depiction of Hayward as a radical theorist. A royalist allegiance was intrinsic to the profession of civil law under Elizabeth and James. In debates about royal power, civil lawyers overwhelmingly supported the monarchy. Indeed, in Elizabeth's reign, as Levack notes, civil lawyers had acquired a reputation as "Her Majesties right and trusty friends," an affiliation with the monarch that continued under James.[59] Working for the bishops, civil lawyers were indirectly controlled by the crown, which partially accounts for their political views. In a famous anecdote in the case against Hayward, Queen Elizabeth doubted that a civil lawyer had written this allegedly seditious text. Recalling his conversation with the queen about Hayward's *Henry IV,* Francis Bacon writes: "when the Queen would not be persuaded that it was his writing whose name was to it, but that it had some more mischievous author, and said with great indignation that she would have him racked to produce his author, I replied, Nay Madam, he is a Doctor, never rack his person, but rack his stile; let him have pen, ink, and paper, and help of books, and be enjoined to continue the story where it breaketh off, and I will undertake by collecting the stiles to judge whether he were the author or no."[60] This anecdote has served as evidence of Elizabeth's despotic willingness to torture an author—"rack his person." More important for this case, the incident raises an obvious yet rarely asked question: why would she doubt Hayward's authorship at all? Why did she have such difficulty being "persuaded that it was his writing whose name was to it"?

Believing that the history was the product of some "more mischievous author," Elizabeth perceives Hayward as an unlikely source for radical political expression. Her hesitation to associate him with mischief strongly argues for her faith in his royalism. A civil lawyer would be expected to support rather than challenge her office, particularly because most civil lawyers worked for the bishops, whom the crown controlled. Bacon's response helps to support this reading, for he also views Hayward in terms of his profession, claiming "he is a Doctor, never rack his person, but rack his stile." Unlike other political prisoners, among them resistance writers, this Doctor of Law should be spared torture. Bacon's anecdote serves as evidence that Hayward was defined by his professional role as a lawyer and that this association with the law helped to protect him from torture.[61]

Hayward's legal studies, completed in 1591 when he was awarded the degree of Doctor of Law from Cambridge, verifies Elizabeth's perception of him as a "right and trusty friend." Trained in the law of

Mile End Library

Borrowed Items 02/02/2012 14:37
XXXXXX6020

Item Title	Due Date
S...	01/03/2012
...	18/02/2012

Amount Outstanding : £1.50

Rome, civil lawyers like Hayward differed from their professional rivals, the common lawyers (among them Coke) who insisted upon the primacy of the common law or ancient constitution. Unlike the common law, Roman law consisted primarily of the Justinianic code, which at the time was believed to support the autocratic power of the monarch, as claimed in the *Institutes*: "quod principi placuit legis habet vigorem" (what pleases the prince has the force of the law).[62] Civil lawyers trained in the Justinianic code applied this legal theory to defend the king's prerogative in England; specifically, they applied the attributes of the Roman emperor's office to English monarchy. The legal delineation of the office of emperor in the *Corpus Juris Civilis* argued against any form of disobedience, since the emperor was neither elected nor subject to popular critique. As Levack notes, "the Justinianic code stated unequivocally that the Roman people had transferred their authority and power to the emperor."[63] Like the emperor, the civilians argued, the English monarch inherits the throne by birthright or royal election, and therefore he or she rules independent of public opinion.

Hence civil lawyers were a political asset to the state, providing a legal defense against resistance theory arguments.[64] Hayward was no exception. His first publication after his release from imprisonment, a 1603 pamphlet, entitled *An Answer to a Conference concerning Succession*, offers a royalist argument, applying the Justinianic code to support English monarchy. Its strident royalism has led to its wholesale dismissal as mere propaganda. As one critic has argued, the pamphlet, like Hayward's other texts produced following his imprisonment, are "mere ambitious attempts to draw upon their author some share of court notice and favour."[65] Certainly Hayward had an unmistakable motive for seeking royal support, having been imprisoned by the former monarch and recently freed by James. Although he undoubtedly attempted to please the king with *An Answer*, scholars are misguided when they interpret his pamphlet solely in terms of its relation to the monarch. *An Answer* offers more than opportunistic propaganda, engaging instead with complex source material from the Justinianic code. Moreover, the pamphlet helps to illuminate the political variety of *Henry IV*, given that it displays a similar debt to legal and political texts as the earlier history. Rather than merely change camps, Hayward offers polemical arguments in *An Answer* that complement the earlier political theory in the prose history. The pamphlet thus serves as evidence in assessing the earlier history, offering a fascinating articulation of the author's views of his own condemned text.

The complementary relation between *Henry IV* and *An Answer* first appears when Hayward's pamphlet returns to the contentious matter of the prose history: the deposition of Richard II. In the dedication to *An Answer,* Hayward claims that his pamphlet presents the same central argument as his earlier history: resistance has no legal justification. In both texts he writes to support the "authoritie of Princes, and of succession according to proximitie of bloud: wherein is maintained, that the people have no lawfull power, to remove the one, or repell the other: In which two points I have heretofore also declared my opinion, by publishing the tragicall events which ensued the deposition of King Richard, and usurpation of King Henrie the fourth."[66] By revisiting the contentious material of *Henry IV,* he risks reminding his audience of his suspected sedition under Elizabeth. He takes this risk, apparently, in the interest of asserting his misunderstood viewpoint. Just as the current pamphlet proves "that the people have no lawfull power" to remove the king, so, too, he claims, did *Henry IV* where he "also declared [his] opinion." His prose history was a publication on "tragicall events," supporting the "authority of princes." Ignoring Elizabeth's suspicions about the history, he recuperates his misinterpreted and censored text by insisting on its royalist arguments.

In his retrospective reading of *Henry IV,* Hayward insists that both his history and his pamphlet argue against deposition with equal force. Yet, despite his claims, the prose history lacks the power of the didactic voice that distinguishes *An Answer.* Thus, when he returns to the issue of Richard's deposition later in the pamphlet, he does so with clarity that is absent from his earlier history. He writes, "the deposition of King Richard the second was a tempestuous rage, neither led nor restrained by any rules of reason or of state; not sodainely raised and at once, but by very cunning and artificiall degrees."[67] The nobility, by the "evil-guided strength of their will" in deposing Richard, produce "their owne headlong destruction" since upon the "occasion of this disorder more English blood was spent then was in all the forren wars which had ben since the conquest."[68] Chronologically, Hayward extends his analysis far beyond the material covered in the first part of *Henry IV.* He argues (as he does in the unpublished manuscript version of the second half of *Henry IV*) that the "usurpation" of Henry IV brought a scourge on his house in the form of the ensuing civil war. If

Richard II's fiscal extravagance is traditionally one of the most telling charges leveled against him, Hayward counters that Henry spent not money but "English blood," a far more precious commodity. As J. J. Manning writes, "the sequel text reveals an historian as cheerless about Henry as he had been in *The First Part* about Richard and his flatterers."[69] In *An Answer,* Hayward adopts the polemical style appropriate for political pamphleteering, wielding hyperbole and vitriol to depict the tragedy of deposition.

If *Henry IV* addresses the reign of Richard II without the vitriol of *An Answer,* nevertheless both writings exhibit a similar debt to legal and political theories drawn from civilian training. Like Carlisle's speech in *Henry IV, An Answer* relies on a Bodinian conception of sovereignty. Specifically *An Answer* challenges Persons's *Conference.* Like Canterbury, Carlisle's polemical opposite in *Henry IV,* Persons persuades his listeners that subjects may lawfully depose an incompetent prince, given that loyalty belongs to the state, not to the crown. When Persons claims, as noted by Hayward, that "the common wealth is superior to the prince," he is employing logic similar to that of Canterbury's speech in the prose history. Like Carlisle, Hayward, in *An Answer,* refutes this resistance theory with the legal argument supporting monarchy. He condemns Persons in claiming that "in a word, to the contrary of this your impudent untruth, our laws do acknowledge supreme authority in the prince within the realme and dominions of england, neither can subjects beare themselves either superior or equall to their soveraigne; or attempt violence either against his person or estate, but as well the civill law, as the particulare lawes and customes of all countries do adjudge it high and hainous treason."[70] By combining the classical tradition of civil law with the "particular lawes and customes" of England, Hayward offers a comprehensive legal defense of the right of kings. Any challenge to the "supreme authority in the prince" constitutes "high and hainous treason." His forceful defense in *An Answer* does not necessarily position the king above the law, yet he claims that "our laws do acknowledge the supreme authority in the prince," a phrase that defers to the law in creating the office of the monarch. Therefore, in order to obey the law, one must respect the superiority of the monarch's office. Legally undercutting the assertions of his opponent, Hayward's case hinges on the same logic as Carlisle's: authority derives from the sovereign and cannot be challenged by his subjects. As Carlisle asks, "what subjecte can attempt . . . violence against hys prince, and not incurre the high and heynous crime of treason?" Following Bodin both in *Henry IV* and *An Answer,* Hayward supports the power of the sovereign over resistance because he believes that a state avoids disorder and violence only when it has a strong ruler. He offers the deposition of Richard II as a case study in the dangers of resistance: out of his deposition emerged the civil war of the following century.

Hayward gained political capital in writing *An Answer,* but the pamphlet also exhibits his intellectual investment as much as his political one. Comparing *Henry IV* and *An Answer* helps us to forge a new understanding of Hayward as a man consistently engaged with his professional source texts. Both works argue in favor of absolute sovereignty by exposing the dangers of deposition. Rejecting the interpretation of Elizabeth's council, Hayward uses *An Answer* to insist on his own royalist intentions in the earlier debacle over *Henry IV.* Both texts also display a methodological debt to civilian models of debate. Indeed, *Henry IV* offers, in the figures of Carlisle and Canterbury, a dramatic anticipation of Hayward's future challenge to Persons. This later debate with Persons, in which Hayward clearly favors the royalist argument, contrasts with the prose history where he balances political theories. Not surprisingly, his intellectual interest in weighing political philosophies resonant with both Bodin and resistance writers, exhibited in *Henry IV,* ceded by 1603 to a more savvy public articulation of his personal investments. Although the pamphlet, published later, announces Hayward's political allegiance and the earlier prose history does not, the strength of this later articulation should not prevent us from recognizing the common interest in political theory and civilian argument that helps shape these two texts. Hayward's intellectual engagement in his field marks both his Elizabethan and Jacobean writing, proving a long-term interest in civilian matters that transcends the division between his earlier, "seditious" prose history and his later "royalist" polemic.

In the case of "The Crown v. John Hayward," however, the author's practice of imitating civilian modes of argument proved only a liability. In writing for an audience outside his profession, Hayward found that his civilian methods of debating sovereignty alarmed his royal readership. His invented speeches, read out of context, served as evidence against him. Provoking in part the bishop's ban of 1599, as Clegg has argued, the Hayward case exposes how an apparently royalist author was interpreted as seditious by addressing sensitive issues without declaring his own allegiance.[71] Fortunately for Hayward, an influential legal colleague recognized his methods and intervened on his behalf: Francis Bacon, one of the few common lawyers who shared the political affiliation of civilians.[72] Bacon was widely read in the source texts of the civil law, familiar with Justinianic legal codes and the Roman history of Tacitus, and thus able to insist on the influence of these Roman sources on Hayward's form of history. When Queen Elizabeth famously voiced her suspicion that Hayward's *Henry IV* was treasonous, Bacon instead joked of the text "for treason surely I found none, but for felony very many." Asked to elaborate, Bacon added "the author had committed very apparent theft, for he had taken most of the sentences of Cornelius Tacitus, and translated them into English, and put them into his text."[73]

Bacon here interprets *Henry IV* within the context that had framed Hayward's perspective, that of Roman history. In doing so he saves the civilian from the charge of treason. Astute enough to recognize Hayward's debt to Tacitean history, Bacon clears his colleague with a legal defense presented as a witty jest.[74] Presumably Hayward learned better than to rely on one subtle reader to save his life, subsequently producing arguments, as he did with *An Answer,* that explicitly announce his political investment.

Following Bacon's lead in interpreting Hayward in relation to his civilian training encourages modern critics to acknowledge his work as simultaneously royalist and oppositional. For, if *Henry IV* was read by Queen Elizabeth as treasonous, supporting resistance theory against the monarchy, and if much recent criticism has echoed her interpretation, reexamining Hayward within his professional context as a civil lawyer reveals that he, like his colleagues, both supported royal prerogative, as indicated in his first publication under James, and followed the civilian practice of debating the terms and limits of sovereignty. If this practice was exercised in support of the monarch, in Hayward's case it nevertheless excited Elizabeth and her council to such a degree that they imprisoned him for the rest of her reign. Ignorant perhaps of the methods of civil lawyers, Elizabeth's council failed to recognize what was obvious to fellow lawyer Bacon: Hayward's offense in *Henry IV* lay not in inventing speeches, as the state had charged, but instead in failing to invent them. After all, as Bacon claimed, "he had taken most of the sentences of Cornelius Tacitus."

Treason and Interpretation

But what about the apparently damning evidence that the earl, as the crown alleged, not only permitted "underhand that treasonable book of Henry IV to be printed and published," but also was "often present at the playing thereof, and with great applause giving countenance and liking to the same"?[75]

Returning to this accusation against *Henry IV*, rehearsed at the start of this chapter, we can now recognize how a decisive, but critically ignored, interpretive shift took place in 1600 and produced the above reading of Hayward's text. Hayward engaged potentially treasonous ideas within the context of a broader debate on sovereignty, and his historical and legal interest was shared by the earl of Essex and his allies, who themselves had pursued questions of sovereignty through Tacitus earlier in the decade. Such interests had not been deemed treasonous by early 1599, but by 1600 the mere articulation of such a debate in the increasingly militaristic context of the Essex circle drew Elizabeth's suspicions. She now read the activities of the earl of Essex's allies, both intellectual and otherwise, as a threat to her authority. As a result, she made an example of one of them, interrogating Hayward and indefinitely detaining him.

This interpretive shift of 1600, evident in Hayward's detention in that year, also prompted the burning of many of the earl of Essex's books and papers, "lest (as he said) they should tell tales."[76] This image of speaking books that tell tales beyond their own scripted narratives highlights the earl's difficulties; now all words speak against him in the interpretive environment constructed by the state. Indeed, in 1600 the crown exposed the seditious potential of those histories that Essex himself, with Elizabeth's own blessing, had supported throughout the 1590s. Once fallen, the earl was now deemed to have, precisely through such association with tale-telling books, "too much knowledge": as Essex tells the earl of Southampton from prison, "make profitt of my wretched and fearful example. . . . I had too much knowledge, while I performed too little obedience."[77] Essex's advice to Southampton, to "make profitt" of his example, recalls Hayward's own defense of the genre of history as full of "lively patterns . . . wherein young men may be instructed." In his demise, the earl offers himself as a form of historical instruction, cautioning his readers to avoid his own fate and instead value obedience over knowledge.

Alienated as a result of his military defeat and intellectual interests, Essex finally confirmed the queen's suspicions by heading into London with a small crew of armed men on February 8, 1601. As Wallace MacCaffrey describes the event, "depressed and half-mad, obsessed with a persecution mania, fearing for his life—Essex led a tiny band of followers in a pathetic attempt to storm the court."[78] What MacCaffrey dismisses as Essex's "persecution mania" may well have resulted not from his overreaching desires but instead from the sudden, violent shift in the queen's interpretive practices. In her suspicion of classical and domestic history, Elizabeth exposed the radical potential in texts that had formerly circulated in support of the monarch. Following a deconstructive reading initiated by Elizabeth herself, the earl now chose to employ analogical history, which formerly supported his royal military ventures, in his fight against the queen.

Reducing imaginative and historical texts to treasonous manifestos, the state spurred sedition in its potential allies. Elizabeth's dealings with Essex thus reveal the political risks involved in exercising treason law, since her suspicion itself may have prompted, rather than discovered, seditious activity. The very practices that earlier confirmed his loyalty, such as his military ventures in the name of the state and his literary interest in the classical historian favored by Elizabeth herself, now appeared as evidence against him. With no political or economic prospects left at court, Essex capitulated to the queen's reading of events and pursued the treasonous activities she clearly expected. In doing so, Essex's followers reputedly commissioned a play "of Henry IV and of the killing on Richard II," precisely the topic suspected by the crown. This performance, however, has an ironic more than evidentiary status. Having vigorously pursued her own treasonous interpretation of analogical history throughout 1600, Elizabeth herself both constructed and reinforced the famous parallel that her subjects might otherwise never have seen: after all, it is she who claims, "I am Richard II, know ye not that?"[79]

CHAPTER THREE

Shakespeare's Anatomy of Resistance
in Richard II

Queen Elizabeth's famous remark, invoked at the end of the last chapter, brings us to the era's fullest examination of the deposed medieval king: Shakespeare's *Richard II.* This play appeared in an atmosphere where politic histories on Richard II were far from neutral, even before February 7, 1601, the night when the earl of Essex's allies commissioned a performance of "King Henry the Fourth and of the killing of Richard the Second, played by the Lord Chamberlain's players."[1] The rebels' precise relation to Shakespeare's play remains elusive: while the scholarship of Leeds Barroll and Blair Worden has helped to turn our attention away from Shakespeare's play toward Hayward's *Henry IV* as the more likely candidate for the February 7 performance, Shakespeare's version is the only dramatic text on Richard II that stages the king's murder.[2] Furthermore, Hayward's apparent guilt before the Elizabethan regime does not in itself prove that his text is at issue since, as discussed in the previous chapter, the state's charge of sedition relies on ignoring much of his text's argumentation.

While the question of the text performed on February 7 remains unresolved, preoccupation with it obscures the important political work of representations of Richard II in the years before 1601, as Barroll powerfully argues and Margaret Shewring recently discusses.[3] The 1590s was a decade when Essex served as dedicatee for two incendiary texts on Richard II, as analyzed in the previous chapter: Persons's *Conference about the Next Succession to the Crown of England* (1594) and Hayward's *Henry IV* (1599). Placing Shakespeare's play next to these texts helps to illuminate how his representation of the king complements and challenges the polemical representation of Richard II in Persons, while anticipating Hayward's subsequent, more subtle depiction of an arguably tyrannical king illegally deposed by rebellious subjects.

Shakespeare's *Richard II* appeared onstage approximately one year after the publication of Robert Persons's *Conference about the Next Succession*.[4] Surprisingly resonant with Persons's polemical tract, the play's first two acts hint at Richard's alleged murder of Gloucester, and depict his banishment of Bolingbroke and Mowbray, as well as his seizure of Gaunt's estate. The rapid succession of events produces a sense of lawless monarchy evocative of depictions of the king by Shakespeare's more radical contemporaries. Indeed, as Donna Hamilton has argued, Shakespeare's Richard is a tyrant who makes law his bondslave, and thereby opens a path for legitimate resistance to his monarchy.[5] Yet Richard's alleged tyranny, as this chapter claims, has an ironic effect: through his legal infractions, Richard functions as traitor to himself, producing his own opposition through his overzealous use of the law. He thus creates and exonerates the opposition that topples him.

Richard's role in producing treason frustrates readings of him, propounded most vigorously by Richard himself, as a sanctified king tragically unseated from his office. At the same time, Shakespeare does not readily endorse Bolingbroke's rebellion, despite strong critical efforts to highlight the play's radical argument. Instead, the issue of justified resistance proves one of the thorniest in the play. The play's duality clearly anticipates Hayward's 1599 history, which equally divides around its portrait of tyranny and treason, with Hayward defending his text's loyalist arguments against deposition and the state insisting on his treasonous support for rebellion. Shakespeare and Hayward further share a multi-textual approach to the telling of history. The incendiary arguments of Hayward's *Henry IV* stretch into additional installments that help to clarify his authorial focus. The unpublished second half of *Henry IV*, like *The Three Lives of the Norman Kings*, works to complete his more contentious representations introduced in the 1599 history. Hayward's addition could have been written or edited, of course, to clear his name before James after his debacle with Elizabeth. But Shakespeare, too, produces such multi-textual renderings of history, without the prompting of jail or censorship.[6] Both writers position their texts within a long view of civil war history: they explore causes and effects of discord rather than stage an argument for unrest.

In Shakespeare's case, *Richard II* is a drama that argues forcefully against tyranny while at the same time representing the dangers and limitations of violent resistance. Both arguments find fulfillment in portions of the *Henriad*: Richard II's deposition initiates the high road to civil war of the three *Henry VI* plays, as well as the more immediate path to comedy in *I Henry IV*. Given these alternate narrative arcs, Shakespeare's play might seem in danger of fracturing over its discordant impulses. On the one hand, in its depiction of Henry IV's successful bid for the throne, the play represents the arguments of radical theorists who justify resistance to monarchical tyranny, such as Robert Persons and Edmund Campion. On the other hand, especially in its prophetic language on civil discord, it also rehearses political truisms on submission to royal authority familiar to audiences from the Elizabethan *An Homily on Obedience*, read regularly to churchgoers. Rather than fracturing, however, the play produces a meditation on rulership itself, engaging with questions of rule through imaginative expression and inventive conceit. As with *King Lear* and *The Tempest*, Shakespeare dramatizes the problem of obedience raised by difficult leadership: how, the play asks, can subjects respond to bad or tyrannical rule?

In contrast to political polemic, with its exploitation of arguments against tyranny and terror, the play stages the effect of tyranny on a wide range of characters, spanning from gardener to courtier, from child to parent. The political chaos that results as fighting erupts within families and on the battlefield offers more highly defined layers of representation than that available to Shakespeare's contemporary polemicists. We witness the struggles of York, Gaunt, Northumberland, Carlisle, Mowbray, and others to restore some form of legitimate monarchy, however differently each figure may define it. The end result is, most obviously, civil war, and undoubtedly the Wars of the Roses shadow the play. This distant threat hardly compromises the comic plot of Henry's rise to power, however. So Shakespeare highlights a more short-term consequence of monarchical bad rule: he uses the play to represent an anatomy of forms of resistance, none of them entirely effective. These responses range from blind obedience to moderate counsel to strong rebuke to violent action. As will become apparent, the resulting instability caused by both tyranny and rebellion tragically turns moderate and loyal subjects into submissive fools, a transformation that anticipates, and resonates powerfully with, the frustrations, accusations, and arrests that culminate in the Earl of Essex's 1600–1601 treasons.

The Historical Richard II and the Abuse of Law

The deposition of Richard II was an action based on historical and legal precedent. Faced with an allegedly incompetent ruler who increasingly disobeyed the country's laws, Edward II's subjects responded by defending the "crown" or state from the person of the king and his followers. The Declaration of 1308 states that, "homage and oath of allegiance are more by reason of the Crown than by reason of the king's person, and are more bound to the Crown than to the person."[7] Articulating what Bertie Wilkinson calls "the rights of the Crown," the declaration provoked "the consequent development of the concept of an impersonal Crown to which both the king and his subjects owed duties and loyalties."[8]

As a result of this Declaration, ninety years later the historical Bolingbroke and his allies stood on precedent in claiming to protect the "crown" or state against Richard II himself. By the terms of the 1308 Declaration, it was Richard who, in breaking his coronation oath, had threatened the office of the king, a point explored in Richard Firth Green's compelling study of medieval *tresoun* and *trouthe*."[9] As the articles from the Assembly of 1399 read, "the same king refused to keep and defend the just laws and customs of his kingdom, but [wished] at his own arbitrary will to do whatever appealed to his desires. . . . he expressly said, with an austere and determined countenance, that his laws were in his own mouth, or occasionally, in his own breast; and that he alone could establish and change the laws of his realm."[10] Will does not rule over custom, as the 1308 Declaration established, and thus Richard's belief in a Justinianic model of prerogative put him in danger of deposition. As John Bellamy elaborates, "the only king who may have had ideas of extending the law of treason was Richard II. He sought to preserve, define and even increase the royal prerogative."[11] Condemning such increased royal prerogative, the king's adversaries in 1399 repeated and legitimated the 1308 assertion of constitutional rights against absolute sovereignty. J. N. Figgis defines this legal shift as the "Revolution of 1399."[12] The articles of deposition against Richard, he argues, articulate "a theory of constitutionalism as uncompromising as the absolutist doctrine of the king."[13]

Viewed in this historical light, representing the deposition of Richard II is not simply about staging the successful toppling of a legitimate sovereign. It is, more powerfully, about the assertion of one model of monarchy over another: one based in the rights of the state and rule of law, the other in the supremacy of royal prerogative. Shakespeare's source texts, including the chronicles of Holinshed, Hall, and the anonymous *Mirror for Magistrates*, emphasize these constitutional stakes of Richard II's reign and deposition. The king ignores the law: he "renteth ryght and law a sunder," he ignored "vertue, ryght, or lawe," and he governed so "neither law, justice nor equitie could take place."[14] Ignoring law and right, Richard glories in his own will instead. He "always put false Flatterers most in trust," he indulged his "willful will."[15] Replacing law with will, Richard governs from his own mouth and devises, as Holinshed writes, a "new oath" for his leige people to gain "further assurance of their due obedience." As a result, many of his subjects were, "through spite, envie, and malice, accused, apprehended, and put in prison" (496). Crime emerges from the shifting and unstable monarchical act of naming (Richard's "envie and malice") rather than from a subject's act of violence under the law. Dermot Cavanagh highlights this aspect of Holinshed, writing that treason is made "to accommodate changes in the disposition of power, rather than embody a consistent concept of justice."[16] Historians such as Holinshed, in representing Richard's abuse of law, custom, and right, demonstrate how laws, as Annabel Patterson writes, "particularly at this stage in history were subject to sudden and continuous change."[17] Such change under Richard often occurred in the interest of bolstering royal prerogative at the expense of custom.

Shakespeare's source texts are nuanced, however, in criticizing Richard's abuse of law. Emphasizing Richard's suspension or manipulation of law and his willful rule, these historical chronicles equally stress the horrors of deposition. These English historians are never polemical or univocal in their depictions of Richard. As a result, as is the case later with Hayward, historical accounts betray competing impulses, as Phyllis Rackin illuminates: they depict Richard's deposition both as "a transgression against God for which the entire country would have to suffer" and as a product of "Richard's faults and errors as a ruler."[18] Yet while Rackin, like Cavanagh and Patterson, teases out the crucial complexities of English historical chronicles, the resistance theorist Robert Persons just uses such historical chronicles as rich fodder for his oppositional theory. As a result, he politicizes the representation of Richard's reign, turning the balanced portrait of constitutional versus absolute monarchy into the material of resistance.

Seeking to prove the contractual nature of the coronation oath, Persons turns to Stowe: "(saith Stowe) 'to remember the oath which he [Henry IV] voluntarily made . . .' hereby we come to learne, what oath the kings of England do make at their coronations" (115–16); proving monarchical debt to law, he turns to Holinshed: "both Holinshead and others do testify, in these English stories, in these very words, to wit 'That he [the king] will during his life . . . administer law and justice equally to all and take away all unjust lawes'" (116); on the issue of Yorkist support for Richard's deposition, he cites a host of historians: "so do write both Stow Hollingshead and other chroniclers of Ingland, that those princes of the house of Yorke, did principally assist Henry duke of Lancaster in getting the crown" (2:63). To this Persons concludes, "all this, I say, is an evident argument that these princes of the house of Yorke were then the chiefe doers in this deposition and consequently cannot alleage now with reason that the said Richard was deposed unjustly" (2:64).

Persons's technique here is easily recognized. He frames each quote with his polemical stance, be it on Richard's lawful deposition or the Lancastrian's legitimate claim to the throne. He then cites a small portion of these English histories and ends by restating his argument as theirs: "all this . . . is an evident argument," "as both Holinshed and others do testify." This tactic turns historical sources into political polemics. He cites them as if his own argument were contained entirely within their pages, despite the fact that these histories show no interest in the specific and highly incendiary issue that fuels Persons's pamphlet: forwarding a Spanish Catholic successor to the throne.

Texts that are multivocal on the issues of succession, deposition, and legitimate resistance become, in his hands, support for deposition of tyrannical kings and the succession of the Infanta. Furthermore, Persons schematizes Richard and Bolingbroke to such a degree that they represent two entirely oppositional political poles: Richard is "a tyrant, a Tiger, a fearse Lion, a ravening wolfe, a publique enemy, and a bloody murtherer" (2:61), whereas Lancaster is a force of God, "to do justice in His name" (2:68), appointed "by universal consent of the parliament and people there present" (2:60): thanks "that God hath seemed to prosper and allow much more of those of Lancaster than those of York" (2:97–98). Given such an opposition, Richard's subjects have every right to depose him: "the common wealth which gave them [princes] ther authority for the common good of al, may also restrayne or take the same away agayne, if they abuse it to the common evil" (2:72).

Persons offers the constitutional argument writ large and radicalized, shaping monarchical rule as a contract drawn up for the "common good." This contract lies in the hands of the commonwealth itself, meaning that subjects determine not only when to "give" and when to "restrayne or take away" monarchical power, but also what constitutes "common good" and "common evil." Persons employs an inexorable logic: if Richard rules by will, not law (as Holinshed and others verify), then he breaks the oath of office (an oath also invoked in these historical sources); if Richard breaks this oath, the commonwealth can "take away" his office in the name of the common good. As a result of such logic, Persons unavoidably politicizes stories of Richard II. After 1594, no sooner does Richard appear as "a tyrant, a Tiger, a fearse Lion, a ravening wolfe," but the solution to this crisis—deposition—becomes inevitable, customary, and logical. Indeed, Persons's solution is powerful enough to break down multivalent texts for use in his own reapplications. It is into this popular polemical master plot that Shakespeare enters one year later with his play on Richard II.

Born to Command: Shakespeare's Richard

Richard II opens with the notorious event that led to the king's downfall: the confrontation of Richard, Mowbray, and Bolingbroke over the earl of Gloucester's death.[19] Opening with this compromising incident, Shakespeare does little to recuperate the king from the attacks against him lodged in Persons's polemic. Even if ignorant of Persons's text, Shakespeare creates a play so strongly resonant with the pamphlet that it seems to stack the deck in favor of resistance.

First, Shakespeare draws attention to this opening conflict as a constitutional crisis concerning the nature of treason, law, and obedience, as Persons had done the year before him. The first speeches of the play, as Mowbray, Bolingbroke, and Richard confront one another over the death of Gloucester, question the definition of treason. Each views the other as a challenge to the peace, and they forward competing definitions of loyalty and treason in their accusations. To Bolingbroke, Mowbray is the traitor for murdering Gloucester: "thou art a traitor and a miscreant" (1.1.39), "with a foul traitor's name stuff I thy throat" (44), "false traitor" (91), "traitor, foul and dangerous" (1.3.39). To Mowbray, Bolingbroke is the traitor for bringing this charge before the king: "these terms of treason" are "doubled down his throat" (2.2.57); Bolingbroke is "a recreant and most degenerate traitor" (144), "a traitor to my God, my king and me" (1.3.24). Indeed, the play's competing definitions of treason are so prevalent that, as Cavanagh argues, the play's "principal conflict might well be characterized as a struggle over the authority to define the offense."[20] Treason is not a clearly defined legal category in the play. Instead, the crime shifts with sovereign power, as Cavanaugh illuminates, and its definition expands to include attacks on king, state, and subjects committed either in action or language.

Opening the play with this legal crisis, Shakespeare then depicts Richard's tyranny, again echoing Persons. Believing he was "not born to sue but to command" (1.1.196), he interrupts the trial-by-battle in the third scene and thus disregards legal ceremony.[21] Having commissioned Gloucester's murder, Richard cannot have his courtiers raise the issue in a court of law: to preempt the legal proceedings, the king banishes these men. Richard might attempt to justify such extralegal action on Justinianic grounds: the laws are in his mouth.[22] Yet other characters repeatedly remind us that the laws in England should not be the creation of the king alone. Bolingbroke, in demanding his legal rights, claims to "challenge law" (2.3.134), while Gaunt tells Richard, "thy state of law is bondslave to the law" (2.1.114), highlighting the interdependence of monarchical government and common law. In trespassing law, Richard enslaves or, as Gaunt elaborates, binds himself: England under Richard is "bound in with shame, / With inky blots and rotten parchment bonds" (2.1.63–64). Shame and servitude, not custom, define the state of law in Richardian England.

Such tyranny arguably pales in significance next to Richard's tragic fall. Forker, for example, argues that the play "enacts a martyrdom, however partially self-induced—a 'passion' that makes the comparisons to Christ and Pilate something more than childish or absurd hyperboles."[23] Forker's emphasis on Richard's Christological martyrdom is surprising given his comparison of the play with Marlowe's Edward

II precisely along the lines of kingly culpability. In both plays the audiences are "alienated by the willful irresponsibility of the title figure in the early scenes and then gradually drawn into sympathy with him as he loses first his crown and then his life" (81–82). These readings evoke how Richard is both culpable and beyond reproach. In other words, the sympathy he evokes at the end of the play has the effect of rendering his earlier infractions irrelevant: he is a martyr no matter how irresponsibly he governs. As Naomi Conn Liebler puts it, even if the king's cancellation of the scheduled joust "appears to illustrate his inability to rule," he cannot be culpable for the rebellion that follows: "It is frivolous to attribute the toppling of whole social and political structures to one individual, even to a king."[24]

Liebler's depiction of Richard as an "individual" deflects attention from the legal foundation of sovereign power that shapes Richard as a representative, not an individual. But both she and Forker articulate a central problem for scholars of Richard II: how can we reconcile the play's representation of Richard in the first half as a tyrannical, incapable ruler with the second half, when the king appears, largely through his own imaginative conceits, as a singularly tragic hero? In other words, where should we place our scholarly emphasis: on the culpable king who provokes and indeed justifies rebellion or on the anointed king who is martyred by traitors?

"A thousand well-disposed hearts": Obedient Resistance in Richard's England

These questions draw attention to the affective opposition between the earlier and later portraits of Richard: as the audience, we find ourselves increasingly moved by this errant king, experiencing his fall as tragedy. This affective or emotional shift does not, however, represent a shift in Richard's political philosophy. Indeed, Richard's final scenes are much more resonant with his initial ones than the play's fractured structure might invite us to believe. Before his fall, Richard attempts to exercise a hyperbolic model of divine right kingship. This exercise continues, under wildly different circumstances, even after his fall.[25] From the first act to the last, Richard lies, he abuses the law, he murders, and he banishes his courtiers. In short, he continues his tyranny to the end. Christopher Highley draws attention to this destructive arc, writing that "Shakespeare presents Richard's Irish sojourn as one more of the king's 'fierce blaze of riot[s]' and a prelude to his wanton self-destruction."[26]

Of course, given the play's emotional and poetic range, interest in the king's political consistency might seem misplaced. Yet it is worth paying attention to the play's political rather than emotive trajectory because, in depicting Richard's tyranny as consistent and unwavering, the play's political solutions to such abuse of power are surprisingly imaginative. These solutions are also quite easily overlooked, since they are found not through the drama of Richard but through the struggles of the host of minor characters adapting to or challenging the king's rule. Shakespeare's use of such secondary characters contrasts with Persons's own technique in *A Conference,* where he simply points to Lancaster as the historical and political solution to the crisis of tyranny. Shakespeare follows Persons's argumentation to a degree. Read one way, the play opens with a culpable Richard as a means of building its argument for Bolingbroke: tyranny provokes legitimate, active resistance. But unlike Persons, who focuses solely on the active resistance typified by Bolingbroke, Shakespeare both refuses to dismiss Richard as a mere tyrant and radically expands notions of resistance through use of other courtiers whose responses to the king range from passive to vocal to violent. The dramatic form supports, and indeed requires, such imaginative experimentation. Here, characters' speeches are not merely set pieces, articulating positions from political philosophy. Instead, these characters shape a more moving drama, a poetics, about the causes and effects of political chaos. Beyond the polar opposition of Bolingbroke and Richard, other subjects offer various methods of resistance in an attempt to influence the wayward king through more moderate means. Shakespeare, as a result, shapes what one might call an anatomy of resistance: resistance represented in multiple forms, through characters more minor than Bolingbroke but nevertheless crucial to the play's form.

The play begins to sketch such an anatomy by locating attempts at resistance in the tongue rather than the sword. Good counsel and frank expression are offered as risky, loyal, and courageous forms of opposition. Such speech is not easy, as the play repeatedly reminds us. Indeed, difficulties in speaking might be seen naturally to dominate the play: at the level of plot, characters plan an illegal rebellion against tyrannical sovereignty, and therefore guard their speech; at the level of performance, Shakespeare stages a play on the deposition of a king to popular audiences, a potentially incendiary activity requiring tact and caution.

Yet one of the more surprising features of Shakespeare's play is precisely the degree to which characters *do* speak freely, even when they deliver unpopular or dangerous news; that is, characters speak freely even against their own immediate political welfare, continually taking chances with their speech. This is not only the case with the oppositional Bolingbroke. Ross vows to "break with silence" before he indulges his "liberal tongue" (2.1.229), and yet he proceeds nevertheless to catalogue the king's bankruptcy. Mowbray, curbed "from giving reigns and spurs to [his] free speech" (1.1.55), proceeds to accuse Bolingbroke and complains to the king. By staging characters who acknowledge the difficulty of speaking freely while doing precisely that, Shakespeare manages to have it both ways. He indicates the dangers of free speech even as he practices it, both through the individual characters and through the activity of staging the play in the first place.

In Gaunt and York, Shakespeare fully develops this model of courageous speech. Each man acknowledges the difficulty of speaking only to deliver his notorious criticisms of the king. Gaunt hopes that his pain will make his words more potent: "they breath truth that breathe their words in pain" (2.1.8).[27] Gaunt decries how,

> This blessed plot, this earth, this realm, this England
> This nurse, this teeming womb of royal kings,
>
> . . . .
>
> This land of such dear souls, this dear dear land,
> Dear for her reputation throughout the world,
> Is now leased out—I die pronouncing it—
> Like to a tenement or a pelting farm.
>
> (2.1.50–60)

Gaunt's images of fertile reproduction ("teeming womb") and fallen commerce ("leased out . . . like to a tenement or a pelting farm") supply the vocabulary over which Richard and Bolingbroke will wrangle for the remainder of the play. Here, Gaunt contrasts his nostalgic vision of noble, fertile England, a pre-lapsarian land that his predecessors, like himself, cherished, with his current view of England as a commercially bankrupt state, a fallen, modern world created by Richard.

Gaunt's vocabulary evolves over the course of the play, however, in a manner that surprisingly alters his ideological and temporal oppositions. Although Gaunt celebrates, in a fashion that upholds the Kantorowiczian model of sanctified kingship, the formerly "blessed plot" over the current "pelting farm," the play increasingly associates the "teeming womb" with Richard's contaminated generativity. Plotting to farm the realm and institute blank charters, Richard's admittedly "liberal largess" and "too great . . . court" suggest a reign based in desire, rather than on law or custom. Gaunt's verbal daring provokes Richard to proclaim that, were it not for Gaunt's lineage, "This tongue that runs so roundly in thy head / Should run thy head from thy unreverent shoulders!" (2.1.122–23), a reminder of the precise stakes in speaking boldly in an atmosphere of tyranny.

The transgression of law and custom condemned by Gaunt preoccupies York in the play's second, most hard-hitting criticism of Richard. Initially speaking in an aside, reluctant to "bend one wrinkle on [his] sovereign's face" (2.1.170), York describes how he is "too far gone with grief" (184) and thus speaks more freely and with less restraint than he would like. York's resulting speech seems at once a heartfelt yet reluctantly expressed counsel in which he tells Richard exactly how he undermines his crown by seizing Bolingbroke's estate. York ends by saying,

If you do wrongfully seize Hereford's rights,
Call in the letters patents that he hath
By his attorneys-general to sue
His livery, and deny his offered homage,
You pluck a thousand dangers on your head,
You lose a thousand well-disposed hearts
And prick my tender patience to those thoughts
Which honour and allegiance cannot think.
                                        (2.1.201–8)

The ways in which these lines inversely resonate with Gaunt's earlier speech on bankruptcy foregrounds the destructive generativity of Richard's rule: by pricking York's patience, Richard fathers the thoughts that York's mind reluctantly births.[28] David Norbrook has termed York's speech a "moment of anti-climax" before Northumberland's more dramatic speech. Further, Norbrook claims, York's "often-protested patience . . . is coming to seem more and more like cowardice," particularly when compared to Northumberland, who represents "the agent of a different policy, crossing the threshold to active resistance."[29] Furthermore, to Peter Ure, York's speech offers less content than legal filler: "These lines would not be immediately intelligible to an audience, but Shakespeare, copying Holinshed, did not worry about this: a little legal jargon sounds well on the stage."[30]

Yet this dismissal of York's speech discounts the value of such legal language. First, York's speech participates in the discourse of inheritance running throughout the play, as William O. Scott establishes.[31] Furthermore, this speech articulates a radical theory of treason: the counselor locates the crime in the monarch's own extralegal actions. Specifically, when Shakespeare's Richard claims Bolingbroke's inheritance, the king punishes the duke as if he were a traitor, condemned to relinquish his property not by a court ruling but instead by forfeiture of war.[32] York's speech, importantly, informs Richard, and the lay audience, that by ignoring the legal parameters governing the charge of treason the king creates the very criminal who will topple him. Exiled and disinherited, Bolingbroke will have, in attacking Richard, little left to lose. Richard's extralegal policy also, as York claims, undermines his own right to the throne, which is established through the process of lawful succession. This connection of the king and law resonates not only with theories of sovereignty that are familiar from Bracton but also with the resistance theories of Persons: "to seize property," he writes, is to "overthroweth the whole nature of a commonwealth itself, and maketh al subjects to be but very slaves" (68). Here, Persons's civil lawyer argues that the right to private property, to "dominion" over one's estate, constitutes the founding principle of a commonwealth, and to seize such property is to threaten the state itself.

Provoking a constitutional crisis, Richard nonetheless ignores York and Gaunt, and instead names traitor after traitor. In doing so, he effectively produces the army of his own opposition. First, when Bolingbroke is "gelded of his patrimony" (2.1.237) and thus suffers the fate of disinherited traitors, Northumberland, Ross, and Willoughby revolt.[33] When they, too, like Bolingbroke, are "proclaimed traitors" (2.2.56–57), Worcester then deserts the king and turns traitor. Instead of stunting the growth of opposition, Richard's use of the treason charge has the very opposite effect: where it should prevent treason, it encourages it; where it should destroy opposition, it creates it.[34]

Richard's perverse productivity in generating traitors is the opposite of true succession, as its name in legal theory suggests: the bad ruler is *ipsa impotentia,* or impotency itself. In a text analyzing the political turmoil of the Wars of the Roses occasioned by Richard II's deposition, the lawyer and political theorist John Fortescue writes:

> All the power of a king ought to be applied to the good of his realm. . . . But if he is so overcome by his own passions or by such poverty that he cannot keep his hands from despoiling his subjects, so that he impoverishes them, and does not allow them to live and be supported by their own goods . . . such a king ought to be called not only impotent, but also impotence itself."[35]

The impotence that Fortescue condemns in a king is not simply a reference to his failure to produce and support healthy subjects, although Shakespeare's play highlights such a literal failure of the childless Richard through the two father-son foils of Gaunt and Bolingbroke, and York and Aumerle.[36] Instead, impotency refers to an economic state of affairs that holds political consequences. A king overcome with poverty, Fortescue elaborates, necessarily reigns badly: "the greatest harm that comes of a king's poverty is that he shall by necessity be compelled to find extreme means of getting goods; such as to accuse some of his subjects who are innocent" (53).

When Richard accuses innocent men, or denies them the right of trial, he fails to rule for "the good of his realm." Richard's lawlessness contrasts with York's equations that connect sovereignty and law, Richard's succession to the crown and Bolingbroke's inheritance of his father's possessions. York essentially asserts common law against canon law, Bracton and Fortescue against Justinian. Whereas Richard behaves as if the laws are in his own mouth, York responds, as Bracton's familiar adage goes, that "there is no *rex* where will rules rather than *lex.*"[37] York acknowledges the legal crisis precipitated by the king's actions: as he tells Richard, by transgressing the common law that establishes his office, "be not thyself." While Norbrook reads the speech as an act of "self-censorship" (44) which allows Richard's absolutism to continue untouched, everyone knows precisely what the "thoughts / which honour and allegiance cannot think" are. York's final lines signal how he now cannot help but contemplate, while condemning, the act of treason.

York manages simultaneously to invoke his treasonous thoughts and to stand apart from them, a move that underscores his attempt to persuade the tyrannical king rather than simply overturn him as Northumberland and Bolingbroke do. In contrast to Northumberland, who ends the scene plotting revolt, York and Gaunt offer persuasive counsel. Yet just as Gaunt's famous lines are to no purpose—they result instead in Richard's seizure of his estate—Richard similarly ignores York to such a degree that, immediately after York's critique, he jarringly names him Lord Governor on the grounds that "he is just and always loved us well" (2.1.221). Both men accuse the king of bankrupting the country and transgressing the law, but their speeches have little effect on Richard other than stimulating his impulsive will.

The speeches, however, do have a powerful effect on the shape and vocabulary of the play and, as a result, are more persuasive as a form of resistance than their failure before Richard might suggest. Gaunt's images of the "pelting farm" and "teeming womb" resonate throughout subsequent scenes: generation and commerce become the two axes along which Richard and Bolingbroke oppose each other. Further, York's legal critique of Richard initiates and justifies legitimate opposition to the king, despite York's own hesitancy to commit treason. Put another way, Richard might ignore these speeches of counsel, but his failure to take either Gaunt or York seriously does not diminish their theatrical power for the play's audience. We are able to see, as Richard cannot, that these prophetic speeches anticipate the crucial terms of the fall that awaits the king. Indeed, the gardeners later voice precisely this vocabulary of law and generation, introduced by York and Gaunt, when they consider the king's upcoming deposition: the king, they claim, has lacked "law and form and due proportion" (3.4.41), and allowed the growth of "noisesome weeds, which without profit suck / The soil's fertility" (38–39). In their penetrating critique, the gardeners, along with Gaunt and York, offer the king a form of loyal opposition that he refuses to acknowledge. The play thus invites the audience, through these minor characters, to recognize what Richard cannot: slavish loyalty and violent resistance are not our only political options.

Richard's Treason and Bolingbroke's Resistance

Highlighting Richard's "impotency" on the Welsh coast, where the king attempts—and fails—to conjure soldiers, angels, and the landscape around him to fight on his side, Shakespeare then introduces Bolingbroke's model of active resistance. The duke downplays the violence of his opposition by articulating his claims in a vocabulary of fiscal responsibility and contractual obligation ("I come but for mine own" [3.3.196]). He thus presents the usurpation as a form of book-keeping. If the king ignores political economy, the usurper repeatedly expresses his awareness of how economic relations undergird political ones. To the king's opponents, Richard has "pilled" and "fined" his subjects (2.1.246–47); he has, as Willoughby states, "grown bankrupt like a broken man" (257), "robbing" (261) his subjects since "he hath not money for these Irish wars" (259). Like Fortescue's impotent king, Richard appears to his subjects as impoverished and "degenerate" (262), undoing the process of generation and filling Gaunt's prophecy of England's "hollow womb."[38]

Adopting the language of bankruptcy to depict Richard's transgressions, Bolingbroke's allies proceed to justify their claim to govern the body politic on the basis of their skill in the marketplace. Northumberland seeks to "redeem from broking pawn the blemished crown, / Wipe off the dust that hides our sceptre's gilt, / And make high majesty look like itself" (2.1.293–95). His image of the crown being pawned locates the specifically economic dangers of Richard's kingship, and, as a result, usurpation seems to save rather than endanger the kingdom. Northumberland's image does additional political work in separating the crown from the king's person in the manner of the 1308 Declaration. Forced to pawn the crown because of bankruptcy, the kingdom is essentially available to the highest bidder, namely, the fiscally prudent Bolingbroke.

The economic terminology increases on Bolingbroke's return to the realm. The duke tells Northumberland, his riding companion on the journey to Berkeley, "Of much less value is my company / Than your good words" (2.3.19–20), and Harry Percy tells Bolingbroke "I tender you my service" (41), prompting the duke's reply, "I count myself in nothing else so happy / As in a soul rememb'ring my good friends; / And as my fortune ripens with thy love, / It shall be thy true love's recompense" (46–49). Bolingbroke tallies his relations with others, "counting" and "rememb'ring" his debts, acknowledging his "less[er] value." Although the verb "ripens" retains the residue of the play's earlier birthing images, the duke insistently presents an economic frame for such images; when Ross and Willoughby enter the scene a few lines later, he echoes his former statement on debt and recompense, claiming to these new allies, "All my treasury / Is yet but unfelt thanks, which, more enriched, / Shall be your love and labour's recompense" (60–62), to which Ross replies, "Your presence makes us rich, most noble lord" (63).

While the Richardian language of divinity would have undercut Bolingbroke's bid for the throne, this newly adopted commercial discourse alters the ideological ground, shifting conceptions of kingship away from familial territory. Indeed, the two opponents speak in distinct vocabularies, using language that corresponds to their alternate theories of sovereignty. As Richard attempts to uphold a crumbling model of godly monarchy, using the treason charge and the rhetoric of divine right to bolster his cause—only, as we have seen, to undermine it—Bolingbroke develops an alternate model of kingship in his bid for the throne: a model of contractual kingship, according to which he will balance the country's books after Richard's tyrannical pillaging. Like Fortescue, who focuses on economic health as a sign of good government, Bolingbroke and his allies claim that it is precisely by appraising the crown within the marketplace, by balancing the books of the kingdom, that a sovereign can honor Gaunt's "dear, dear land." This model of kingship obeys the laws of the monarchical marketplace or, as Lars Engle puts it in his analysis of Shakespeare's *I Henry IV*, "royal power is pragmatically produced in, and to some extent by, an economy of credit and negotiation."[39] In Bolingbroke, *Richard II* thus charts what Henry Coursen has argued of Hal in *I Henry IV*: the ascendant prince turns to a mode of rule that shifts from "sacramental to commercial premises."[40]

While Bolingbroke employs the language of commerce and contract to legitimate his sovereignty, this vocabulary also betrays him. Suffering disinheritance and exile, Bolingbroke enters England in debt. Despite his promise to recompense his allies, his material dependence on his subjects will, as Richard prophesizes, haunt Bolingbroke: Northumberland, the "ladder wherewithal / The mounting Bolingbroke ascends" (5.1.55–56), does indeed revolt. Between his "unthrifty" son (5.3.1) and his unsettled accounts with Northumberland and other allies, Bolingbroke enters the office of king as a debtor, owing "recompense" to those men who financed his successful bid.

Furthermore, Shakespeare rapidly shifts his representational energy elsewhere precisely at the moment when the play's strain of resistance theory climaxes and Bolingbroke triumphs. He does so on two levels.

First, he directs the play's argument away from Bolingbroke's triumph toward his already compromised position and, in the process, teases out the connections between the former king and his successor. King Henry mirrors Richard in his bankruptcy, circling the audience back to the fiscal irresponsibility that helped fuel the deposition party. Then, like Richard before him, the new king commissions a murder (for Richard it was Gloucester; for Bolingbroke, Richard) and rids himself through exile of the offending agent. As a result of such close parallels, the revolution from Richard to Henry appears neither merely oppositional nor triumphant, neither a move from tyranny to legitimate law-based rule nor from sanctified kingship to treasonous rule. Instead, Shakespeare wastes no time in representing how lawlessness and indebtedness characterize both rulers.

Second, Shakespeare refuses to cede stage time to Bolingbroke. No sooner does he return to England and gain the crown than Shakespeare concentrates not only on the fate of Richard—which is to be expected and for which the play is famous—but also, more surprisingly, on the familial trials of the duke of York. Consequently the play's last act is structured around a juxtaposition: the scenes of Richard alternate with scenes of York. Richard and the queen separate in act 5, scene 1, then York describes the scene to his wife in act 5, scene 2; York and his wife and son confront one another before King Henry in act 5, scene 3, and then Exton plots Richard's death as Richard meditates in jail in act 5, scenes 4 and 5. Just when the play could follow the triumphant Bolingbroke, it instead features these two divergent plots, each hinging on tragedy. Richard's high tragedy is evident, contrasting with York's more pedestrian one. York is a decent figure who might have been better but whose sense of duty and allegiance become compromised in a political atmophere of tyranny and treason. Holding together these two radically different, but equally tragic, plots at the play's close is part of its critical challenge and part of its significant swerve from triumphalist resistance theory.

Richard's deposition represents the play's most evident tragic plot, and we might expect his final scenes to offer a stark contrast to his opening ones. But his speeches during his deposition and in prison betray many of the preoccupations that marked his former tyranny. Richard continues to elaborate his highly exaggerated notion of kingship through fanciful conceits. The belief that his office should protect him from mortality and that he should be subject to nothing, not even the laws of nature, leads to the series of political meditations that begin with the scene on the Welsh coast and culminate in his speeches during his deposition and imprisonment. These speeches are most frequently read psychologically or spiritually: he explores subjectivity, he exhibits narcissism or solipsism, or he becomes a martyr or Christ figure. I examine these scenes, however, as part of the play's continuing interest in political philosophy: what happens to a king whose own theory of sovereignty fails? As he attempts to contemplate kingship differently in these final scenes, Richard struggles movingly with this question.

Richard continues to believe in the absolute singularity of his kingship. From the play's opening, he views the sovereign as a power alone, inviolate, even unearthly. He repeatedly asserts his difference from human subjects and concerns—he is aligned with "God omnipotent" (3.3.85) and should be subject to "no hand of blood and bone" (3.3.79). To Richard, compromise is debasement, and negotiation is subjection. If Richard's refusal to negotiate with traitors seems good political policy, Shakespeare undercuts this hard-line stance by representing an easy solution to the king's crisis: Bolingbroke claims to come only for his seized estate, and Richard initially consents. But to compromise is, as Richard says, to "debase ourselves" (127), to lose what he has been, and to shape a new, abject political identity: "Subjected thus, / How can you say to me I am king?" (3.2.176–77). It is this exaggerated sense of his own superior isolation that prohibits Richard from engaging in the play's political world at all. He inhabits only the extreme end of the political spectrum—if he cannot be absolute king, then he is the opposite, equally removed from the political economy of the kingdom in being a hermit, a palmer, or a monk (3.3.148–57). Or, finally, he claims dramatic singularity in having "no name, no title" (4.1.255), being "nothing" (5.5.38) under "crushing penury" (5.5.34).

But Richard is forced to participate in this new political economy. He cannot retreat to a hermitage. His speeches from the time of his deposition repeatedly detail his conceptual struggles as he begins, for the first time, to examine himself in relation to his subjects. Whereas formerly Richard saw himself as singular, now he tries to connect himself to his subjects through a series of fanciful equations based in an oppositional mathematics. He is one of two buckets on either side of the crown, each moving in opposition to the other. Or, as he puts it in prison, he is the clock that marks time for the new king Henry, counting down hours. The mechanistic simplicity of these equations belies their ideological innovation. Richard has never thought like this. Most remarkable, he deems himself to be just one of a group of traitors threatening the crown: "I find myself a traitor with the rest" (4.1.248). This line is noteworthy not only as a culmination of the play's argument on Richard's tyranny, suggesting how the self-destructive king created the treason that topples him, but also, finally, as an admission of the king's similarity to his own subjects. For once, Richard joins in with the rest. He is part of a larger equation, one based in the inevitability of succession.

No sooner has he grouped himself with his subjects than Richard swings wildly back to memories of his singularity: "was this the face / That like the sun did make beholders wink?" (4.1.283–84). Here Richard returns to the image of himself as the sun, as Phaeton, that characterizes his mode of sovereign rule. Content to gaze at his own image so long as he maintains his fiction of separation from his subjects, Richard dashes the mirror when his own face reminds him that he has been "outfaced" by Bolingbroke.

Even as Richard struggles to come to terms with his fall, then, his lyrical speeches recapitulate precisely the reasons for his failed kingship. His sense of isolation in prison only parallels his former isolation as the face of the sun.[41] As king, Richard refuses to negotiate with his subjects and reigns only through those figures who mirror his desires, and so, too, in the final scenes: Richard's elaborate conceits in prison serve as the residue of his earlier exercise of sovereignty. He uses his own brain to produce a kingdom "of still-breeding thoughts; / And these same thoughts people this little world" (5.5.8–9). But all these thoughts are merely extensions of his own fancy. Similarly, he breaks the mirror and thus creates a kingdom of many faces, all reflections of his own. As Christopher Pye elaborates, "Richard's more overtly theatrical deposition of himself—his mirror game—reflects some of the serious requirements of absolutism."[42] Richard's mind still turns over the remnants of his former philosophy, examining how he remains singular in this new political environment where he has become subject not only to Bolingbroke but, more generally, to mortality.

The Beggar and the King: York's Tragedy

By featuring Richard's rigidly singular rule, the play initially invites us to imagine, along with Bolingbroke, Richard's deposition. Bolingbroke's preliminary claims—to return only for his property—help support this argument in favor of the opposition party. Indeed, in its opening scenes, the play offers a version of what Stanley Fish famously claims of *Paradise Lost*: we are surprised into rebellion. The play depicts resistance in some form as inevitable. In representing successful usurpation, however, Shakespeare shifts his focus to the tragedy of political chaos, and thus, like Adam and Eve, we are counseled away from a celebratory understanding of rebellion toward a tragic one.

It is easy, given Bolingbroke's success, to read his opposition as the only form of resistance in the play. In its anatomy of resistance, the play, of course, does represent Bolingbroke's successful political muscle, but it retains nonetheless a preoccupation with milder forms of dissent. Pursuing the York plot, Shakespeare completes the narrative arc of legitimate, verbal resistance initiated by Gaunt. York struggles to remain loyal to his king, be it Richard or Henry, and he attempts to offer both men the good counsel they need in order to rule effectively. Yet it is through York that, ultimately, the tragic effects of the chaotic political landscape become most evident, as a decent, moderate subject experiences increasing difficulties in a politically unstable commonwealth. York makes us ask, what does it mean to continue to obey the law in an atmosphere in which everyone else suspends it?

York begins as one of the play's most laudable figures. A courtier, like Kent in *Lear*, he counsels the king in the midst of crisis. Yet, as the play unfolds, York is forced to serve as the king's deputy, putting him in the awkward position of defending policies he disagrees with. When Bolingbroke returns to England, York attempts to remain "as neuter" (2.3.159), housing the rebel while maintaining respect for the king. But his professions of neutrality seem increasingly hollow—or emasculated—as he quibbles with Northumberland over his nomenclature for the king. Then, with the treason of his son Aumerle, the true peril of York's political position finally emerges and takes center stage.

York's family conflict should be one of the most serious in the play, since it anticipates the interfamilial fighting of the Wars of the Roses. The pitting of father against son, mother against husband, in act 5, scene 3, sets forth the stakes in this deposition that even now is leading toward civil war. But the scene is cast as comedy: "Our scene is altered from a serious thing, / And now is changed to 'The Beggar and the King'" (78–79). This is comedy not only because Henry himself gives a name to this theatrical interlude, "The Beggar and the King," but also because it has a happy resolution in Aumerle's pardon. Furthermore, the audience is due for a little comic relief and the play offers it, conventionally, at the expense of a woman. Not only does her entrance prompt Henry's comical comment, but her decidedly domestic readings of the political crisis create an aura of ridiculousness to her cause: York, she insists, only condemns his son because he questions his legitimacy, or because he thinks, mistakenly, that his wife can bear more children. The fact of Aumerle's rebellion seems hardly to register with her.

While the duchess of Gloucester and Queen Isabel before her have sued for political assistance from their sons and husbands and retained their dignity, the duchess of York's bid for her own efficacious voice comes at the expense of her seriousness: the king will hear her only to mock her, just as York himself dismisses her: "foolish woman" (5.2.80), "thou fond madwoman" (95), "fond woman" (101), and "unruly woman" (111). On her knees, begging for a pardon, she proves embarrassingly insistent, prompting Henry to repeat, "Rise up, good aunt!" (5.3.91), "Good aunt, stand up" (109), "Good aunt, stand up" (128). These lines reinforce the familial aspect of the crisis, even as they uncomfortably draw attention to Henry's kingship as a disruption in proper sequence: here, the older generation kneels before his feet.

Surprisingly, though, the scene is even more compromising for York. On one level, York's political wisdom appears sound and echoes the gardener's logic of cutting: just as the gardener claims that "superfluous branches / We lop away that bearing boughs may live" (3.4.63–64), so, too, does York tell Henry "this festered joint cut off, the rest rest sound" (5.3.84). York even uses the language of pruning directly, telling his son moments before he learns of his treason, "bear you well in this new spring of time, / Lest you be cropped before you come to prime" (5.2.50–51). Like the gardener, then, York advocates surgery as a means of restoring the country's health, but the correspondence only highlights the clarity of the gardener's political diagnosis in contrast to York's muddled one. Deeming his son a mere "festered joint," he wants to cut off the younger part of himself, interrupting the process of fair sequence and succession which he eloquently defended earlier to Richard.

Denying familial bonds, York resorts to a language of exchange instead, refusing to purchase Aumerle's pardon with his own good name: "so shall my virtue be his vice's bawd, / And he shall spend mine honour with his shame" (5.3.66). In his eagerness to retain rather than spend his "pledge" (5.2.44), "honor, troth" (78), "virtue" (5.3.66) and, again, "honour" (67, 69), he shuns his "thriftless son" (68) even as the new king seeks out his own—the scene begins, in an often noted irony, with Henry asking "can no man tell me of my unthrifty son?" (1). While York's language of exchange accords well with England's new monarchical economy, it uncomfortably contrasts with the language of physical generation employed by the duchess: in contrast to Gaunt's "teeming womb of royal kings" (2.1.51), she mourns her "teeming date drunk up with time" (5.2.91), as she reminds York of the inimitability of their son. York's use of wit also jarringly contrasts with his wife's seriousness. With the duchess begging the king to offer a pardon to their son, York, in his last line in the play, counsels Henry to offer only an equivocating pardon—"Speak it in French, King; say 'Pardonne-moi'" (5.3.118), namely, denying her request by saying "forgive me, but no." This jest underscores his lack of tenderness but also a clever deviousness, a quality absent from his earlier, moving speeches of advice.

Of course, how could York act otherwise, we might reason, since he owes allegiance to the new king and must condemn treason, even if it appears in his own son; Gaunt faced a similar dilemma in banishing his son Bolingbroke. Indeed, York's and Gaunt's political efforts are entirely parallel. While York tries to counsel Richard away from his abuses of office, like Gaunt he fails. When he is pressed by a woman to uphold family loyalties over royal obedience, like Gaunt he refuses. Like Gaunt, then, York takes the political risk of offering verbal counsel while remaining a dutiful subject. But Gaunt repeatedly communicates his difficulties with competing political and familial allegiances: he complains to the king and duchess of Gloucester about his torn loyalty. York, who attempts to walk a similar path, fails to win audience sympathy. Having initially challenged Bolingbroke on his return to England, York now stands behind the new king without question, never even registering grief about his son's treason, as Gaunt so powerfully does. Indeed, York's unwavering commitment to Henry at the expense of his son appears perverse. The loyalty to Henry seems misplaced, performative, overstated; it signals York's abandonment of the still living Richard and of his own family. By refusing to acknowledge the depth of the dilemma, York demonstrates a new-found allegiance too quickly, losing audience support in the process.

We could dismiss York as a weak or heartless character in comparison with Gaunt. A more productive way of looking at these doubled characters, however, is to recognize what York's failure tells us about the shifting political landscape. If Shakespeare represented the deposition scene as lawful and legitimate, York's position would be laudable. He would have been an advocate of law throughout the play. York, after all, upheld law both against Richard (2.1.163–214) and against Bolingbroke on his initial return (2.3.87–147). By this point, however, the category of law itself has been drawn into question. In the play's first half, Richard distorts the law, misapplying the charge of treason to his political opponents; in its second half, Bolingbroke returns to England in the name of law, only to depose the legitimate monarch. Tyranny and rebellion are thus both undertaken in the name of the law, undermining the stability of York's position. Furthermore, Northumberland's transparent and desperate attempts to satisfy the commons by following so-called procedure expose the lawlessness of the deposition spectacle—Richard's reading of his "grievous crimes" hardly would prove that he is "worthily deposed" (4.1.223; 227). Since Shakespeare's representation stages questions about the legality of deposition, York's participation in the process undercuts his claim, held rigidly against his son, to obey custom and sovereignty over rebellion. He seems no longer consistent but merely slavishly obedient to a new authority.

The transformational representation of York, shifting from loyal counselor to blindly submissive subject, dramatizes the more broadly shifting views on loyalty and moderation in the play. Whereas to Persons, York is simply the "chief prince assistant to the deposing of king Richard" (2:63), to Shakespeare York's dilemma is much more nuanced, dramatizing the untenable status of the middle ground in a situation where compromise is no longer considered possible. Unlike Kent, whose service to Lear makes him one of that play's most admirable characters, York offers initially dutiful counsel that cedes to political wavering when he shifts from Richard to Bolingbroke. Critical of Richard's tyranny—just as Kent challenged Lear—York then capitulates to the stronger power of the rebel. The tragedy of *Richard II* as it unfolds through York lies as much in the demise of decent subjects as in the fall of an errant king. York struggles to remain decent, obedient, and neutral in an environment in which competing stories and allegiances compromise objectivity. As he tells Gaunt early in the play, "all too late comes Counsel to be heard, / Where Will doth mutiny with Wit's regard" (2.1.27–28). While York refers here to the intractable Richard, his lines resonate with the perennial position of the counselor in the play, arriving belatedly only to face the stubborn will of Richard, Aumerle, or Bolingbroke.

York is also ineffectual and passive. Despite his own sympathy for Richard, York continually functions as a mere observer rather than active political participant. This position is typified in his speech on the entrances of Bolingbroke and Richard into London. The popular support for Bolingbroke creates pathos for the fallen Richard, who enters London alone and uncelebrated. As York puts it,

> As in a theatre the eyes of men
> After a well-graced actor leaves the stage,
> Are idly bent on him that enters next,
> Thinking his prattle to be tedious,
> Even so, or with much more contempt, men's eyes
> Did scowl on gentle Richard.
>
> (5.2.23–28)

If York's speech provokes audience sympathy for Richard, at the same time it also raises the question of York's own role in the spectacle: "no man cried God save him! / No joyful tongue gave him his welcome home" (28–29). His own silence suggests the awkward position of the reporter—neutral, without comments, ineffectual. Furthermore, York's description perfectly fits his own role in the play. As the drama shifts between Richard and York in these final scenes, our eyes are bent on York as "him that enters next." He is the minor character who is known precisely for his "prattle," for offering words over deeds. York offers, then, not only a moving speech about the deposed king but an embedded theatrical caricature of his own role.

York thus functions as a figure akin to the author. In his role as political moderate, York offers corrective commentary on the situation that surrounds him. In doing so, he dramatizes the challenges facing the author during a time of treasonous crisis when an increasingly fractured political environment presses on definitions of obedience, law, and legitimate rulership. Figuring the role of a creative writer in late 1590s England, York attempts to comment on a situation, to serve as the political historian, as the custodian of custom, but instead finds himself drawn into the political fray.

If York's dilemma evokes the difficulties of writers and other subjects positioned in a treasonous environment, it is important to note how Shakespeare's character is not entirely sympathetic. Shakespeare certainly demonstrates with compassion the eroding middle ground and York's resulting struggle, but the play also exposes York's inefficacy with some derision. Recognizing this mixture of sympathy and scorn, we can see how the portrait of York as the writer, who only comments on action rather than undertake any himself, functions as a form of self-reproach for a writer living under tyranny. What had seemed to be the initially praiseworthy position of critic quickly cedes to the more questionable stance of the parrot of authority, willing to sacrifice his own family line to maintain his status at court, favoring public recognition over private allegiances. York thus shifts before our eyes from a figure akin to Lear's Kent or his Fool, to a figure more like Hamlet's Osric—a blindly submissive courtier, a fool without will or wit.

York's fate in the play signals a parallel series of shifts both within and surrounding Shakespeare's text: his is the fate of Catholic fathers such as Tresham and Percy, whose sons turn traitor by participating in the Essex Rebellion, and later the Gunpowder Plot. Equally, his struggle anticipates Hayward's, whose loyal support for the crown converts to tragic condemnation when the political environment radically changes. Further, this transformation of a loyal and moderate subject into a compromised participant in a rebellion he does not clearly support proves prophetic of the play's own production history, and, indeed, of tales of Richard II in the 1590s more generally. If at the time of its initial production, in 1595, the play appeared to be popular and acceptable, by 1600 it had become associated with Essexian politics and rebellion, just as, more dramatically, Hayward's *Henry IV,* a text this author defends as balanced in its portrait, was censored on the grounds of its seditious viewpoints. With Shakespeare's company interrogated by the state, and with Hayward's imprisonment, Essexian treason fractured the political landscape to such a degree that historical texts suddenly seemed to take sides.

This contraction of interpretive possibility characterizes the time of treasonous crisis when texts, like people, fall on one side or the other of a divide carved by legislation and distrust as much as criminal activity itself. Texts formerly perceived as moderate, popular, scholarly, or at least unremarkable are suspected of prompting, in a time of crisis, the treasonous action of the state's opponents. Essex's fear that his books would tell tales, noted in chapter 2, stems precisely from his awareness of such retrospective interpretation. Convinced of his guilt, Elizabeth's counselors turn the materials signifying Essex's learning, patronage, and courtly status into the weapons of his alleged treason.

Tracing this process of interpretive contraction before treason naturally poses questions about the other side of criminal textuality: what happens to textual engagements with treason in the aftermath of the contemporary event? Once the dividing line between traitor and loyalist has been starkly drawn—through prosecutions and executions, through new legislation and proclamation—how do imaginative and polemic writers respond? Do they, as the fate of Hayward might encourage, announce their political loyalty to the monarch more boldly? It is to these questions the remaining chapters turn.

CHAPTER FOUR

Scaffolds of Treason in Shakespeare's Macbeth

The threat posed by the Essex Rebellion prompted no new legislation, no draconian measures. Instead, rather than function as a triumph for Elizabeth, the prosecution of Essex's treason proved to be one of the more traumatic moments of her reign. The period after the rebellion produced neither a literature of condemnation nor of celebration of treason—which was Elizabeth's focus during the two years leading up to the rebellion—but rather tragic accounts of the earl's fall.[1] Mourned as one whose "excellent parts were so great," the earl seemed a victim of his enemies at court: "the envy which attends such excellency is so boundless."[2] Essex's recuperation begins from the time of his much reproduced scaffold speech. Provoking "many teares, loud sighs, and lamentations," his masterful scaffold performance also functions, more aptly for this book, as a rendering of himself as misinterpreted text.[3] He becomes—like the Tacitean history with which he was associated —condemned, censored, arrested, but, as he insists, innocent: "I entreat that all men would have a charitable opinion of me. We never, I protest to God, intended violence or harm to her Majesties person or dignity."[4]

While not persuaded by Essex's claims to innocence, Elizabeth nevertheless spared many of his followers and their families. Indeed, what MacCaffrey calls the "tiny band of followers" proves important enough to the Elizabethan regime that the queen reintegrates most of the soldiers into her service, relying on their military or financial contributions. Sir Edward Wintour, for example, was appointed the deputy lieutenant for Gloucester on August 16, 1601, even though his son participated in the Essex Rebellion and would later be executed for his role in the Gunpowder Plot. Similarly, on October 13, 1601, Arthur Throckmorton and Thomas Tresham were requested to provide light-horses to the earl of Northampton to help bolster the cavalry against the dual Spanish and Irish threat, although Tresham's son, Francis, had just been arrested for his role in the Essex Rebellion.[5] And while the queen prohibited the earls of Rutland and Bedford, and the Lords Sandies and Cromwell from attending Parliament because of their participation in the Essex uprising, at the same time she reassured these men that, as members, they could vote by proxy during their absence.[6]

Saving Essex's men such as Francis Tresham, Robert Catesby, Thomas Percy, and Thomas Winter from execution, Elizabeth proved accommodating over the course of their imprisonments as well. When Tresham fell "into dangerous sickeness by loathsomeness of Newgate," as recorded on March 29, 1601, the queen allowed him to be bailed out with 2,000 pounds and removed to his house to recover.[7] Similarly, Catesby was removed from the Fleet and Thomas Percy, a devoted follower of Essex who visited King James in the time before Elizabeth's death, was granted, along with his brother, greater "liberty of the house . . . to enlarge their close imprisonment" on March 1, 1601.[8]

As a result of Elizabeth's clemency, the earl's legacy came to haunt the newly crowned King James: several of his followers turned, with James's accession, to treason. Once released from prison after the Essex uprising—having paid enormous fines to the state and with little hope for advancement—Catesby and Tresham, along with Winter, immediately sought funding from treasonable sources. In his interrogations after the Gunpowder Plot, Winter recounts how, with the aid of Catesby and Tresham, he traveled to Spain to recruit Philip III "for the general good of the Romanish Catholic cause" in Britain.[9] Winter met with Philip on June 30, 1602, and asked the king "to bestow some pensions here in England upon sundry persons, who making use of the general discontent that young gentlemen and soldiers were in by reason of my Lord of Essex's death, and the want of his purse to maintain them, might no doubt by relieving their necessities have them all at his devotion."[10]

Winter's suggestion that English Catholics, wanting Essex's "purse to maintain them," now might receive pensions from the Spanish king upset entirely the relationship between England and Spain as imagined by Essex himself: the earl strove to prevent "Spanish servitude" and, at his uprising, proclaimed that "his life was saught and the kingdom sold to the king of Spain."[11] Essex's strong allegiance was instead to King James VI as successor; after all, in the "little black bag, wherein was contayned the whole plot, which the Earl wore about his neck," he supposedly had a note from James, who would succeed to the English throne after Elizabeth's capture.[12] Joined with Essex in supporting the claim of James against Philip, the earl's Catholic allies fought against the Spanish state since, despite their religious faith, they strove to defend England against an invading foreign ruler. Such men, in aligning themselves with a Protestant nobleman, also preserved an interest in fighting against the radical and treasonous elements of Catholicism; distancing themselves from Jesuit missionaries and monarchomachs seemed a possible route to securing toleration.

It is a testimony to the increasing isolation and radicalism of some of Essex's former Catholic allies that they now lobbied, as a result of his execution, for precisely the Spanish domination that the earl had spent his military career fighting against. Initially, like many Catholics, these men had been hopeful of a clement ruler in James. Father Henry Garnet—the famous "farmer" associated with the plot and referenced by *Macbeth*'s Porter—expresses this sense of hopeful expectation in a letter to Robert Persons in the weeks after Elizabeth's death: "The Catholics have great cause to hope for great respect, in that the nobility all almost labour for it and have promise thereof from his majesty [King James]."[13] Fellow Catholic John Gerard elaborates this sentiment, writing that "most Catholics had great hope and expectation of King James. . . . And this hope did bring some comfort with it amidst the many discomforts sustained under the long-continued reign of Elizabeth." He adds further, "how ready Catholics were in all countries to receive him, yea, how joyful to entertain and welcome him. . . . But now what shall we think to have been the state of all Catholic minds when all these hopes did vanish away, as a flash of lightning, giving for the time a pale light unto those that sit in darkness, doth afterwards leave them in more desolation?"[14]

Certainly James viewed himself as a voice of temperance in contrast to many Puritans in Parliament. As *Rex Pacificus*, James strove to unite rather than divide subjects in his new nation, Derek Hirst reminds us.[15] Out of fiscal considerations, security concerns, or deference to the state counselors of Elizabeth's late regime, however, the new king retained England's recusancy legislation.[16] Furthermore, he clarified that he had no intention of offering blanket toleration for Catholicism, as on May 4, 1603, when he "made a long and vehement apology for himself in the Council Chamber against the Papists who flatter themselves with a vague hope of toleration, declaring that he never had any such intention and if he thought his sons would condescend to any such course he would wish the kingdom translated to his daughter."[17] A discussion in the Star Chamber on February 13, 1605, further reveals the new king's frustration with Catholic expectations. According to the report of the Star Chamber exchange, English Catholics accused James of ruling "without law, against law, and injustely," and the state faced "petitioners that either come in multitudes, or presume of multitudes of subscription of hands, as papists and sectaryes or puritanes . . . who say that the king's high commissioners have no warrant by law to do as they do." But James responded blandly that "the king's majesty" is "inheritable and descended from god," and further that he "hathe absolutelye monarchicall power annexed inseperablye to his Crowne and diademe, not by common law or statute law, but more ancient than either of them."[18] This appeal "in multitudes" to "law"—recalling the claim of Shakespeare's Bolingbroke who sues "for law"—was deemed "seditious" by the members of the Star Chamber.[19]

Disappointed and alienated, radical English Catholics criticized the new king for double-crossing those supporters who had lobbied for him as successor throughout Elizabeth's reign. A letter in Lord Egerton's papers, written by a Catholic and endorsed as "a most sawcy insolent and presumptuous narrative," notes that the king could

> have staied his hand a while from taxinge the people with any paymentes and to have help them up in the oppinion that now they were entered into the land of promise wherein they should take breath from the egyptian impositions, wherewith for so many yeares they were oppressed; but behold how unfortunately all things have succeeded. No sooner was his Majestie possessed of this realme but presently he . . . picked them [Catholics] out for the men whom he would expose to all maner of persecution.[20]

If this letter exaggerates the conditions for Catholics in early Jacobean England (James was more lenient in enforcing recusancy legislation than Elizabeth), it offers an important reminder of the "persecution," "oppression," and betrayal that recusants nonetheless felt after his ascension to the English throne. Retaining Elizabethan recusancy legislation, James then began to pursue peace with the Spanish monarch, traditionally an ally of alienated English Catholics. The resulting disappointment to the English Catholic community turned some believers, Derek Hirst notes, to desperation: "alienated and alone, they turned their thoughts to a 'sudden blow'" (106). More broadly, Philip Caramon writes, "the failure of James, on reaching London, to honor his promise of limited toleration for Catholics was the principal cause of the Gunpowder plot" (308).[21]

In May 1604, polarized by recusancy legislation and England's unexpected peace with Spain, five men took the notorious oath that initiated the November 5 treason: Robert Catesby, Thomas Percy, Christopher Wright, Thomas Winter, and Guy Fawkes. In the final three chapters of the book I use the phenomenon of this plot to explore the questions posed at the end of the last chapter: how do literary writers imagine the categories of sovereignty, treason, and tyranny at stake in a contemporary treasonous event? In turning to the Gunpowder Plot, I examine the textual aftermath of a treason that might seem the mirror reflection of the Essex Rebellion: whereas the representations of treason associated with Essex were interpreted by the state, reductively, as an aid to the crime in the years before the Essex Rebellion, now the depictions of treason in the aftermath of the 1605 plot appear univocal in their condemnations of crime and celebrations of the victorious state. In both cases, however, the imaginative possibilities of these texts on treason expand beyond the contracted interpretive environment marking the treasonous crisis. Readings of Shakespeare's *Macbeth*, Donne's *Pseudo-Martyr*, and Jonson's *Catiline* expose how, through the familiar genres of domestic and Roman history, political polemic, and state proclamation, writers continue to represent their conceptual struggles through a poetics of political philosophy. Particularly after 1605, such representations increasingly question restrictive state policies and refuse to endorse the contraction of interpretive possibility that characterizes a state's response to the crime. As a result, these writers forge, through their imaginative engagements, public meditations on questions of emergency power, sovereign prerogative, and active obedience at stake in treason.

Treason in *Macbeth*

The play most immediately associated with the 1605 Gunpowder Plot is Shakespeare's *Macbeth*. On August 7, 1606, *Macbeth* was allegedly performed before Queen Anne and her visiting brother, King Christian of Denmark, to celebrate James's triumph over the Gunpowder Plot traitors.[22] Although the play's role in the royal celebrations that followed the discovery of the plot may be merely apocryphal, *Macbeth*'s Porter directly refers to one of the plotters, Father Henry Garnet, suggesting that Shakespeare's portrait of treason emerged partly from the contemporary event.[23] As Henry Paul argues in *The Royal Play of Macbeth*, the play celebrates James's exposure of the plot, serving as a contemporary compliment to the king, and educating audiences in the ideology of legitimate sovereignty. Leonard Tennenhouse also analyzes *Macbeth* as a panegyric celebrating sovereign power, suggesting that Shakespeare "mystifies the notion of kingship, reinvigorates the signs and symbols associated with the exercise of legitimate power, and makes the theatre speak a more conservative ideology."[24]

The spectacle of Macbeth's severed head at the end of the play serves this didactic purpose precisely and, as a result, arguably serves to contain the traumatic events of the Gunpowder Plot. With the death of the villainous hero at the play's end, his head, as Marjorie Garber reminds us, will be displayed "painted upon a pole, and underwrit, / 'Here may you see the tyrant'" (5.7.26–27). She notes how Macbeth "is to become an object lesson, a spectacle, a warning against tyranny."[25] Closing with bloody death and didactic speech, the play opens with it as well. In scene 4 of the play, Malcolm confirms the first Thane of Cawdor's execution for treason. Reporting on the event, Malcolm declares of Cawdor that "very frankly he confess'd his treasons, / Implor'd your Highness' pardon, and set forth / A deep repentance" (1.4.3–5).[26] These lines reveal the dying last words of a traitor, familiar to its Jacobean audience as a monologue spoken from the scaffold by hundreds of prisoners, including those executed for their roles in the Gunpowder Plot just months before the staging of *Macbeth*.[27] Unlike in the Essex Rebellion, where traitors Catesby, Tresham, Percy, and Winter lived to continue their treasonous activities, the aftermath of the Gunpowder Plot saw a slew of executions and resulting scaffold speeches. Such speeches were characterized by a confession of guilt and a prayer to the monarch as illustrated by Cawdor's own words. Recorded in pamphlets and state papers, the "scaffold speech" was delivered by prisoners prior to execution. These speeches were meant to serve, as many scholars have contended, as a site for the affirmation of the monarch and a reestablishment of public order.[28]

Indeed, these speeches, in their ideal form, were didactic. First, the spectacle of the prisoner on the scaffold itself instructed the audience to avoid such crime and thus its gruesome punishment. Second, the prisoner's speech often directly admonished the audience not to engage in criminal activity. Cawdor's scaffold speech within *Macbeth* thus serves as a warning within a warning: English Renaissance theories of tragedy, offered by writers such as George Puttenham and Sir Philip Sidney, stress the didactic effect of tragedy in cautioning its audience members against crime and tyranny. In his *Defense of Poesy* (ca. 1581), for example, Sidney offers a theory of tragedy that, although based primarily on the classical model of Seneca and the contemporary model of *Gorboduc* (1562), nevertheless both influences and anticipates the tragic playwriting of the next decades. He defines "high and excellent tragedy, that openeth the greatest wounds, and showeth forth the ulcers that are covered with tissue; that maketh kings fear to be tyrants, and tyrants manifest their tyrannical humors."[29] Sidney's theory posits tragedy as the exposure of "wounds" and "ulcers," suggesting that the genre reveals faults in characters so as, in turn, to reveal or prevent such faults in the audience. While the Aristotelian model of tragedy both provokes emotion in the audience and then purges this emotion through catharsis, Sidney's model either teaches its audience to avoid vice or exposes those viewers guilty of it: like *Hamlet's* mousetrap play, tragedy causes abusive kings to "manifest their tyrannical humors."

If *Macbeth* appears to confirm this exemplary model of tragedy, then the early representation of Cawdor's scaffold speech could be read as a foreshadowing of the events of the play: a hero turns traitor and, in dying, teaches the audience to avoid his own treachery. On another level, however, the play opens with treason that as much teaches Macbeth as deters him. Indeed, Cawdor's penitent death produces not an aversion to but an attraction toward the crime. Upsetting tragedy's didactic purpose, *Macbeth* returns us to Sidney's phrase for the genre: it "showeth forth the ulcers." Although tragedy serves as an exemplum, Sidney describes tragedy as a genre that turns things inside out: what should be inside the body protrudes for external, public view in the form of an ulcer or wound. Specifically, tragedy externalizes inward, transgressive desire for all to see, and this simple mechanism of exposure produces complex results in terms of audience reaction and interpretive possibility. As Garber argues, for example, Macbeth's success as an object lesson is complicated by his uncanny role as a type of male Medusa: he is both familiar and monstrous, both male and female.[30] He is also, notably, both traitor and tyrant. Rather than fulfill Sidney's definition of exemplary tragedy which should teach kings to fear tyranny, then, *Macbeth* provocatively illuminates how tragedy "showeth forth the ulcers" by depicting, through the titular character, the seepage between the office of king and the tricks of the traitor. At the moment when the state in its post-plot propaganda attempts to produce treason's demise before an audience, and tries to distinguish most starkly between loyalist and traitor, *Macbeth* instead demonstrates the uncanny dependence of traitor and monarch.

While Macbeth produces the horror of treason before its audience, helping them to imagine the violent plot that never took place in 1605, its effect in doing so is not didactic. Instead, as this chapter will argue, *Macbeth*'s anti-didactic impulses, evident initially in the scene of Cawdor's death, more broadly drive the play's portrait of treason. Specifically, the play imagines treason beyond ideologically confining polemical discourses that proliferated at the time of its production. While the rhetoric of scaffold speeches and post–Gunpowder Plot accounts of the treason resound with triumphalism, Shakespeare's play simultaneously replicates such rhetoric, by initially opposing the demonic Macbeths with sanctified kingship, and exposes its fictional nature, by later drawing not only the audience but also the future king into league with the traitor. The play thus explores the charismatic power of treason: staging the crime charms audiences on and off stage with apparent truths or sheer imagination, infecting the ways in which we perceive the social and political world. In the context of the play this infectious representation proves, ultimately and tragically, productive for Scotland's future king. Learning from both the charismatic traitor Macbeth and his legitimate but limited predecessor Duncan, Malcolm evinces deceptive tactics that secure his triumphant leadership.

Wilbur Sanders and David Scott Kastan rightly note that Malcolm is a man of "smaller stature" and "reductive vision" in comparison with his father, Duncan.[31] He nevertheless represents the negotiable model of kingship the play deems necessary in Scotland's (and perhaps Jacobean England's) own fair and foul landscape: Malcolm adopts the villainous characteristics of Macbeth's own reign, employing the deceptive mechanisms alleged of traitors in order to rule his kingdom effectively. As Janet Adelman and Peter Stallybrass have argued, the promised efficacy of Malcolm's rule emerges out of his association with the reactionary, patriarchal politics of "consolidating male power." Malcolm also, however, consolidates the power of king and traitor.[32] He, as Alan Sinfield argues, "indicates the circumspection that will prove useful to the lawful good king, as much as to the tyrant."[33] As a result the play ends with a double tragedy: the death of one traitorous King and the ascension of another.

To explore the play's challenge to didacticism and its emerging portrait of what I call pragmatic sovereignty, this chapter first discusses the characteristics of historical scaffold speeches to elucidate their interpretive complexity. Turning to the episode of Cawdor's execution, I then demonstrate that the duplicitous language at stake in the historical scaffold speech typifies the speech of traitors as represented in *Macbeth*, first in Cawdor's scaffold speech and subsequently in the witches' prophecies. Macbeth's and the witches' treasonous language reappears, I argue, in the mouth of Malcolm. He adopts the hero's traitorous speech and, in doing so, exhibits how the verbal duplicity, typical of traitors, proves necessary in sustaining Scotland's monarchs as well. His pragmatic leadership contrasts with Duncan's ineptitude and Macbeth's corrupt ambition, offering a model of literally mixed monarchy that stabilizes the country while evacuating it of the charismatic, imaginative energy that drives the play's portrait of treason.

The Scaffold Speeches of Traitors

On May 3, 1606, Father Henry Garnet, a Catholic minister arrested for his role in the Gunpowder Plot, was brought to the scaffold for execution. The official account published by the king's printer, Robert Barker, records Garnet's speech from the scaffold erected at the west end of St. Paul's Church:

Then Garnet said, "Good countreymen, I am come hither this blessed day of the Invention of the holy Crosse, to end all my crosses in this life. The cause of my suffering is not unknown to you; I confesse I have offended the King, and am sorry for it, so farre as I was guilty, which was in concealing it, and for that I ask pardon of his Majestie; the treason intended against the King and State was bloody, My self should have detested it, had it taken effect . . . I pray God the Catholics may not fare the worse for my sake, and I exhort them all to take heede they enter not into any Treasons, Rebellions, or Insurrections against the King," and with this, ended speaking and fell to praying.[34]

Here Garnet confesses his offense, asks the king's pardon, and ends with a prayer, following the model of confession undertaken by the penitent soul. With Elizabeth having abolished the Catholic method of confession in 1563 with the establishment of the Anglican Church, the scaffold speech itself functions as a secular form of this confessional, a point explored by Peter Lake and Michael Questier who examine the dense mixture of "state, religion and ideology" in the scaffold genre.[35] Moving beyond the subversion-containment model of dying last words, Lake and Questier instead establish how Catholic subjects, in particular, claimed agency through dying words and, in doing so, demonstrate how categories such as state and religion were neither stable nor monolithic.

The formula evident in Garnet's last dying words appears in hundreds of speeches recorded in the sixteenth and seventeenth centuries. Even in the most sensational instances of treason in early modern England, most prisoners begin with a confession of guilt and end with a plea to God, following the conventional rhetoric that ostensibly convinces the audience of the criminal's wrongdoing while warning them against committing treasonous acts.[36] In analyzing English scaffold speeches, scholars have drawn attention to their contradictory history. On the one hand, as the historians J. A. Sharpe and Lacey Baldwin Smith argue, such strict conventions of execution speech served to validate the monarch and control the audience. Here, Garnet's warning to fellow Catholics is exemplary: "I exhort them all to take heed they enter not into any Treasons, Rebellions, or Insurrections against the King." On the other hand, Thomas Laqueur and Frances Dolan expose another phenomenon evident on the scaffold: the unruly prisoner who breaks with convention and defies the state. As a result of such transgression, Dolan writes, "the scaffold becomes not only a locus of dom-

ination and oppression, but also an arena of boundary crossing, negotiation, and possibilities for agency."[37]

My own contribution to this critical conversation on scaffold
speeches focuses not on oppositional speeches—those moments when
the event unraveled—but instead on utterly conventional speeches to
draw attention to the instability of the genre even when offered in its
most ideal form. Influenced by Laqueur, Dolan, Lake, and Questier in
their analyses of unruly speakers, I focus on the apparently docile
speeches delivered by the recent Gunpowder plotters in order to reveal how even the formulaic scaffold speech produced interpretive
chaos rather than upholding state power. Certainly these speeches appeared to justify the state's punishment, and, not surprisingly, they
were used as propaganda in support of the monarch. Printed with the
monarch's permission, and often by his or her own printer, traitors'
speeches circulated in pamphlets that narrated events from the prisoner's arraignment to his or her execution, reminding the audience not
to sympathize with the traitor. The didactic power of the scaffold
speech is put forth in Henry Goodcole's record of the execution of
Francis Robinson in 1618. Goodcole's preface states that "dying men's
wordes are ever remarkable, and their last deeds memorable for succeeding posterities, by them to be instructed, what vertues or vices
they followed and imbraced, and by them to learne to imitate that
which was good, and to eschew evill."[38] He defends his own practice
of circulating scaffold speeches, insisting on his interest in education
over sensation. He is confident that "succeeding posterities" will learn
the proper lesson from these prisoners, rather than mistakenly follow
their corrupt example: they will "learne to imitate that which was
good, and to eschew evill."

While the state or author may have manufactured a prisoner's last
words for propaganda purposes, a point to which I return below, a
prisoner may well have uttered a formulaic speech because he or she
was pressured by political, economic, and spiritual concerns during
imprisonment; and when the audience was aware of such concerns,
the reliability of the confession was clearly compromised. Rather than
capitulate to the state's version of events out of obedience, the prisoner
may instead have uttered formulaic words to save family members, an
estate, or his or her soul. First, a prisoner could protect his family eco-
nomically if he confessed his crime. According to the statute law, the
sentence for treason included forfeiture of the prisoner's entire estate

to the monarch.[39] Since the state occasionally returned the wife's jointure to her, this possibility effectively forced the prisoner to comply with the state's judgment in the hope of securing the estate for his surviving family and saving them from destitution. Before his execution for treason for his participation in the Gunpowder Plot, for example, Ambrose Ruckwood offered the conventional formula of confession, apology, and prayer, and he ended his speech by "beseeching the King to bee good to his wife and children."[40] Likewise, the Gunpowder conspirator Sir Everard Digby requested that "his wife might have her jointer, his children the lands intailed, by his father; his sisters their legasies in his hand unpaid."[41]

In addition to the economic pressure exerted on a prisoner to deliver a conventional scaffold speech, he or she was also subject to spiritual pressure to do so. Once in prison, the captive would receive visits from Anglican ministers intent on tending to the state of his or her soul. In a culture committed to the Christian belief in the afterlife, the confession of sins and the expression of penitence were vital to gaining salvation after death.[42] Further, the long tradition of the *ars moriendi* helped prisoners to shape their deaths (and their scaffold speeches) according to a conventional model of penitence. The prayer reveals the prisoner's contrition before God, and hence his potential for salvation ("that my soule may be lifted uppe by faith"), a formula that evokes the *ars moriendi*, found in such devotional texts such as Thomas Beacon's *Sicke Manne's Salve* (1561), William Perkin's *Salve for a Sicke Man* (1595), and Christopher Sutton's *Disce Mori* (1600). Salvation comes as a result of penitence, as Beacon writes in his popular text: "I being sure that the thing cannot perish, which is committed unto thy mercy, most humbly beseech thee (O Lord) to give me grace, that I may now willingly leave this fraile and wicked flesh."[43] The body of the dying criminal, despite its villainy, cannot prevent its penitent soul from reaching heaven, enabling the prisoner to prompt his own spiritual ascension, and erecting the scaffold as a site of religious faith. As a stage on which both secular punishment and Christian promise are performed, the scaffold witnesses the prisoner physically destroyed by earthly authority while potentially ascending to heaven.

These pressures served largely to ensure that scaffold speeches conformed to the formula of confession, apology, and prayer. Yet the utterly formulaic quality of such speeches could have raised doubts among audience members, who were aware of such pressures, regarding a given speech's authenticity. The audience might understand the performance on the scaffold as a false repentance born of a sincere desire to protect one's family. As condemned subjects endlessly performed the same role on the scaffold, the crowd's faith in the authenticity of each confession may well have dwindled. Indeed, early modern pamphleteers occasionally voice suspicions about the authenticity of a traitor's sentiments on the scaffold. In "A True and Perfect Relation of the Whole Proceedings against the late most barbarous Traitors" (1606), for example, the author reports a phrase made by Sir Edward Coke at the arraignment of the Gunpowder plotters: "true repentance is indeed never too late: but late repentance is seldome found true."[44] Coke's pithy saying, which may have been a common expression, draws into question the sincerity of a prisoner's eleventh hour confession and prayer on the scaffold. Coke's doubt about the authenticity of scaffold repentances mirrors that of the author F.W., who condemns the prisoner Ambrose Ruckwood for insincerity in "The Arraignment and Execution of the late Traytors," a pamphlet circulated after the Gunpowder Plot. The author claims that Ruckwood, "out of a studied speech would faine have made his bringing uppe and breeding in idolatrie, to have been some excuse to his villanie, but a faire talke, could not helpe a fowle deed."[45] He condemns Ruckwood's speech as "studied," a term suggesting that the speech is a fictional expression akin to the memorized speech of an actor onstage. Such "faire talke" does not impress the author, who reminds his readers of Ruckwood's "fowle deed." Scaffold speeches are therefore problematic not only because of their use as propaganda but also because the insincerity of the confession could be patently obvious to an audience. While the speeches may appear to reconstitute monarchical power, then, in the case of the scaffold genre a significant gap exists between the mouthing of the scaffold conventions and a full confirmation of the state's position.

As well as questioning the sincerity of formulaic repentance, these pamphleteers may have occasionally fabricated a prisoner's dying words. Given the propagandistic value of such pamphlets in justifying the state's case, the authors would themselves have experienced pressure to record speeches according to the conventional formula. In an account of the scaffold speech of Henry Cuffe, the earl of Essex's former secretary who was executed in March 1601 for his role in the rebellion, the author condemns the prisoner for refusing to repent, only to report his utterly conventional final words on the scaffold. Cuffe initially reiterates his innocence on the scaffold, claiming, "I do here call God, his angels, and my own conscience to witness, that I was not in the least concerned therein, but was shut up that whole day within the house, where I spent time in very melancholy reflections."[46] Despite Cuffe's self-defense, however, the account, switching to third person, then records that he "began to apply himself to his devotions, which he managed with a great deal of furvor, and then making a solemn profession of his Creed, and asking pardon of God and the queen, he was dispatched by the executioner."[47]

Similarly, in an account of the Gunpowder plotters, F.W. tells his readers that the prisoners "seemed to feele no part of feare, either of the wrath of God, the doome of Justice, or the shame of sinne; but as it were with seared Consciences, senceles of grace, lived, as not looking to die."[48] The prisoners "took Tobacco out of measure" and generally expressed little concern for their treason. When brought to court they continued to be insolent, "craving mercy of neyther God nor the king for their offences" (sig. B3r-v). Yet F.W. reports that, on the scaffold, Edward Digby and Francis Bates asked forgiveness "of God, of the king, and the whole kingdom." Indeed, Bates, the writer notes, "seemed sorie for his offence" and "prayed to God for the preservation of them all" (sig. C1r; C2r). The discrepancy between prisoners' indifference or claims of innocence in jail and their subsequent repentance on the scaffold may have raised doubts in readers' minds about the pamphlet's accuracy, since the author manages both to condemn the obstinacy of the men and to confirm their guilt through their own scaffold confessions. Of course, in the case of the Gunpowder Plot, the most notorious conspirators, namely, Catesby, Tresham, Wright, and the Percy brothers, all died before reaching the scaffold, either in the fighting immediately after the plot or, in Tresham's case, in prison. A repentant speech from Catesby might have pushed the boundaries of belief just too far, highlighting, in a particularly bare fashion, the fictional nature of scaffold speech pamphlets.

The accounts of the Essex Rebellion and the Gunpowder Plot openly acknowledge the frequent opposition of sinful deeds and pious speech: as F.W. claims above, "faire talke could not help a fowle deed." Explicitly arguing that a reported speech might be insincere, these pamphlets question the very formulaic, artful language that is the stock and trade of their own profession. If such speeches were meant to instruct the audience to avoid vice and to fear sovereign authority, the reports convey these repentant dying words with the recognition that they are a convenient fiction. This sense of the scaffold speech impels the vital work of Steven Mullaney, who stresses the opposition of the state and theater scaffolds. According to Mullaney, the last dying speech is "an exemplary manifestation of the power of the state to foster internalized obedience even among its most retrograde members," while the "power of the stage was precisely the power of fiction."[49] Yet the scaffold speech, as I argued above, is itself a powerful fiction. Aware of audience skepticism, the pamphleteers nevertheless practiced their trade under the encouragement of an avid reader who may have been the only audience member willing to mistake the fiction for reality: the crown itself. Attempting to rely on the illusory sincerity of the speech to validate its punishment, the state's scaffold instead produced a spectacle of physical violence and interpretive riddles, uncomfortably mingling "fowle" and "faire" in a manner that recalls the foggy heath of the witches in Shakespeare's *Macbeth*.

Interpreting Cawdor's Scaffold Speech

The witches' phrase in the first scene of *Macbeth* famously announces the play's interpretive ambiguity in terms that match F.W.'s condemnation of Ruckwood: "Fair is foul, and foul is fair: / Hover through the fog and filthy air" (1.1.11–12). The play's next scenes, alternating between Duncan's bloody battlefield and the witches' foggy heath, swiftly confirm this interpenetration of foul and fair by presenting two treasonous spectacles: the treachery of the Thane of Cawdor, which Rosse reports to Duncan in scene 2, and the witches' seditious prophecies to Macbeth in scene 3.[50] In both cases, fair news accompanies foul deeds or desires: first, the triumph of Scotland against Norway comes with the announcement of the first Thane of Cawdor's treason; second, the promotion of Macbeth to Thane of Cawdor provokes the birth of his treasonous desire. As Macbeth asks himself on hearing the witches' prophecy, "Why do I yield to that suggestion / Whose horrid image doth unfix my hair, / And make my seated heart knock at my ribs, / Against the use of nature?" (1.3.134–37). This alteration between triumph and treason helps to establish the play's unsettled atmosphere in which oppositional forces appear in tangled relation to one another.

The play powerfully establishes the parallelism between the heath and battlefield: in both scenes, an onstage audience of two noblemen struggles to comprehend treasonous language. In one instance, Banquo and Macbeth hear the witches' prophecies, and, in the other, Duncan and Malcolm respond to the report of Cawdor's treachery. While the witches' words provoke the birth of treason in Macbeth, however, Cawdor's scaffold speech presents the other end of the trajectory, reporting the voice of the condemned traitor. Having seen Macbeth lured by "instruments of darkness," we now witness the first Cawdor denouncing his treasonous acts in a conventional, didactic speech. Malcolm announces Cawdor's death to his father:

> I have spoke
> With one that saw him die: who did report,
> That very frankly he confess'd his treasons,
> Implor'd your Highness' pardon, and set forth
> A deep repentance. Nothing in his life
> Became him like the leaving it: he died
> As one that had been studied in his death
> To throw away the dearest thing he ow'd
> As 'twere a careless trifle.
>
> (1.4.3–11)

According to Malcolm's report, Cawdor's final words consist of his confession of treason, his plea to the monarch and his repentant prayer. This correspondence of Cawdor's lines with extant speeches of historical traitors, and the circulation of the Gunpowder plotters' speeches in pamphlets during the year before the production of *Macbeth*, strongly suggest that Shakespeare drew on such material in depicting Cawdor's last moments. This episode with Cawdor has received limited critical attention, however, possibly because scholars concur on its dramatic function: it foreshadows Macbeth's later treason in granting him the traitor Cawdor's title, and it alerts the audience to the accuracy of at least part of the witches' prophecy in the following scene, where they hail Macbeth as the Thane of Cawdor. Although these lines may not strike a modern audience as problematic, this scaffold speech presented Shakespeare's contemporary audience with a familiar, yet complex, genre. Karin S. Coddon has helped to illuminate the scene's interpretive richness; as she argues, Cawdor's reported lines "paint a typical enough tableau, but it is ironized both by its narrative prematurity and by the fact that the new Thane of Cawdor is already contemplating treason."[51] Such formulaic repentance should accompany tragic closure rather than occur in the play's first scene.

Indeed, Malcolm's report acknowledges the interpretive challenge of Cawdor's model of repentance. Despite the "frankness" of Cawdor's speech, Malcolm expresses his reservation at the traitor's performance. Malcolm's first line, "nothing in his life became him like the leaving it," dances between disdain and compliment for the traitor. Although he wryly dismisses the traitor, suggesting that death suits the treacherous Cawdor more than life ever did, he equally implies that the traitor earned an unprecedented glory in his final moment, making it the greatest achievement in his life. Malcolm maintains this tenuous balance between praise and contempt for Cawdor in his next line: "he died / As one that had been studied in his death." Expressed through a simile, the line compares Cawdor's end to a stock death, "one that had been studied," suggesting that the traitor appropriately prepared himself according to the tradition of the *ars moriendi*. The phrase "studied in his death" equally implies, however, an artful or dissembling end, one of mouthing forms without belief, as F.W. suggests in his report of Ruckwood's death, analyzed above. The use of "studied" in Malcolm's phrase could insinuate an even less favorable portrait if we interpret the line "the dearest thing he ow'd" not as the body but instead as the soul, as suggested by Kenneth Muir.[52]

The conventional scaffold speech should educate the audience away from treason, but Cawdor's speech instead defies easy characterization since Malcolm appears to question the sincerity of the prisoner's "studied" lines. Moreover, when considered in light of early modern scaffold speech pamphlets, such a formulaic account raises doubts about the authenticity of the report itself. If these pamphlets of dying last words elicited skepticism, then Malcolm's report may have provoked equal suspicion from theater audiences. Like a pamphleteer, Malcolm demonstrates his ability to manipulate language, creating a convenient fiction for the benefit of the state, a point I return to below.

If Malcolm's report on the execution highlights the insidious power of treason to confuse truthful speech and "studied" falsehood, then Duncan is perhaps the only viewer who fails to learn this lesson. In response to the report, the king offers a short commentary, laced with dramatic irony: "There's no art / To find the mind's construction in the face: / He was a gentleman on whom I built / An absolute trust—[Enter Macbeth . . .]" (1.4.11–14). Unable to detect the "mind" in the "face," the king becomes a victim of Macbeth's false hospitality at Inverness where he is murdered, as many critics have noted. On one level, Duncan here serves as a symbol of untarnished monarchy, unable to see, and therefore untainted by, treason. The play appears to reinforce Duncan's sanctified rule by highlighting his baffled response to Cawdor's treason, in contrast to the ambitious Macbeths: in the scene after Cawdor's execution, and immediately following Macbeth's promotion, Lady Macbeth recommends the treasonous duplicity between "mind" and "face" to her husband, urging him to "only look up clear" as he welcomes, and contemplates killing, Duncan (1.5.71). While Duncan's "gentle senses" (1.6.3) celebrate the sweet air at Inverness, Lady Macbeth summons an atmosphere of "thick Night," filled with the "dunnest smoke of Hell" (1.5.50–51), anticipating Macbeth's own "Come, seeling Night" speech (3.2.46–55). In its portrait of the Macbeths, the play thus rehearses the most sensational portraits of treason, familiar from propagandistic pamphlets that chronicle the "fearfull Chaos" of the treason: it would have "sent forth of the bottome of the Stygian lake such sulphured smoke, furious flames, and fearefull thunder, as should have by their diobolicall Domesday destroyed and defaced" the country.[53] William Barlow's sermon after the plot also employs such language: the "false-hearted rebels" dwell in "the lowest pit," while the king's "resplendent brightness" shines so that "all the kingdomes of Christendome may receive their light."[54] With the attempted treason, "these lights thus gloriouslie shining in this golden candlesticke . . . would have at once blowne out" (3r).

This stark rhetorical opposition between the legitimate Duncan and the murderous Macbeth has worked, however, to obscure the play's exposure of the king's weak rule and its resulting exploration of other, rival models of sovereignty. First, the opening scenes of the play depict Duncan's political ineptitude, born of his inability to read the political landscape that surrounds him.[55] One may object that Duncan's struggle with treason does not suggest his inadequate leadership but implies instead the fallen state of Macbeth's Scotland. But such an emphasis on Macbeth as the sole source of treason ignores the political turmoil that opens the play: at war with Norway, the Scottish troops have only recently succeeded in freeing Malcolm from captivity (1.2.4–

5). Furthermore, Harry Berger reminds us that by the fourth scene of the play Duncan has encountered two rebels, and "these facts have to be set against the persistent praise of Duncan as an ideal king, the head of a harmonious state."[56] Jonathan Goldberg advances a related point: while Duncan's language may appear to support the play's propagandistic opposition of sovereign and traitor, his lines find their source in Holinshed's witches; as a result, Goldberg claims, "the absolute differences and moral clarity that critics have found to be Shakespeare's are [instead] . . . Duncan's."[57]

Duncan is further culpable if we consider, following the example of the scaffold speech pamphlets, that Malcolm's report itself may be a fabrication. Since pamphleteers sought royal license and approval by producing the speeches of penitent traitors, then the very spectacle that should help reassert royal authority over the state's subjects instead serves the opposite function: the subjects, in this case the pamphleteers, reassure the crown of its own authority through an arguably fictional genre.[58] Duncan, a king threatened by treason from within and rebellion from without, attempts to reestablish his own political authority through his swift execution of Cawdor. Instead, not only does Cawdor's execution provoke Macbeth's treason, but it also exhibits Duncan's excessive dependence on his loyal subjects, including Rosse, who informs him of Cawdor's treason, and Malcolm, who informs him of the execution. Rather than lead his subjects, Duncan, as Berger so persuasively argues, is continually in their debt, as when he proclaims to Macbeth immediately after the execution of Cawdor, "more is thy due than more than all can pay" (1.4.21). Duncan does not protect his country but requires protection himself, and Malcolm's comforting but possibly fictive report of Cawdor's death only further highlights the king's profound dependence on his own subjects.

Duncan's inadequacies appear even more striking when compared to an example of monarchical reading—discussed at the opening of this book—contemporaneous with the play: James's sensational discovery, upon reading a cryptic letter delivered to Lord Monteagle, of the Gunpowder Plot. The letter reads:

> My Lord, out of the love I bear to some of your friends, I have a care of your preservation. Therefore I would advise you, as you tender your life, to devise some excuse to shift of your attendance at this Parliament. . . .

For though there be no appearance of any stir, yet I say they shall receive a terrible blow this Parliament; and yet they shall not see who hurts them. This counsel is not to be condemned because it may do you good and can do you no harm; for the danger is passed as soon as you have burnt the letter, and I hope God will give you the grace to make good use of it, to whose holy protection I commend you.[59]

While the note's clues may be obvious to an informed reader ("terrible blow this Parliament"), nevertheless, according to the narrative of events in *The King's Book,* the note was intelligible neither to Lord Monteagle nor to the earls of Salisbury, Suffolk, Worcester, and Northampton with whom he consulted.[60] At a loss, they turned to King James upon his return, "for the expectation and experience they had of His Majesty's fortunate judgment, in clearing and solving obscure riddles and doubtful mysteries."[61] Only James, strikingly like Oedipus in his riddle reading, had the ability to decipher this note: "After the reading of it, the king made a pause, and then, reading it again, . . . did conclude, as he was walking and musing in the gallery, that the danger must be sudden, like the blowing up by gunpowder."[62]

At pains to draw out the moment of reading, the pamphlet recreates the king's triumphal discovery. The performance of reading skeptically in these lines (he "made a pause," "musing," "considering," "concluding") highlights the connection between reading and revelation in the world of politics. In the report circulating after the plot, James's interpretive ability was called "extraordinary, being against the common construction, far from what any other did apprehend by it."[63] Rather than locate treason in violent action, here the crime lies in cryptic language: to protect the country, the king defends himself not with arms but with interpretive skill. His distinction from the "common construction" verifies James's rightful position as king, singular in his ability to interpret "far from others" and thereby save Parliament.

If James's skillful reading saves England from treason, so, too, does Malcolm's interpretive power in the Cawdor scene offer the promise of effective rule beyond that of his allegedly idealized father. Duncan's failure to interpret treasonous language endangers himself and his country. In his reading of both Cawdor and, as I suggest below, Macduff, Malcolm demonstrates the verbal skepticism required to rule in Scotland.

"I am as I have spoken": Malcolm's Sovereignty

Malcolm's emergent leadership owes more to the deceitful tactics of Cawdor and Macbeth than to his vulnerable father's example. First, Malcolm's revolt against Macbeth is of questionable legitimacy, a point illuminated more clearly in Shakespeare's historical sources than in his play.[64] On one level, as both the nominated Prince of Cumberland and Duncan's son, Malcolm appears to satisfy two systems of inheritance: tanistry, the traditional, Scottish system of indirect inheritance, and primogeniture, the newer system based on direct succession. Yet, in nominating Malcolm as Prince of Cumberland, Duncan ignores Macbeth's equal claim to the throne through indirect succession, thereby complicating issues of legitimate inheritance in the play. As David Norbrook argues: "there were still noblemen whose allegiance was to the older system according to which Macbeth, son of Malcolm's other daughter, would have had a strong claim" (88). In the case of Shakespeare's play, Norbrook notes that "if Duncan has to nominate his son, presumably the implication is that he could have nominated someone else, that the system is not one of pure primogeniture" (94). Further, as both Michael Hawkins and David Scott Kastan perceptively maintain, despite Macbeth's usurpation of the crown, he nevertheless reigns as an anointed king and thus Malcolm remains bound to obey his rule.[65] The doctrine of nonresistance, upheld by James himself in *Trew Law of Free Monarchies* (1598), forbids rebellion: "a wicked king is sent by God for a curse to his people, and a plague for their sinnes: but that it is lawfull to them to shake off that curse at their owne hand, which God hath laid on them, that I deny and may do so justly."[66]

Malcolm emerges, then, as a Cawdor and Macbeth figure himself. Most obviously, according to the doctrine of nonresistance, he treasonously attacks a legitimate monarch. Yet the play occludes this issue in depicting his rebellion. Instead, Malcolm's role as a Cawdor figure develops more subtly: in each of Malcolm's appearances between his father's murder and his own ascension as king, he increasingly exploits the opposition of "mind" and "face" so that, like Macbeth, he deceives his audiences onstage to protect himself and eventually gain the throne. First, immediately after his father's murder he separates speech from sincerity, claiming that "to show an unfelt sorrow is an office / Which the false man does easy" (2.3.134–35). His connection of performance ("to show") and falsity ("unfelt sorrow") recalls his ambiguity toward Cawdor's studied speech, since in both cases he retains a skeptical distance from sirenic speech. Here Malcolm and Donalbain remain silent, causing Malcolm to ask his brother in an aside, "Why do we hold our tongues, that may most claim / This argument for ours?" (2.3.118–19). The image of the held, or controlled, tongue powerfully contrasts with the overflow of the scene, occurring at the level both of the body, seen in Duncan's blood and Lady Macbeth's emotion, and of the tongue itself, evident in the emotion of Macduff and the Macbeths. Malcolm's initial image of the held tongue could stand as a symbol for the virginal prince who is, as Janet Adelman has noted in her influential reading of the representation of masculine power in the play, "yet / Unknown to women" (4.3.125–16).[67]

Initially questioning the association of speech and sincerity, Malcolm then begins to exploit the duplicitous potential of language as he establishes his allies in the fight against Macbeth. His exchange with Macduff in act 4, scene 3, most clearly reveals this linguistic deception; here, as Norbrook argues of Malcolm, "paradoxically, it is only by modeling himself on Macbeth's own strategies of dissimulation (4.3.117–19) that he can prove Macduff's virtue" (111). Characterizing himself to Macduff as an uncontrolled libertine who would "pour the sweet milk of concord into Hell" (98), Malcolm claims that his own vices are so heinous that "when they shall be open'd, black Macbeth / Will seem as pure as snow" (52–53). He ends his list of multitudinous sins by insisting, to Macduff's disbelief, that "I am as I have spoken" (102). Malcolm's self-characterization directly contradicts his own behavior in the play (he is a man who is known more through silence than speech) inverting his identity in a manner parallel to the equation plaguing Scotland: "fair is foul and foul is fair." His own statement, "I am as I have spoken," ironically recalls Duncan's belief in authentic speech, invoking the earlier faith in the correspondence of speech and intent as a ruse to expose deceit.[68]

Having manipulated his audience through false speech, Malcolm ends by tricking Macbeth's troops with his illusionist battle tactics. According to the witches' prophecy, Macbeth is safe "until / Great Birnam wood to high Dunsinane hill / Shall come against him" (4.1.92–94). This statement reassures Macbeth, who cannot imagine this geographical impossibility: "That will never be: / Who can impress the forest; bid the tree / Unfix his earth-bound root?" (94–96). By the next act, however, we learn that it is Malcolm who "can impress the forest" and "bid the tree / Unfix" its root, when he tells his troops, "Let every soldier hew him down a bough, / And bear't before him: thereby shall we shadow / The numbers of our host" (5.4.4–6). While Malcolm is ignorant of the witches' speech to Macbeth, his command nevertheless fulfills their prophecy. In attempting to "shadow / The numbers," he implements devious tactics in order to conquer treason, since he, like the Macbeths, proves willing to haunt the darkened shadows in order to obtain royal power.

Using deception to test Macduff's loyalty and triumph over Macbeth, Malcolm adopts the traitor's art. Ironically, while the Macbeths began the play by using language as a medium through which to deceive Duncan, as the play continues they increasingly betray themselves by speaking frankly of their treasons. Macbeth unwittingly discloses his murder of Duncan and Banquo to his nobles in the banquet scene, and Lady Macbeth famously confesses her crimes to her doctor and maid while sleepwalking. Further, unable or unwilling to recognize the witches' prophecies as misleading half-truths, Macbeth desperately clings to their speeches as authentic statements about his future, repeating the lines "I will not be afraid of death and bane, / Till Birnam forest come to Dunsinane" as a means of consoling himself (5.3.59–60; see also 1–10). If Macbeth's demise comes in part from his unwillingness to recognize the witches' prophecies as riddles, Malcolm acknowledges and employs the riddles of language, both in the opening scene where, as I have argued, he highlights the indecipherability of Cawdor's dying words, and in the closing scenes with Macduff.

In addition to exposing Malcolm's use of treasonous deception in gaining the throne, the play also reinforces his distance from pious kingship, thereby frustrating attempts to read his victory as a restoration, or establishment, of sovereign order. The scene of his misleading exchange with Macduff, for example, ends with the portrait of England's saintly King Edward whose methods deeply contrast with Malcolm's own. Describing Edward's god-given power to cure, known as "the king's touch," the doctor reports how, "at [Edward's] touch, / Such sanctity hath Heaven given his hand, / They [the ill] presently amend" (4.3.143–45). Malcolm elaborates, saying to Macduff that the king can heal the Evil:

A most miraculous work in this good King,
Which often, since my here-remain in England,
I have seen him do. How he solicits Heaven,
Himself best knows; but strangely-visited people,
All swoln and ulcerous, pitiful to the eye,
The mere despair of surgery, he cures.

(4.3.146–52)

In treating "the Evil," namely, the physical malady of scrofula, the king heals "strangely-visited people," a descriptive phrase that recalls Scotland's own trauma under Macbeth, himself the object of strange visitations in the form of the witches, ghosts, and visions. Indeed, the description of England's "Evil" powerfully resonates in the context of Scotland's own plague with the crime of treason, a point persuasively argued by Susanne L. Wofford, who writes that the play "nostalgically invokes the English King as healer of the body private and politic—the successful doctor missing in Scotland is found in the English King who can heal by the laying on of hands."[69] While Duncan attempts to excise the treasonous plague through violent surgery, executing the treasonous criminal Cawdor, "the Evil" only multiplies, becoming "the mere despair of surgery." Edward's ability to heal through the divine gift of touch imaginatively provides a cure, fulfilling Duncan's earlier longing for an art to cure the Evil that haunted his kingdom and resulted in his death.

The model of monarchy presented in this short, idealized portrait of Edward's reign offers a powerful antidote to the bloody tyranny of Macbeth, suggesting a form of pious rule for beleaguered Scotland. Although Edward receives Malcolm in England and therefore symbolically purifies the Scottish heir, nevertheless the connection of monarchy and treason established with Cawdor's opening scaffold speech argues against the possibility of a divine monarch, independent of treasonous machinations. Juxtaposing the two episodes of act 4, scene 3, one of deception, in which Malcolm slanders himself before Macduff, and one of healing, in which Malcolm depicts Edward's curative powers, throws into high relief the contrast between the English and Scottish contexts. Malcolm's testing of Macduff exposes the tragic condition of Scotland's monarchy, which combines strong rule with traitorous arts. The contrasting portrait of Edward thus represents the illusion of divine kingship that Malcolm and his countrymen can no longer experience.

Although the play struggles to assert a model of divine kingship in the figures of Duncan and Edward the Confessor, it ultimately challenges the ideological opposition of monarch and traitor by intertwining these roles. Macbeth's own rule most clearly undermines the distinction by combining the tactics of traitor and king. Yet even before he succeeds to the throne, Scottish kingship appears compromised by Duncan's imperceptive, vulnerable rule. Duncan dismisses interpretive arts partly because he sees his political landscape in terms of absolutes, dividing his soldier friends from his foreign enemies. Such oppositions fail to account for the conceptual fog that hovers over Scotland, blurring the distinction between male and female, as with the witches and Lady Macbeth, and ally and traitor, as with Macbeth himself. If material, gendered bodies become indistinguishable in the play, as Marjorie Garber has so effectively argued, so, too, do the immaterial categories of truth and falsity lose their definition: the witches' speeches defy such rigid characterization, hovering between accurate prophecy and alluring deceit. As a result, the nation's successful king combines the attributes of monarch and traitor, negotiating between legitimacy and fabrication in order to establish his rule. Despite Norbrook's astute analysis that the play ends with the recuperation of authentic, public language, evident when "Macduff is able to proclaim an end to dissimulation" (111), Malcolm's trajectory from silent witness of his father's murder to deceptive leader who tricks Macbeth undermines such assurances. Rather than offer, as Norbrook suggests, "not just a restoration but the foundation of a new and more stable order" (112), Malcolm's accession in the play tragically demonstrates that only by adopting the tools of the traitor can the king triumph on Scotland's foggy heath.

Ironically, if state spectacles should instruct potential traitors to abstain from transgressing, in the case of *Macbeth* the traitor's tricks instead educate the country's future rulers. Specifically, the initial spectacle of Cawdor's execution backfires, since, rather than inspire loyalty, it teaches Malcolm the value of deceptive rhetoric and bolsters Macbeth's ambition for the crown. Staging Malcolm's tragic education at the hands of Cawdor and Macbeth, the play presses on the boundaries of the English Renaissance model of tragedy. Rather than confirm the didacticism implied in Sidney's definition, the play instead reinforces the more radical implications of his model: tragedy imagines a theatrical world in which the political and epistemological oppositions between king and traitor, innocent and guilty, internal and external, bleed into each other. The tragic genre as represented in *Macbeth* thus exposes how the transgressions of witches and traitors lie in the tissue of each spectator as well, hidden just beneath the surface and waiting to be exposed on the tragic scaffold.

Macbeth's Dying Speech

Such a frightening political insight—based in the inevitability of violence, dissimulation, and treason—is palatable to the play's audience only because history is on our side. Malcolm becomes a traitor only temporarily. However much he might dissimulate and act like a traitor, the play's final scenes allow us to believe that he, finally, is not one. Instead, he seeks to preserve the common good and restore legitimate order during a time of treasonous crisis, and he succeeds. Lest we forget this, the play embeds a reminder: when Macbeth asks about Banquo's "issue," the witches show him a line of eight kings, stretching all the way to James himself with the "two-fold balls and treble sceptres" of monarchy (4.1.121). This line of kings powerfully reasserts a distinction between monarch and traitor, blurred in the play. Succession, in this fantasy at least, is clear, natural, and inevitable.[70] We might hesitate to take solace in the witches' spectacle (we could, like Macbeth, end up cursing in frustration, "damn'd all those that trust them" (139)), and we might register the rejection of Scottish noble succession for an English model, as Malcolm turns thanes to earls. Nevertheless, with the benefit of history, we know that Banquo's issue does in fact end with James, that the king did indeed survive a treasonous attack, and that England and Scotland will, eventually as modern audiences realize, be united. Scotland's crisis under Macbeth does not have to be England's own, a comforting final fantasy that the play conjures for its contemporary audience. Having entangled treason and sovereignty, truth and lies, for four acts, Shakespeare ends with the fantasy of uncontested restoration.

Opening with the failed didacticism of Cawdor, then, *Macbeth* ends with Malcolm's alleged triumph over treason. But amid the celebration of Malcolm's victory lies a ghost plot, haunting the final scene. This ghost plot concerns the manner of Macbeth's death, a topic that plagues him for the second half of the play. Given the doubling of Macbeth and Cawdor, both in name and in deed, Macbeth's death has already been written in Cawdor's in the first act. To make the spectral relation complete, and to reinforce the distinctions between traitor and sovereign reestablished in the play's last act, Macbeth should follow his namesake's example, didactically confessing in the final scene. This plot-not-taken remains a possibility until the end, a possibility that seems all the stronger given the historical precedent of traitors who, despite their fierce challenges to authority, appear to repent in their final moments.

Juxtaposing the deaths of the two Cawdors highlights the tragic power of Macbeth's decision to embrace bloodshed as a means of carving his own end. His manner of dying opposes that of his earlier namesake: while Cawdor's speech recalls the dying last words of the vast majority of traitors, Macbeth becomes a bestial fighter who defies human expectation. His death betrays a fiendish intensity challenging not only the state that the king had formerly ruled but also the religious faith to which he is expected to turn. Realizing that the riddling prophecies of the witches are fulfilled, Macbeth, like Marlowe's Faustus, condemns himself to hell onstage, presenting the audience with a vision of terror: the transgressive subject refuses or is unable to repent, therefore damning himself before our eyes. In a play staged after a failed but frightening treason, this spectacle figures James's triumph: in the fashion of Gunpowder plotters Catesby, Wright, and Percy, Macbeth dies unrepentant, fighting, and damned.

Yet even at the end, as the play attempts to foreclose Macbeth's treasonous charisma by condemning his "usurper's cursed head" (5.9.21), he continues to lure his audiences away from the didactic toward the dangerously criminal. Cawdor, in the conventional manner of scaffold performance, offers himself to a theater of spectators watching rapt as he utters his dying last words, be they authentic, insincere, or entirely fictional. In violent contrast to this allegedly docile subject on the scaffold, Macbeth cries "before my body / I throw my warlike shield" (5.8.32–33). In doing so, he challenges the relation of spectator and actor that operates on the scaffold by forcing us to examine our own generic expectations for repentance and restoration even as we gaze at him. As with Perseus's triumph over Medusa, Macbeth turns his spectral shield to the audience, opposing the conventions for pious death and allowing himself, momentarily, to triumph. Denying expectation, damning himself, yet famously inventing his own plot, Macbeth reveals Cawdor's submissive and familiar formula to be weak art indeed.

CHAPTER FIVE

Donne's Pseudo-Martyr
and Post–Gunpowder Plot Law

Having investigated, in the previous chapter, Malcolm's pragmatic sovereignty in his fight against demonic treason in *Macbeth*, this chapter turns to King James's own response to treason in the aftermath of the Gunpowder Plot. Here, James's own form of pragmatic sovereignty emerges, and to questionable effect. Amid scaffold speakers, criminal investigations, and the atmosphere of "fog and filthy air" characteristic of treason, James conducted the opening session of Parliament that had been the target of the Gunpowder plotters.

This 1606 meeting naturally provoked fears among the king's Catholic allies, as suggested in a letter by the Venetian ambassador to England, Nicolò Molin. He writes to his Senate, "the meeting of Parliament is approaching. . . . Parliament is full of Puritans, who desire new laws against the Catholics. The King is said to share this desire; and so, unless the good God stretch out his holy hand, we must look for great calamity."[1] Molin's fears seem justified in that the English Parliament immediately began a discussion on recusancy laws, considering how to expand and better enforce them.[2] The result was sweeping, new legislation on recusancy, including "An Act for the Attainder of divers Offenders in the late most barbarous, monstrous, detestable, and damnable Treasons," "An Act against seditious Speeches, Words, and Rumours, against the King's most excellent Majesty," "An Act for the avoiding of unnecessary delays of executions," and "An Act to preserve and restore to the Crown the true and ancient Regalities appertaining to the same," among others.[3]

Most notably, on May 27, 1606, James and his Parliament passed the oath of allegiance, which required all subjects over the age of eighteen to swear their allegiance to the king in all temporal matters.[4] Specifically the oath dismissed the deposing power of the pope, claimed against the English monarchy. The oath asked subjects to swear,

> I A.B. do truly and sincerely acknowledge, professe, testifie, and declare in my conscience before God and the world that our Sovereigne Lord King James is lawful and rightful King of this Realme, and of all other his Majesties Dominions and Countries: and that the Pope neither of himself nor by any authority of the Church or Sea of Rome, or by any other meanes with any other, hath any power or Authoritie to depose the King, or to dispose any of his Majesties Kingdoms or Dominions, or to authorize any foreign Prince to invade or annoy him or his Countries, or to discharge any of his Subjects of their Allegiance and obedience to his Majesty, or to give licence or leave to any of them to bear arms, raise tumult, or to offer any violence or hurt to his Majesties royal person, state or government, or to any of his Majesties subjects within his Majesties dominions. . . . Also I do further sweare, That I do from my heart . . . abhor, detest and abjure, as impious and hereticall, this damnable doctrine and position, That princes which be Excommunicated or deprived by the Pope, may be deposed or murthered by their Subjects, or any other whatsoever.[5]

As discussed in chapter 1, treason had been associated with Catholicism throughout Queen Elizabeth's reign. This Jacobean oath, however, established into law for the first time the coupling of treason and popery: now all subjects were required to swear their allegiance to the king and denounce the papal deposing power or else suffer the penalty for *praemunire* or treason.[6] The oath, as Stefania Tutino convincingly argues, "redefined the question of the relationship between religion and politics."[7]

This oath has been called either a justifiable, and indeed fair, means of dealing with Catholic traitors in England or, alternately, a new form of economic and political persecution for recusant subjects under James, a debate that continues in current scholarship. On one level, scholars argue that post–Gunpowder Plot policies, combined with the fearful atmosphere following the discovery of the plot, helped to establish the king's claims to absolute sovereignty. First, James interpreted his discovery of the plot as an indication of his divine appointment, as Derek Hirst writes: "The greater intensity after 1606 of his rhetoric of lieutenancy to God, which at least some MPs came to find distasteful, can be traced to the conspiracy."[8] The 1606 Parliament helped to legally reinforce such rhetoric through its legislation against Catholicism, a point Alan Haynes makes in his study of the Gunpowder Plot: "The theory of the Divine Right of Kings so passionately upheld by James was a very important item in the struggle for national rights against the papacy, and these new [1606] statutes were props for this over-arching notion."[9] As an allegedly divinely appointed ruler, James particularly condemned theories of legitimate resistance for implying that a king could be deposed by his subjects. David Wootton has shown how "in James's reign, particularly after the Gunpowder Plot of 1605, tyrannicide was a doctrine that only Catholics dared defend: to deny the absolute authority of the king appeared to open the way to the legitimation of Catholic plotting."[10]

James may have used the opportunity of post–Gunpowder Plot legislation to help secure this royal authority. The 1606 Jacobean oath of allegiance seemed to have been especially designed to increase state control of Catholic subjects. The oath was not a simple profession of civil allegiance to which the pope and his allies responded with paranoia; instead, the oath, as M. C. Questier writes, was "an exceptionally subtle and well-constructed rhetorical essay in the exercise of state power."[11] Further, he writes, "the ideological foundations of the oath of allegiance were potentially a model for the royal supremacy."[12] Johann P. Sommerville also interprets the oath of allegiance and James's contributions to the ensuing debate as an articulation of his absolutist ideology:

> James and his supporters in this [oath of allegiance] controversy claimed that kings derived their powers from God alone and were therefore accountable to neither pope nor people. They portrayed kings as sovereign lawmakers, not as bound by the law of the land.[13]

By defining kings above the law in his defenses of the oath of allegiance, James articulates a theory of absolute sovereignty.

While James's policies effectively articulated the king's sovereign authority as these historians suggest, the king equally insisted on his clemency and toleration toward Catholic subjects. He took immense pride in his newly established peace with Spain and emphasized his role internationally as a pacific prince. In attempting to defend his new policies toward Catholics before a continental audience and thereby maintain peaceful relations with Catholic countries, he claimed that such policies represented a moderate, reasonable attempt to govern the actions of his more extreme subjects. The regulation of the Catholic minority proved an immediate political necessity; it did not represent a programmatic attempt to expand his prerogative at the expense of his subjects.

Following King James, several historians develop a more sympathetic portrait of James's post–Gunpowder Plot policies. Specifically the oath seemed to offer loyal Catholics the ability to declare their obedience to the state while continuing to live as recusants. At the same time James's call for temporal obedience among his subjects functioned simply to defend the state from resistance theorists and traitors. Roger Lockyer writes, "The Oath of Allegiance demonstrates the consistency of James's policy of splitting the radicals from the moderate majority, and is evidence that he preserved a balanced and unfanatical approach to the catholic problem, even in the turbulent wake of the Gunpowder Plot."[14] Mark Nicholls also supports this view in his study of the Gunpowder Plot, noting that the "legislation passed was hardly severe."[15] Furthermore, as Glenn Burgess posits, the oath of allegiance controversy attracted a European audience, and James's polemics in the controversy, in which he articulates a theory of the divine right of kings, should be read in this context: the debate "was increasingly carried out before a European audience, and so took on a degree of abstraction and removal from the specifics of the ancient constitution of England."[16] Burgess emphasizes the European context to the oath debates, suggesting that James's policy and polemics emerged out of a pragmatic attempt to communicate his point in a non-English context.

This Jacobean oath of allegiance, as Charles Howard McIlwain notes, gave "rise to a paper warfare in Europe the likes of which has never been seen since."[17] The oath elicited multiple, conflicting responses not only from the pope, Cardinal Bellarmine, and English Archpriest George Blackwell, to which James himself replied, but also from Francesco Suárez and Nicolas Coeffeteau, as well as from the English Catholics Robert Persons, Humphrey Leech, and Thomas Fitzherbert. Further contributions from James and his allies, including Pierre de Moulin, Bishop Lancelot Andrews, William Barlow, William Barclay, John Donne, and Thomas Preston led to polemics from Martin Becan and Jacques Davis, the Cardinal du Perron. Yet, in assessing the nature of this "paper warfare," historiographical debate continues: does this explosion of polemic reveal James's ideological commitment to absolutist forms of sovereignty, as Sommerville argues? Or, as Burgess claims, is the atmosphere of political consensus in early Stuart England unaffected by this predominantly European controversy? M. C. Questier's analysis of the oath of allegiance begins to answer such questions, offering a critique of the revisionist position on the oath while at the same time acknowledging James's overt defense of the policy as moderate and consensual. Writing of the oath that "in intention and even in form it advertised itself as a profession of merely civil allegiance," Questier goes on to examine how the oath effectively divided Catholics against one another: "Nothing that the Elizabethan authorities had done caused the chaos and division that the 1606 oath managed so effortlessly, and under a convincing guise of moderation, to introduce among English papists."[18] Such an effect, Questier argues, suggests the oath's genius in simultaneously undermining the cohesion of Catholics in England while claiming to monitor only temporal obedience.

This chapter and the next build on Questier's analysis of the oath of allegiance by examining the literary and polemical texts engaged in the controversy. While Questier traces the various responses of Catholics to the crisis, these chapters expand his investigation to address a selection of Protestant responses as well, such as those offered by the only recently converted writers John Donne and Ben Jonson, and the more vociferous polemic of James and his allies. Furthermore, while Questier emphasizes the genius of the Jacobean regime in crafting an oath that produced chaos among Catholic subjects, I interpret such proliferation of discourse as a sign not of political chaos over consensus but of a level of public debate extending beyond and independently of the monarch. By emphasizing chaos, Questier implies a limited efficacy to the Catholic polemic against James, presenting an image of disorder rather than one of legitimate opposition. This chapter instead charts the political agency exercised in the mixed response of both Catholics and Protestants. Through printed pamphlets and books, a variety of rulers and subjects debated "the general rules governing relations," to use Habermas's description of the public sphere.[19]

This argument about public debate on treason in the post–Gunpowder Plot era develops in two sections. In the first I examine the state's position on the Gunpowder plot and the oath of allegiance by investigating the post-plot propaganda and James's own writings, including *Triplici Nodo, triplex ceneus, or an Apologie for the Oath of Allegiance* (1608) and its second edition (1609), with a long introduction entitled *A Premonition to all most mighty Monarches, Kings, free Princes, and States of Christendom*. In the second section I turn to John Donne's 1611 *Pseudo-Martyr, wherein . . . those which are of the Romane religion in this Kingdome, may and ought to take the Oath of Allegiance*. Donne's prose work marshals historical and scriptural support for James's oath of allegiance policy, repeating many of James's arguments from *Triplici Nodo*, and, as a result, literary critics have frequently characterized Donne's argument as absolutist.[20] As a former Catholic, however, Donne expressed sympathy for his Catholic readers and discouraged blind submission to either James or the pope, modifying James's claim to absolute authority by insisting on the sovereignty of one's own conscience.[21] This simultaneous support for James's policy and qualification of his absolutist pretensions appears in Ben Jonson's *Catiline*, produced the same year as Donne's polemic, to which I turn in the book's final chapter.

Plot, Polemic, and Policy

Post–Gunpowder Plot propaganda exposes the charged political atmosphere in which James's supporters celebrated the king's sovereignty while vilifying the Catholic faith—a provocative combination that would attract international attention. In discovering the plot and saving the state from its enemies, the king claimed to benefit from God's intervention, as discussed in chapter 4. William Barlow's sermon preached at St. Paul's Cross on the Sunday after the Gunpowder Plot, as well as propagandistic pamphlets like Omerod's "Picture of a Papist" (1606), the anonymous "A True and Perfect Relation" (1606), and "The Arraignment and Execution of the late Traytors" (1606) helped to bolster James's claims to godly kingship.[22] Like the biblical King David, such pamphlets proclaim, James is *"God's king"*: he has "all the partes that may concur either in a king, or in a good King, to whom that title, first attributed to *David* . . . the *light of Israel*, principally appertaineth, as one from whose resplendent brightnesse, al the kingdomes of Christendome may receive their light."[23] Robert Cecil, the sober defender of law against James's divine pretensions, also invokes this David parallel after the plot, in this case to signal the king's inviolability: traitors "make murder spirituall resolution, and openly threaten the lives of Kings that are Gods breathing Images" while "the Prophet David trembled to violate the skirt of King Sauls garment."[24]

Professions of godliness after the plot had an obvious political edge. In his first speech to Parliament after the plot, James celebrates God's protection of him while paralleling God and himself as two rulers holding dominion: he claims, "And now I must crave a little pardon of you, that since Kings are in the word of GOD itself called Gods, as being his Lieutenants and Vicegerents [*sic*] on earth, and so adorned and furnished with some sparkles of the Divinitie, to compare some of the workes of God the great King, towards the whole and generall world, to some of his workes towards me, and this little world of my Dominions."[25] This language continues in subsequent speeches, as when James tells Parliament in 1609 that "the state of Monarchie is the supremest thing upon the earth. For Kings are not onely Gods Lieutenants upon earth, and sit upon Gods throne, but even by God himselfe they are called Gods."[26] He repeats this reasoning throughout his speech, reiterating that "Kings are justly called Gods, for that they exercise a manner or resemblance of Divine power upon earth." More than serving as the *pater patria*, James has "sparkles of the Divinitie" and, the passage implies, an intimate relationship with God, who at once governs "the whole and generall world" and exercises special "workes towards" James. The king's apparent modesty, as he "crave[s] a little pardon" to govern his "little world," hardly masks the political work of the speech in equating God and the king in the context of Parliament, precisely the "little world" where he claims "dominion."

James develops the political ramifications of such godliness in other post–Gunpowder Plot writings. Here he voices familiar claims, for example, that kings are "God his Lieutenants in earth" or that kings represent "the image of God in earth."[27] But he invokes these phrases in his arguments for complete obedience and for the related doctrine of nonresistance: citing St. Paul, he writes that "all powers are ordained of God" and that "resisting of powers is resisting the ordinance of God: because the Magistrate beares the sword to execute justice: because obediance and subjection to the Magistrate is necessary."[28] Even in the case of a tyrannical or heretical ruler, subjects must continue to obey him: "I will not deny that an heretical Prince is a plague . . . but a breach made by one mischief must not be filled up with greater inconvenience: an error must not be shocked and shouldered with disloyalty."[29] While waiting for divine intervention against a tyrannical ruler, subjects should remain in "obediance and subjection," rather than contemplate resistance.

In his 1615 defense of the oath of allegiance, *A Remonstrance for the Right of Kings,* James offers kings as the instruments of such divine intervention. Here he employs poetic license in depicting his role as an instrument of God, on the one hand, and the bane of traitors, on the other. He writes, against his Jesuit opponents, "how long shall Kings whom the Lord hath called his Anointed, Kings the breathing Images of God upon earth; Kings that with a wry or frowning looke, are able to crush these earth-wormes in pieces; how long shall they suffer this viperous brood, scotfree and without punishment, to spit in their faces?" (248). Here James, like Shakespeare's Richard II, condemns the "villians" and "vipers" (3.2.129), the "earth-worms" and "viperous brood," who challenge legitimate kings such as himself. As Richard would say, "A puny subject strikes / At thy great glory. Look not to the ground, / Ye favorites of a king. Are we not high?" (3.2.86–88). Indeed, James marshals theories of sacred kingship, familiar from the reigns of medieval kings such as Richard II. While such medieval theories asserted, in general and undefined terms, the connection of the monarch and God, James presses on the political edges of such theories: in doing so, he asserts the main planks in the theory of divine right, namely, the king's position above the law, his command of obedience without resistance, and his appointment by God and not earthly contract.

It is precisely this political edge to James's use of divine rhetoric that helps fuel the post–Gunpowder Plot debates. Asserting James's status as "God's king," the post-plot writings then proceed to condemn Catholicism as a religion grounded in treason, and thus further develop the political rather than merely religious nature of the conflict. In the sensationalist "The Arraignment and Execution of the late Traytors" (1606), the author pits treasonous Catholics against pious Protestants: "The trayterous Papist will pull downe princes, and subvert Kingdomes; murther and poyson whome they cannot commaund; The faithfull protestant praieth for princes, and the peace of the people, and will endure banishment, but hate rebellion: The proud papist will shewe intemperancie in passion, while the humble protestant will embrace affliction with patience."[30] Schooling his readers in a model of pious obedience, the author praises the Protestant subject for enduring tyranny through prayer, while condemning those Catholics who practice violent rebellion against authority. In an equally violent depiction, the anonymous author of "A True and Perfect Relation" portrays Catholics as vicious hunters seeking to kill their Protestant prey. Quoting from David's *Psalms* 124, the pamphleteer writes that "if the Lord himself had not been on our side, when men rose up against us, they had swallowed us up quicke, when they were so wrathfully displeased at us: But praised be the Lord, which hath not given us over for a pray [*sic*] unto their teeth" (G4v). The author of "The Arraignment and Execution" also mocks the Catholic methods of prayer to "wooden Ladies," claiming that "Papistrie is meere Idolatrie, the Pope an incarnate Devill, his Church a Synagogue of Satan, and his priestes the verie locustes of the earth" (D1v). This inflammatory rhetoric fills the pamphlet, uncomfortably mingling calls for passive obedience with aggressive attacks on England's enemies. Such rhetoric contributes to an environment that politicizes Catholicism in England to a degree that recusants would be viewed as traitors by virtue of their faith alone.

Father Robert Persons comments on precisely this vilification of Catholics after the Gunpowder Plot when he asks, "Is there no end of exprobriation against the Innocent, for the nocent? No compassion? No commiseration?"[31] Here he attempts to separate innocent from traitorous Catholics, urging his readers toward a type of charity absent in post–Gunpowder Plot propaganda. Yet Persons also sympathizes with the desperation of the plotters themselves. He writes how "the powder-treason was not a cause of these afflictions but an effect rather: that is to say, that those gentlemen foreseeing or knowing the course that was designed to be taken, and partly also put in practice, resolved upon that miserable medium to their own destruction and publick calamity."[32] Highlighting the relation between repressive state policies towards Catholics and the resulting treasonous designs of the afflicted, Persons nevertheless helps reinforce the image of a Catholic population sympathetic with the plotters.

In this post-plot atmosphere, marked by hyperbolic rhetoric of divinity and treason, Pope Paul V issued a breve in September 1606, in which he forbade Catholics from taking the Jacobean oath of allegiance. He writes, "Such an Oath cannot be taken without hurting of the Catholike Faith and the salvation of your soules; seeing it conteines many things which are flat contrary to Faith and salvation."[33] The pope condemns James's policy as heretical and invites his Catholic readers toward the glory of martyrdom in their fight against this Jacobean oath: the "singular vertue, valour, and fortitude in which these last times doeth no lesse shine in your Martyrs, then it did in the first beginning of the Church. Stand therefore, your loynes being girt about with veritie, and having on the brest-plate of righteousnesse, taking the shield of Faith."[34] The pope encourages the devout to continue this spiritual warfare in the historical style of the original church converts, who defended the fledgling religion against its enemies. In his breve, he clearly presents the oath as a test of faith. James's condemnation of papal deposing power challenged the indefectibility of the Catholic Church, according to which it could not lead its members astray in matters of faith or morality.[35]

Despite these papal orders, however, some Catholics took the oath in England, particularly after Archpriest Blackwell issued a letter encouraging fellow Catholics to consent to it. In his "Letter to the Romish Catholiques," he writes: "be not dismayed therefore I beseech you, with any letters or Briefes, which doe after a sort insinuate, that the taking of the Oath of Allegiance is either repugnant to any point of Faith," since the "kingdom of heaven" is distinct from "kingdomes terrene."[36] Given Blackwell's authority over English Catholics, his direct contradiction of the papal breve provoked a crisis among Catholics, who were torn between the instructions of the pope and those of the archpriest. To the surprise of the Venetian ambassador, many Catholics resolved this controversy by taking the oath. As the ambassador wrote to his senate in September 1606: "Almost all Catholics have made up their minds to take the oath. This is quite contrary to the expectation of the Council."[37]

Responding to this widespread disobedience to his orders, the pope dismissed Blackwell from his position and recruited Archpriest Robert Bellarmine, the Cardinal of the Church of Rome, in his paper war against Blackwell and James. In his 1606 open letter to Blackwell, Bellarmine encourages English Catholics to sacrifice themselves by embracing "the glory of Martyrdom" as a "gift of God" while ridiculing the former archpriest's "imbecillitie" of "old age," his "humane infirmity" and "feare of punishment and imprisonment."[38] Bellarmine reinforces the imagery of masculinist warfare deployed in the papal breve when he encourages the archpriest to die bravely: "Quite you like a man."[39] Furthermore, like the pope, Bellarmine attacks James's pretext in passing the oath, arguing that the king's policies are "but the traps and stratagemes of Satan."[40] Like Satan, James lures Catholics to take the oath "where they may indamage the Faith."[41]

Blackwell's defense of the oath continued, however. He reiterated his position, perhaps after coercion, in his examinations before the state in 1607. Published by the crown's printer, Robert Barker, these examinations reassure Catholics that they can take the oath in good conscience. Yet these texts also reveal Blackwell's efforts to restore the legitimacy of loyal English Catholics within the Jacobean state. Specifically, he claims that before the Gunpowder Plot he worked "to stay all unlawfull attempts so farre as he was able."[42] He and his English Catholic allies are not, he claims, treasonous plotters. Instead, he strives to "execute his Office for peace and for restraint of the stubbornness of some."[43]

By acknowledging the "unlawfull attempts" and "stubbornness of some," Blackwell aligns himself with the Jacobean state in condemning treason even as he works to establish a form of toleration for Catholics hitherto absent from James's policy. Key to this attempt is his attitude toward the incendiary papal deposing power. He reassures the state that he, in contrast to Robert Bellarmine, challenges such papal power. In "Mr Blackwels answer to Cardinal Bellarmine's Letter," the priest writes how "the supreme Bishop hath not an Imperiall and Civill power to depose our king, at his own pleasure and appetite."[44] This defense of the oath and, more broadly, James's absolute authority continues in "The Examination." Here, Blackwell claims that "it is lawful for all Catholickes in England to take the said oath of Allegeance," and further adds that "if the Pope should command any thing that doth sapere peccatum, savour of sin, were it but a veniall sinne, (the Pope supposing his commandement to be just) he were not to be obeyed therein, when those that are so commanded by him, doe know his commandement to be unjust."[45] Since Catholics who refused to take the oath would be executed or exiled by James, thus ensuring the extinction of Catholicism in England, Blackwell argues that the pope's orders should be ignored as unjust. The pope, who is required to protect his church, cannot prescribe behavior that would lead instead to the church's demise.

In response to this oath crisis and the insubordination of his former archpriest, the pope issued a second breve in August 1607. Here he reiterates that Catholics "are bound fully to observe [the Apostolic Letters], rejecting all interpretation perswading to the contrary."[46] James also entered the debate, vigorously challenging Bellarmine and the pope with *Triplici Nodo,* and the expanded second edition, including *A Premonition to all most mighty monarchies, kings, free princes, and states of Christendome.* The oath does not persecute Catholics, James argues in these texts; instead, it merely distinguishes loyal subjects from traitorous ones, those subjects who "although they were otherwise Popishly affected, yet retained in their hearts the print of their naturall duetie to their Soveraigne" from "those who being caried away with the like fanaticall zeale that the Powder-Traitors were, could not conteine themselves within the bounds of their naturall Allegiance."[47] Throughout these texts James maintains that he cares for his subjects' political rather than spiritual obedience. Rehearsing the statute defining treason in England, he argues that no subject is ever in danger of arrest for treason "if hee breake not out in some outward acte expresly against the words of the Law."[48] Treason law concerns only the outward act, be it in words or deeds, against the king, rather than the inward conscience of the individual subject. Indeed, James claims, he has no interest in persecuting subjects for their consciences: "all my labour and intention in this errand, was onely to meddle with that due temporall Obedience which my subjects owe unto mee; and not to intrap or inthrall their Consciences, as hee most falsely affirmes."[49] No subject in England "died here for his conscience."[50] He allows for the privacy of conscience and he tolerates individual faith, he claims, so long as the Catholic believer remains a loyal and obedient subject in temporal affairs.

In *Triplici Nodo,* he repeatedly stresses the temporal nature of his policy, claiming that the pope and Bellarmine have no right to "meddle betweene me and my Subjects, especially in matters that meerely and onely concerne civill obedience."[51] He contrasts his own clemency with the papacy, which perverts justice by defending traitors such as the Gunpowder plotter Henry Garnet in the name of religion: to the Catholic Church, it is "lawfull, or rather meritorious (as the Romish Catholicks call it) to murther Princes or people for quarrel of religion," James argues in his post–Gunpowder Plot speech to Parliament.[52] Elaborating in "A Premonition," James writes how "treasonable practices" are "accounted workes of pietie," and traitors "inrolled in the list of Martyrs and Saints."[53] Pierre du Moulin reinforces James's point in his defense of the oath, writing that, with the Catholic support for king killing, "the murdering therefore of kings will ere long turne into a custome; and the naturall respect that the French were wont to have of their Soveraigne bee choaked by superstition."[54]

At the same time that the king insists on a split between temporal and spiritual power, however, he uses the occasion of the crisis to establish his own sovereignty in Britain against papal authority. In *Triplici Nodo* and the *Premonition* James attempts, as J. P. Sommerville notes, "to protect the rights of kings everywhere against the assaults of Jesuits and puritans."[55] Following theories of natural law, James further argues that allegiance to one's king, being natural, is therefore the law of God.[56] Scripture supports the divinity of kings: the "word of God" attests to the "Supremacie of Kings" within their own dominions.[57] Such supremacy finds support in a long list of scriptural and temporal authorities, all of whom assert the doctrine of obedience to kings. James writes: "What example is there in all the Scripture, in which disobedience to the Oath of the King, or want of Allegiance is allowed?" an argument he expands in his later "Remonstrance for the right of kings" (1615), written against the arguments of Cardinal du Perron.[58]

Finally, James notes the traditional authority of secular princes over the papacy itself, tracing how emperors created, and later deposed, popes, having ordained the Apostolic See and established the Roman principality of the papacy.[59] Indeed, European monarchs continued to assert their temporal power over popes; James's English predecessors, even before the Reformation, "spared not to punish any of their Subjects, that would preferre the *Popes* Obedience to theirs, even in Church-matters: So farre were they then from either acknowledging the *Pope* for their temporall Superiour, or yet from doubting that their owne Church-men were not their Subjects."[60]

Studying James's writings against the papal breves and Bellarmine's letter exposes the contradictions inherent to his argument: he disavows meddling in spiritual affairs, even as he claims divine authority over his subjects. His practice of administering the oath of allegiance only reinforces Catholic fears about the king's expanding prerogative. As a means of assisting the justices of the peace who had been charged with administering the oath, in May 1608 James's Privy Council issued a list of more than a hundred chief officers, customers, controllers, and searchers of the country's ports, giving them license to administer the oath to any subjects or foreigners entering the country:

> forasmuch as the audaciousness of divers persons of disloyall affection and malitious entention toward his Majetie and the State in presuming (notwithstanding the said statute) to come into this Realme with mindes corrupted by Traitors and fugitives beyond the Seas, hath given his Majestie greate cause to require a very straight observance and execution of the said lawe and thereupon hath not onely declared his pleasure for the due performance of the said statute but also (for supply of other fitt persons besides the Justices of the peace to bee alwaies at hand to minister the said Oath) hath geven warrant to your Lordship: to graunt Commission from time to time to any of the Officers of the Portes as any such of us of his privy Councell should under our handes signify unto your Honor.[61]

Striving to administer the oath as effectively as possible, the king significantly expanded the officers involved in surveillance and arrest, even as he argued of the oath in *Premonition* that "almost never one of those sharpe additions to the former Lawes hath ever bene put in execution."[62] The Privy Council defends this expansion of oath officers as a necessary measure in response to "the audaciousness of divers persons of disloyall affection," but this vague allegation against corrupting foreigners echoes the rhetoric of anti-Catholic propaganda. Ultimately, despite his alleged separation of temporal and ecclesiastical authority, James continued to enforce anti-Catholic legislation while refusing to concede spiritual power to Rome.

Even as the king claimed to undertake political rather than spiritual regulation of his subjects, then, Catholics experienced no such distinction; as a result, some firmly protested his newly formed policies. Specifically English Catholics claimed that, with the oath of allegiance, obedience to the king and the pope proved to be mutually exclusive. Although dual allegiances had long been acknowledged by Catholics in England, never had a monarch instituted a policy that systematically forced subjects to choose between excommunication and poverty, or, in certain cases, execution. To the Venetian ambassador, the oath appeared devastating to the Catholic cause in England; as he writes in February 1606, "I am informed that in Parliament they will enforce an oath to be taken without exception by all, that they do not believe the Pope has authority to depose or excommunicate a Sovereign. If any refuse he will be held for a Catholic forthwith, and they will proceed against him . . . for the entire two-thirds of his income. This will render the position of Catholics intolerable."[63]

Many Catholics shared the ambassador's fears. One writer summarizes the situation concisely in a manuscript headed "Whether the late Parliament Oath may bee lawfully taken, or no." He writes,

> this last oath enjoyned by act of Parliament unto all Catholics under most grevious penalties hath bred no smal difficulty, and given an occasion of some breach, & dissention in opinion: while as some regarding the temporal danger ensuring thereby unto the Recusants, have practised their witts, & enclined their judgements, every one almost by different devises to approve the admittance of it; others having respect rather, to the integrity of faith, and the bond of Christian Confession, have censured the same as a thing, most injurious to the Catholic Profession & damnable in al those who presume to swear it. The case is lamentable, when as the loss of either side seemeth exceeding. If we take it, we endanger our souls; if we refuse it the Exchequer & hungry persons ar readie to leap upon your Goods & liberty; & one of these two extremities we must of necessity undergoe, but in choice the losse of the soule is principally to be avoided, whatsoever become of our Goods; for what availeth it a man to winne ye whole world if he wrack his own Soule.[64]

As this writer suggests, the oath frustrated the attempts of loyal Catholics to balance their faith with their political allegiance. The last phrases of the oath, in particular, presented Catholics with a spiritual dilemma: no believer could describe the pope's policies as "damnable" and "hereticall" without risking excommunication. As Father Robert Persons writes in a series of letters, "the present affliction of Catholic people here" is both owing to "new statutes" and to "the oath lately devised to afflict men's consciences."[65]

Split between two forms of loyalty, to the church and king, Catholic subjects confronted an intractable problem. While the oath initially seemed to be a policy borne of a desire to protect the Jacobean state from a religious population that threatened it, the policy instead had the effect of vilifying subjects who had traditionally been loyal to the state. Post-plot writing thus exposed, to use Peter Lake's phrase, "the ideology of consensus."[66] The post-plot propaganda attempts to construct a consensual community, notably as writers echo one another's calls for obedience, piety, and the celebration of James's divine authority while consigning opposition onto their fictive creation of the hungry papist traitor. This extreme portrait of the Catholic traitor creates the illusion of domestic consensus by forcing recusants either into the position of English subject, expressing pious loyalty to the English monarch, or foreign traitor, upholding papal authority over James. This polemical maneuver positions the king's opponents outside England, establishing an apparent consensus within the borders.

Yet, as exhibited by the controversy surrounding the oath of allegiance, the Catholic recusants could not be so easily converted or condemned, to the apparent surprise of James and his supporters. While propaganda erased the middle ground occupied by loyal English Catholics, the writing of moderate Catholics and Protestants after 1605 reveals the intense struggle taking place on this very middle ground, as writers grapple with the threat of treason, on the one hand, and absolutist authority, on the other. Refusing to concede to either extreme, moderate writers instead produce subtle interrogations of state policy at the same time as condemning criminal attacks on the state. Specifically they argue about the rights of subjects to law *and* conscience, both of which remain independent of familiar, and incendiary, resistance theories. It is perhaps the emergence of such moderate yet forceful voices that offers the most sustained and damaging critique of the king's absolutist pretensions: if James can condemn or ignore radical resistance theorists, he cannot so easily dismiss those writers and readers at home who echo his own language of clemency and obedience while challenging his methods for exacting such obedience.

One polemical contribution to the oath of allegiance debate directly addressed these entangled loyalties of Protestants and Catholics living in England. Written with James's support, John Donne's 1611 *Pseudo-Martyr, wherein . . . those which are of the Romane religion in this Kingdome, may and ought to take the Oath of Allegiance* upheld the king's argument on multiple fronts: first, Donne repeated the king's assertion that Catholic opponents of the state are traitors, rather than martyrs; second, he challenged the pope's claim to temporal authority on historical and scriptural grounds. Rather than exacerbate the tension between Catholics and Protestants as other oath polemicists had before him, however, Donne, a former Catholic, participates in the debate from the perspective of a convert who had himself grappled with issues of faith. He expresses sympathy for the Catholic dilemma by acknowledging the contradictory dictates of royal and spiritual authorities: whom does one obey, given the opposition of James and the pope? His answer to this question hinges, as I suggest below, on the role of conscience.

Donne's *Pseudo-Martyr*

Pseudo-Martyr, Donne's first published prose work, was printed with royal approval in 1610. This long polemic encouraged Catholic readers to take the oath of allegiance. It does so, first, by challenging the Catholic claims to martyrdom at the hands of James, and, second, by presenting scriptural arguments to support the theory of obedience to kings. Condemned by Evelyn Simpson as "the dullest of Donne's works,"[67] it was possibly the result of royal commissioning, as Isaac Walton suggests in his biography of Donne:

> His Majesty discoursing with Mr. Donne, concerning many of the reasons which are usually urged against the taking of those Oaths; apprehended, such a validity and clearness in his stating the Questions, and his Answers to them, that his Majesty commanded him to bestow some time in drawing the Arguments into a method, and then to write his Answers to them. . . . To this he presently applied himself, and, within six weeks brought them to him under his own handwriting, as they be now printed; the Book bearing the name of Pseudo-Martyr.[68]

Most scholars dismiss this account of the composition of *Pseudo-Martyr,* suggesting that Walton misinterpreted Donne's dedication to James. Here, Donne announces his debt to the king's arguments: "The influence of those your Majesties Bookes, as the Sunne, which penetrates all corners, hath wrought uppon me, and drawen up, and exhaled from my poor Meditations, these discourses."[69] Despite his obvious flattery of a patron and monarch in writing the text, Donne had both personal and professional reasons for his interest in the oath of allegiance controversy. First, just after the passage of the oath of allegiance, his Catholic mother returned to England from the continent. Although Donne had recently converted to Anglicanism, his family's suffering after their return would have made him sensible to the costs of recusancy and the oath for loyal Catholics. Second, the oath controversy concerned both legal and spiritual issues to which Donne, having been trained in the law and encouraged toward the ministry, was qualified to speak. By demonstrating his polemical skills to a broad audience including the king, to whom he presented a copy of the book on January 24, 1610, Donne may have hoped to advance himself professionally, as his biographers R. C. Bald and John Carey suggest.[70] As a result of this tract, James persuaded him to enter the ministry, a decision that was perhaps a disappointment to Donne who had hoped for preferment at court.

Partly because of the text's royal dedication, Annabel Patterson has called *Pseudo-Martyr* "that remarkable act of submission to the system."[71] The text, she argues, endorses James's royal authority against his Catholic opponents and thus represents Donne's "submission" before the king. As Patterson's description suggests, *Pseudo-Martyr* reiterates James's arguments from *Triplici Nodo* and *Premonition*, supporting the king's case through its significant scholarship. Initially Donne's polemic closely follows the arguments of James's earlier contributions to the oath controversy. The most obvious similarity is that Donne distinguishes, as James does, between the temporal authority of monarchs and the spiritual authority of the church. In doing so, he contends that the oath does not concern issues of religious faith but rather matters of civil obedience, writing "this Oath is not offred as a Symbole or token of our Religion, nor to distinguish Papists from Protestants, but onely for a Declaration and Preservation of such as are well affected in Civille Obedience, from others which either have a rebellious and treacherous disposition already, or may decline and sinke in to it" (177). These lines strongly echo James's own defense of the oath in *Triplici Nodo*, where he distinguishes between those subjects with "naturall Allegiance" and "fanaticall zeale."[72] Loyal Catholics can take the oath, because it concerns only issues of "civill obedience," according to Donne, and therefore does not challenge any article of faith of the Catholic Church; as he puts it, "it can never come to be matter of Faith, that subjects may depart from their Prince" (178). Since the oath does not touch an article of faith, he argues, the Catholic subjects who die in England are only pseudo-martyrs, bereft of the spiritual benefits that accompany martyrdom. By suffering execution in England, Catholics die for a cause unable to elevate them to the status of martyrs in heaven and rendering their deaths suicides.[73]

Like James, Donne levels his strongest attack against the pope's claim to an indirect deposing power. Such a claim produces traitorous Catholics who threaten their sovereigns: "if the temporall jurisdiction (which is the immediate parent of Treason) be the childe of the Romane faith, and begot by it, treason is the Grandchilde" (25). Casting the pope as a grandfather of current treasons, Donne argues that God, despite the pope's claims to the contrary, does not demand submission to papal authority on such temporal issues as the deposing power. Donne thus mocks the pretense to religious war evident in the papal breves: "to offer our lives for defence of the Catholique faith, hath ever beene a religious custome; but to cal every pretence of the pope, Catholique faith, and to bleede to death for it, is a sickenesse and a medicine, which the Primitive Church never understood" (19). Here, he distinguishes papal commands from Catholic doctrine, suggesting that the pope's innovation, requiring temporal obedience from subjects, transgresses the customs of the "Primitive Church."

Pseudo-Martyr, like *Triplici Nodo,* attempts to recast the controversy surrounding the oath as an issue of obedience rather than faith: whom should the devout Catholic obey—the prince or the pope? This question presents difficulties for the Catholic believer, Donne recognizes, because scripture argues for obedience toward princes, but the Catholic Church demands subordination to the pope. Although expressing his sympathy toward Catholics suffering under this split loyalty, Donne nevertheless characterizes those who deny the oath as traitors. He defends this charge by presenting two arguments on the necessity of obedience to kings: kings have "many markes and impressions" of God's power, including divine touch, and God has made obedience to royal power one of the laws of nature. The latter point is central to Donne's thesis and follows the argument of *Triplici Nodo* in asserting that obedience to the monarch proceeds from natural and reasonable laws of society: "This therefore is our first Originary, naturall, and Congenite obedience, *to obey the Prince:* This belongs to us as we are men; and no more changed in us, by being *Christians,* then our *Humanity* is changed" (134). Since the Christian church has been established, God has "infus'd" kings with his natural power and has "testified abundantly, that *Regall Authoritie,* by subordination of *Bishops,* is the best and fittest way" to order society (131). Obedience to royal authority, which is divine, proves a natural condition of living in human society.

Although Donne upholds James's arguments in favor of the oath of allegiance as suggested above, *Pseudo-Martyr* ultimately proves much more nuanced than a mere act of submission. While Donne advocates for and demonstrates his own obedience, he argues vigorously against blind submission, which implies passivity before tyrannical authority. If the distinction between submission and obedience seems a fine one, for Donne's argument it nevertheless signifies the difference between a vulnerable subject, passive in the face of tyranny, and a subject actively subscribing to his or her chosen authority.[74] Between the paths of blind submission and active obedience lies the middle ground of passive obedience, a ground familiar to Catholics from the time of the Reformation but no longer available as a result of the oath crisis in which James and the pope each forward mutually exclusive demands. Recognizing this conflict, Donne stresses the necessity of active exploration, and offers his model of action based in the independent conscience as the navigational tool in charting one's route through the oath debate.

First, however, Donne must wrest the governance of the conscience away from the casuists. In claiming scientific expertise in moral theology, the casuists generated precepts for individual conduct in a given situation. Donne does not want his Catholic readers to defer to these authorities since, in doing so, they would clearly follow the pope and Bellarmine, that is, refuse the oath. Yet he cannot challenge this tradition through an appeal to a set of absolute moral claims, since he would merely be asserting the expertise of his own Reformed theology in doing so. To undermine casuists, then, he argues that the believer must act from his or her conscience independent of external precepts or authorities. One must take responsibility for one's spiritual and temporal welfare, and can only do so in freely governing one's own conscience. Such sovereignty of the mind does not imply a radical relativism in moral judgment; on the contrary, the believer exercises the conscience through knowledge gained from scripture and nature rather than through recourse to the contradictory, labyrinthine, and self-serving logic of earthly authorities.

Before tracing Donne's argument in detail below, a brief outline of his theory may help to clarify its density. He develops his theory in relation to three factors: will, judgment, and knowledge. Our will to act, he claims, emerges from our understanding and judgment (two terms he uses synonymously): how we understand a particular situation determines how we act in relation to it. Where, then, Donne asks, does our judgment come from? From our conscience, he argues. But what is the conscience? Donne's fuzzy answer to this question betrays his attempt to persuade his Catholic readership while retaining his own Protestant faith. If the Protestant answer would suggest that the conscience is the province of the divine, Donne cannot claim this explicitly; to do so, he would then cede the territory of the conscience to the pope, God's authority on earth for Catholic readers. Instead, he develops further steps in his argument, stating that the conscience emerges out of knowledge. What, then, is knowledge? Since the Catholic conscience is conventionally governed through casuistic rules and papal commands, Donne clearly needs to persuade his readers away from this form of knowledge, terming it blind submission to authority. Instead, he argues, in a move betraying his Protestant faith, the pure knowledge necessary for the conscience to govern itself can be gathered directly, only from scripture and nature. Armed with, and indeed constituted by, such knowledge, the conscience gains the proper understanding, thereby directing the will to act. Donne clearly hopes that proper understanding, emerging from a conscience based in knowledge of scripture and nature, will produce consensus among Catholics to take the oath. Yet he outlines a theory of action based in the independent conscience that does not demand such consensus. He shows the reader how to free his or her conscience from external dictates, developing a form of personal sovereignty; he does not himself determine how the reader should exercise this sovereign power. The following section traces this theory through Donne's text in order to suggest how this notion of action based in the independent conscience proves simultaneously essential to, and dangerous for, his polemical argument.

Donne begins *Pseudo-Martyr* by reaching out to his Catholic readers as a former Catholic himself. In his "Preface to the Priests, and Jesuits, and to their Disciples in this Kingdome," he positions himself as an appropriate guide through the oath crisis. Rather than capitulate to the more politically expedient Reformed faith, Donne tells us, he endured the hardships of living as a Catholic in England while he weighed the doctrines of Protestantism and Catholicism against each other. His interest lay in his spiritual welfare, rather than merely "binding my conscience to any locall Religion" (13). He writes:

> although I apprehended well enough, that this irresolution not onely retarded my fortune, but also bred some scandall, and endangered my

spirituall reputation . . . yet all of these respects did not transport me to any violent and sudden determination, till I had, to the measure of my poore wit and judgement, survayed and digested the whole body of Divinity, controverted betweene ours and the Romane Church. (13)

Beyond signaling his sympathy for Catholic readers, Donne's description begins to lay the groundwork for his central argument. He establishes here an opposition between the external world of reputation and fortune, and the internal world of wit and judgment, celebrating the integrity of the latter while also acknowledging its relative vulnerability (his wit, he claims modestly, is a poor faculty). Furthermore, honoring one's judgment over external pressure involves a process of actively educating oneself: employing a metaphor of physical consumption and thus suggesting the individuated nature of the task, Donne claims that he had to both "survey and digest the whole body" of divinity before he could properly act.

For Donne, the current controversy necessitates this turn from external authority to internal wit, since papal and temporal dictates contradict each other. First, Donne argues with a tone of sympathy, his Catholic readers are caught between two definitions of treason, one spiritual and the other political. The faithful Catholic strives, on the one hand, to avoid religious treason, committed through disobedience to the church; as Donne claims, it is "spirituall Treason, not to obey her" (138). In obeying the church against King James, however, Catholics suffer as political traitors to the English state. To make matters worse, rulers continually alter the secular treason law itself, forcing obedient subjects to decipher shifting definitions of the crime. Even if certain treasons, Donne argues, are naturally evident to subjects (such as "what violates or wounds or impeaches the Majestie of the State") (139), other condemnable actions might not seem treasonous at first. As a result, the loyal subject must educate himself in the new laws so that "some things are made to his understanding *Treason*, which by the generall light he apprehended not to be so dangerous before" (139).

In peril of committing either spiritual or secular treason no matter how they resolve the oath of allegiance issue, Catholics further suffer because their spiritual leaders disagree with one another. Catholics cannot have "recourse to their Superior" (232) since their immediate superiors have "beene in different opinions" (233) as to the nature of obedience and spiritual treason. The infighting between the pope and

Cardinal Bellarmine, on the one side, and Archpriest Blackwell and his English Catholic allies, on the other, complicates the question of Catholic allegiance, since English recusants have difficulty determining whom to follow. Rather than employ the rhetoric of Catholic against Protestant, traitor against loyalist, then, Donne instead illuminates the difficulties caused by irresponsible governance: the pope, like temporal leaders, creates chaos and confuses followers in altering law.

The solution to such chaos, as suggested above, lies within.[75] If, as Debora Shuger claims, Donne celebrates "passivity and dependence" in his devotional texts, *Pseudo-Martyr* provides a stark contrast.[76] Here he continually reinforces the importance of actively directing one's spiritual life, rather than passively capitulating to external pressures. In an extended metaphor in the preface, for example, he shifts his conceit of the digesting body, traced above, to one of a house in order to develop his theory of independent action and judgment. Remembering that, for Donne, action or will emerges out of judgment, which itself proceeds from the knowledgeable conscience, helps to follow the logic of metaphor. In a section of his argument defending the Reformed religion, Donne concludes,

> And if you will suffer these things to enter your understanding and judgement, I cannot doubt of your will to conforme your selves: For it is truly said, *Nothing is so contrarie to the will and consent, as Error:* And whatsoever appears true to the Judgment, seemes good to our will, and begets a desire to do it. But if you shut up that dore, and so expose your selves, that men may possesse your Will, without entering by your Judgement, they enter like Theeves at the window, and in the night. For, though the will bee as a window, somewhat capable of light, yet your selves benight your whole house, by drawing these Curtaines upon your judgement. (22)

According to the polemical argument of his text, Donne wishes the truth of the Reformed religion to enter the understanding of the reader. More fundamental, however, the metaphor depicts the vulnerability of the will and argues for the need to protect it through exercising one's own judgment. The will, he reasons, can be stolen from the vulnerable individual. Donne represents the protective force of judgment both as a doorway through which men may legitimately enter to engage with one's will, and as a sun, producing a bright environment that frustrates illegitimate entrance by thieves. Similarly double, the will is both the possession within the individual's house of the soul, which other men seek to capture, and the window of that house through which judgment shines or darkness falls.

The duality in each case hinges on Donne's irresolution concerning the status of these mental faculties: do the judgment and will have material presence that likely eludes our control, as signified by the image of the remote shining sun and the easily stolen will? Or are they alternately, as the images of the doorway and the window suggest, border spaces through which we regulate the entrance of outside forces into the house of the soul? For a poet like Donne, such hesitation in his analogy betrays the conceptual difficulty endemic to his argument. While the image of the sun evokes a sense of divine or royal power, he resists submission to such power throughout the polemic. Our judgment does not, according to Donne's argument, emanate from royal or godly decrees. Instead, in a gesture familiar from his sonnets, his description hinges on a paradox: he acknowledges the apparently absolute power of the sun only to insist on the individual's control over it. As he writes in the sonnets, "Busie old fool, unruly Sun / Why doest thou thus / Through windowes, and through curtaines call on us? / . . . Thy beames, so reverend, and strong / Why shouldst thou thinke? / I could eclipse and cloud them with a winke" (1–13).[77] Like Donne's speaker who famously dismisses the sun as a busy old fool, insisting that he can control its beams through his blinking eye, his polemic both invokes the sun itself as judgment and suggests that the speaker controls such a judgment through his ability to open or close the door. Yet *Pseudo-Martyr* proves much less playful than the sonnet, which teases the reader in both undermining absolute authority and reveling in the speaker's exercise of it. The polemic instead obfuscates the relation between the sun and domestic space occupied by the hypothetical reader. Employing the same vocabulary as the sonnet, and depicting the same struggle between the sun and the speaker/reader, Donne now avoids obvious provocation by having it both ways. Judgment is both the sun and the door, the exterior force of divine or royal power, and the internal faculty that controls the absorption of this power. Here Donne avoids implying, as he does playfully in "The Sun Rising," that the subject controls the king or God. Neither, however, does Donne entirely reject this radical possibility, leaving it alive in his conflicting images.

Such tangled images suggest Donne's conscious hedging on the agency of humans in governing our judgment, a hedging once again born of his desire to articulate, as a sympathetic Protestant, an argument to Catholic readers. How can judgment, according to Donne's tangled metaphor, be both the sun and the door, both beyond human control and within our reach? One way to answer this question is to investigate where, in Donne's view, our judgment comes from. According to the Protestant formula, invoked by Philip Sidney among others, the answer lies in divine grace. In his *Defense of Poesy,* for example, Sidney approaches his "infected will" with suspicion, relying instead on his "erected wit" or judgment for guidance.[78] Donne nods to this Protestant belief in casting the judgment as the sun, a force of the divine. He deviates from this compact equation, however, by extending it, introducing through the metaphor of the door the component of human agency. Resisting an explicit turn toward the divine beyond his metaphor of the sun, Donne later tells us in his slowly unfolding argument that understanding emerges from the conscience, that seat of knowledge from which our decisions emanate. He writes:

> Since the conscience is, by Aquinas his definition, *Ordo scientiae ad aliquid,* and *an Act by which wee apply our knowledge to some particular thing,* the Conscience ever presumes Knowledge: and we may not, (especially in so great dangers as these) doe any thing upon Conscience, if we do it not upon Knowledge. For it is not the Conscience itself that bindes us, but that law which the Conscience takes knowledge of, and presents to our understanding. (237)

Even as he condenses the process he describes in referring to the conscience as an act, Donne argues that the conscience must gather proper knowledge of an issue, present this to the understanding, and only then, as he suggests above, direct the will to act. In this laborious process the conscience strives to present knowledge to the understanding, a formula that again instructs the believer toward active engagement. Donne's theory of proper action, as the conscience gathers the knowledge and directs the will to act, relies on the independent believer who exercises his or her own faculties. Although Donne stresses the importance of obedience throughout the polemic, then, his theory of action functions as a cornerstone of his argument, and it effectively establishes the right of each reader to determine his or her path through contemporary controversy.

The process of gathering knowledge, crucial to action, proves elusive the further we drift from such elemental sources as Nature and Scripture. One's conscience can be easily led astray by faulty arguments not rooted in trustworthy sources. Developing yet another metaphor, now of secure knowledge as a family tree from which arguments extend like branches and the conscience hangs like a leaf, Donne cautions:

> If since, by some arguments of probabilitie and of Conveniencie, or by some propositions propagated and deduced from those first principles of Nature, and Scripture, by so many descents and Generations, that it is hard to trie whether they doe truly come from that roote, or no, any Conscience have slackned it selfe, and so be straied, and dissolved, and scattered, by this remisnesse, and vaciallation, it ought rather to recollect it selfe, and return to those first ingraffed principles, then in this dissolute and loose distraction, to suffer an anxious perplexitie, or desperately to arrest itself upon that part, which their owne Rules given to reduce men in such deviations, and settle them in such waverings, cannot assure him to be well chosen, nor deliver and extricate him, in those laborinths. (165)

This extended metaphor cautions the conscience to return to the roots of knowledge, in scripture and nature, rather than follow the tree's various branches, representing rules. Such rules, for Donne, signify the precepts of the Catholic Church and the casuistic tradition. At a distance from secure knowledge, these rules cause the conscience to waver and vacillate in tangled branches. While this extended metaphor appears in the service of Donne's argument against the Catholic moral theology, it tells the reader, equally and more obviously, to shed external dictates and turn from earthly authority toward one's own judgment. Ultimately the exercise of judgment and conscience is the individual believer's responsibility. Only through direct engagement with natural and biblical roots, rather than through the exterior precepts or rules of various authorities, can we gain the knowledge that fills the conscience. Further, we must know about the authorities that govern us and about our own conditions through independent investigations: "every particular man is bound to know those things which pertaine to his state and office."

Donne's emphasis on conscience, like his emphasis on scripture and nature as pure knowledge, may function as a means of advocating for the Protestant faith over Catholicism. Donne exposes, as Meg Lota

Brown notes, how the Catholic Church "is more concerned with submission to its laws than with explaining the reasons that produce those laws."[79] By contrast, the Protestant God (as typified in Donne's *Essays*) appears to welcome intellectual reasoning, wherein the conscience guides one to act correctly. If *Pseudo-Martyr* favors the Protestant-based conscience, however, it does so in a context that celebrates the active exercise of individual freedom. As Donne writes in his preface, he favors "my Indulgence to my freedome and libertie, as in all other indifferent things, so in my studies also, not to betroth or enthral my selfe to any one science, which should possesse or denominate me" (12). Referring to his scholarly method (as Douglas Trevor elucidates), this passage nevertheless upholds Donne's more general argument about the exercise of "freedom and libertie" over thralldom.[80] Not surprisingly, then, his polemic—even in supporting James's cause—does not simply call the pope's authority into question. Instead, Donne strongly emphasizes the importance of wrestling with one's own conscience, gaining the appropriate knowledge in order to reach a judgment. Conscience for Donne does not serve as a rhetorical wedge with which to pry apart the Catholic faith; rather, it produces in the subject, whether Catholic or Protestant, that seat of sovereignty from which to assess spiritual and temporal dictates.

The above argument, that *Pseudo-Martyr* represents Donne's considered accommodation of both Catholic and reformed believers and his advocacy of action based in the individual conscience, gains support from one of Donne's letters, written against William Barlow, the Bishop of Lincoln and author of the Gunpowder Plot sermon noted above. Barlow's sycophantic pamphlet, entitled "Answer to a Catholike English-man" (1609), appeared at the request of the state in order to counter Robert Persons's pamphlet, "The Judgement of a Catholicke Englishman."[81] In his reply Barlow viciously attacked the Catholic faith, provoking responses by Persons, Fitzherbert, and Coffin who ridiculed Barlow's ignorance and thus rendered his polemic damaging, rather than profitable, to the king's cause. Donne, too, voiced his reservations about Barlow's text both for its poor scholarship and for its sensationalism and self-promotion. In a letter to Goodyer, he writes: "The Book is full of falsifications in words, and in sense, and of falshoods in matter of fact, and of inconsequent and unscholarlike arguings."[82] Further, he condemns Barlow's "silly ridiculous triflings" and "extreme flatteries," dismissing the author as "extremely obnoxious."[83] The term "obnoxious" here signifies not merely Donne's objection to Barlow but, following the term's Latin connotation, his sense of the author's servitude to another's will. As Quentin Skinner has shown, Roman writers including Sallust, Seneca, and Tacitus employ this term to describe a condition of slavery, in which the bodies of people are *obnoxia*, at the mercy of others.[84]

While both Donne and Barlow may have sought the king's favor by participating in the oath controversy, Donne's violent response to Barlow suggests that he refused to enslave himself to the king's cause.[85] Instead, Donne retained freedom of judgment, attempting to assess each side fairly, as he notes in his letter to Goodyer: "in the main point in question, I think truly there is a perplexity (as farre as I see yet) and both sides may be in justice and innocence; and the wounds which they inflict upon the adverse part, are all *se defendendo*."[86] Here Donne acknowledges truth on both sides of the debate: the Jacobean state needs the oath to protect itself from residents who practice treason against the monarchy on the grounds that they are not the king's subjects; the Catholic Church, however, cannot brook a challenge such as the oath, which effectively diminishes its authority. By recognizing the two sides of the debate in his letter, Donne exhibits the same sympathetic response to Catholicism evident in *Pseudo-Martyr*. In fact, such balancing provokes Anthony Raspa to claim of Donne, he manages to "tell everyone that everybody could be right if they tried."[87]

Yet Donne's text is neither a flattering submission nor solely a compromised endorsement of both sides. Instead, as this section has suggested, the polemic both contributes to, and to some extent challenges, the king's cause. Most obvious is that Donne supports the king's case for the oath of allegiance, expanding James's own arguments concerning the divine right of kings and the false claims of Catholic "martyrs." By insisting on the role of conscience in deciding one's religious faith, however, Donne fails to stress the "truth" of the Protestant position and instead favors an individualist response to the crisis of faith and politics. This focus on individual conscience betrays his Protestant faith, based in a personal relationship with God. Further, his challenge to church doctrine and hierarchy poses a threat to the Catholic Church by undermining its faith, based in tradition and obedience. In the more political context of the oath of allegiance controversy, however, this interest in the active conscience over passive deference challenges the assertion of absolute power by either the pope or James.

Donne's anatomy of the dilemma facing Catholics penetrates the oath controversy to such a degree that he exposes, perhaps against the purpose of his own argument, the liberties necessary for thinking subjects to reconcile the crisis. If Donne single-mindedly writes to persuade Catholics to take the oath, his series of arguments against submission, although anti-papal, necessarily grant Catholics the freedom to challenge James's authority as well: Donne can hardly hope to persuade his readers to surrender to the king's will over the pope's. Instead, then, Donne challenges the practice of submission generally, thereby opening the way for potential resistance to both papal and royal policies. While one could argue that this loophole undermines his polemic, permitting resistance as he argues for obedience, more important is that its presence confirms Donne's portrait of James as a tolerant ruler. Unlike the tyrannical pope, he argues, the judicious king exercises only limited claims to temporal power.

Donne produces an argument potentially against his own purposes since he paradoxically articulates the right of conscience in the midst of an argument upholding the king's policy. This paradox, between his support for James and his advocacy of the independent conscience, results in a polemic rife with twisted logic, overlapping and at times contradictory images, and overly determined vocabulary. Attempting to occupy a political middle ground in the oath controversy, Donne instead exposes the fissures that force temperate subjects into conflicted, and possibly oppositional, positions. In doing so, he retains a position of moderation or, as Richard Strier terms it in a different context, a "suspension of commitment."[88] His conflict could be explained differently, through recourse to a model of radical subversion, for example, by which the author sneaks a Trojan horse into James's camp. Emphasizing subversion unsatisfactorily implies, however, both Donne's disingenuousness in claiming to support the king and the king's dimwittedness in failing to see the opposition, obvious to other readers, that marks the polemic. Donne's conflict could be equally explained as an unconscious one, although he clearly articulates his attempt both to appeal to his Catholic readers and to defend the king. Neither model—intentional subversion, on the one hand, and unconscious textual effects, on the other—acknowledges the extent to which Donne's conflict remains both obvious and unresolved in the text.

That James's oath of allegiance encountered papal resistance is not surprising. Nor is the widening opposition between Jesuits and monarchomachs, on one side, and divine-right theorists and Puritan preachers, on the other. What should surprise us instead is the impact of the oath controversy on a moderate thinker like Donne. A Protestant who neither vilifies Catholics nor supports conventional resistance theories, Donne strives to bolster the king's cause among Catholic readers. But in his advocacy of the king's policy, he qualifies James's pretensions to absolute power and challenges the consolidation of sovereign authority that was a feature of post–Gunpowder Plot England. As a result, he produces a polemic that resists the king even in supporting him. The tensions pressing on Donne's text, evident in his insistence on obedience in the context of independent thought, and in his theory of agency articulated amid references to a force definable as divine grace, emerge out of the oath conflict. Such tensions expose how even the flexible imagination of a thinker like Donne cannot produce an argument for consensus among English subjects. Indeed, precisely because of Donne's mental acuity and his attempt to examine the issues in close detail, he exposes the contradictions that characterize the oath crisis, frustrating his attempt to produce an unqualified defense of the king's policy. As a result of taking the king's claims to clemency and non-tyranny seriously while also supporting the oath, Donne produces an argument against submission that James himself may have only gestured toward rhetorically: asserting the very right of conscience that allows Catholic subjects to protect their spiritual lives from the tyrannical claims of temporal princes like James.[89] Wresting Catholics away from the pope by designating conscience as an independent, pure faculty in every subject, Donne surprisingly forges, in the midst of his vigorous defense of the oath, a space for the spiritual and temporal liberty of the English subject.

Treason and Emergency Power
in Jonson's Catiline

The previous chapter traced the philosophical and religious issues raised by King James's post–Gunpowder Plot policy on the oath of allegiance, focusing on John Donne's defense of the right of conscience in his polemical *Pseudo-Martyr.* In this chapter I examine a related right at stake in the oath crisis and the post–Gunpowder Plot era more generally: the rule of law in relation to the king's emergency power. The ideological debate around questions of wartime power, familiar as we shall see from 1606 and 1610 Parliaments, drives Ben Jonson's 1611 Roman play, *Catiline.* In the contentious environment of post–Gunpowder Plot England, Jonson's play returns to issues familiar from the early chapters of this book: Jonson's *Catiline,* like Shakespeare's *Richard II,* and Hayward's *Henry IV,* addresses the relationship of law to prerogative, treason to tyranny, through the lens of history. Yet Jonson's portrait of Cicero, in contrast to Shakespeare's Richard, provides a more idealized figure of the ruling sovereign battling starkly corrupt traitors. The play's clearly fractured landscape evokes that of post–1605 England while also exhibiting Jonson's unwillingness to capitulate to easy or readily available solutions. The pragmatic sovereignty of *Macbeth's* Malcolm no longer satisfies a playwright and audience too familiar with treason to compromise state customs and subjects' rights to fight it.

Perhaps the knowingness of Jonson's play stems from his own experiences as a Catholic in England. Like Donne, Jonson was a practicing Catholic during the years before the Gunpowder Plot. According to his conversations with William Drummond, he had converted to Catholicism in 1598 "by the trust of a priest who Visited him in Prisson," where he lay for the murder of the actor Gabriel Spencer.[1] After his release, Jonson associated with some of the most prominent Gunpowder plotters. Friendly with Robert Catesby, Jonson attended his dinner party a month before the treason, as the state discovered in its investigations. The dinner took place in October 1605, when Jonson visited Catesby's house in the Strand with Sir Joselyn Percy and Francis Tresham, both of whom, along with Catesby, had participated in the Essex Rebellion and would be implicated in the Gunpowder Plot.[2] As discussed in chapter 4, Catesby was one of the primary conspirators in the plot. When Jonson visited Catesby for dinner, the plot lay ready since Parliament had been scheduled to open in October, only to be prorogued until November 5.

The conspirators may have expected a sympathetic audience in Jonson, given that he had already been imprisoned under James for anti-Scottish references in his play, *Eastward Ho.* Moreover, he had earlier been interrogated for *Sejanus*, a play that was deemed by the Privy Council full "both of popperie and treason."[3] Yet, if Catesby wanted Jonson to join the treason, the occasion of the plot, ironically, offered Jonson a chance to prove his loyalty to the state by drawing on his Catholic connections to aid the state's investigations. The Privy Council issued the following warrant on November 7: "A warr^t unto Beniamen Johnson to let a certaine priest knowe that offered to do good service to the State, that he should securely come and goe to and from the LL's, wh^ch they promised in the said warrant upon their honours."[4] Although Jonson could not persuade this unnamed priest to come out of hiding, his letter to Robert Cecil indicates his desire to assist the investigators: "there hath bene no Want in mee, eyther of labor or sincerity in the discharge of this busines, to the satisfaction of yor Lo: and the state."[5] David Riggs writes of this period in 1605 that Jonson's letters express "his loyalty, his patriotism, and his eagerness to do the state some service."[6]

In the wake of the assassination of Henry IV of France by Catholic traitors and James's reassertion of the oath of allegiance, Jonson converted back to Anglicanism in 1610. Given the stiffening of legislation in that year, including the ban of Catholics from court, he may have reconverted in order to maintain his position as a writer of court masques. According to his own account, he "was reconciled with the Church, and left of to be a recusant, at his first communion, in token of true reconciliation, he drank out all the full cup of wyne."[7] His biog-

raphers offer conflicting interpretations of this story, however: W. David Kay claims that Jonson's conversion was sincere and lasting, writing that Jonson's account of the conversion "surely expresses his relief that his intellectual struggle and the political pressures toward conformity had finally been resolved."[8] Here Kay challenges David Riggs, who suggests that, "given Jonson's reputation as a drinker, he may have been speaking with his tongue in his cheek." In any case, this anecdote suggests that he regarded his re-conversion as a symbolic act, or "token," that "signified his reintegration into the body politic."[9]

Jonson's religious and social life between 1598 and 1610 is therefore filled with a range of contradictions: first Protestant, then Catholic, then allegedly Protestant again, he defended his "popish" play before the Privy Council, dined with the Gunpowder plotters, and then assisted the state in its post-plot investigations. Jonson further complicates matters when, in 1611, he constructs a play on treason filled with anachronistic references to the Gunpowder Plot. Performed by the King's Men, the play depicts the treason of Catiline against Republican Rome, a treason exposed by Cicero in a series of famous orations in the Senate (*Orationes in Catilinam*). Jonson's contemporaries had already linked the Gunpowder Plot to this classical treason. "The Picture of a Papist," for example, deems the Gunpowder plotters "worse then Catilinarie conspiracies," while in a speech to Parliament, James termed the same conspirators "worse than Catilines [who] thought to have extirpated us and our memories."[10] Both references to Catiline serve as shorthand for a sensationalist portrait of treason in part because—like the Gunpowder plotters—Catiline and his rebels planned to attack the Senate.

While popular opinion had already linked Catiline's conspiracy and the Gunpowder Plot, Jonson alters his source material in Sallust and Plutarch to increase the connections between the two treasons, making reference to sulfurous attacks on the senate on the fifth of November. Barbara de Luna in her study, *Jonson's Romish Plot*, carefully follows these links to argue that the entire play serves as a "parallelograph" of the Gunpowder Plot, with the plotter Robert Catesby represented by Catiline, Robert Cecil as Cicero, and the earl of Essex's ghost as Sylla.[11] Even without de Luna's allegory, several elements in Jonson's play invite obvious comparison with the Gunpowder Plot. First, although the conspiracy occurred on October 28, Jonson's Cicero describes the treason in terms that evoke instead November 5 when he asks Catiline, "thy purpose / Was, on the fifth, the kalends of November, / T'have slaughter'd this whole order?" (4.2.186–88).[12] Second, the play repeatedly refers to gunpowder and its effects, one of Jonson's innovative additions to his source material. Catiline, for example, will "strike" the senate with a "violent blow" (1.1.529; 438), a description that evokes the accounts of the Gunpowder Plot itself, termed a "deadly blow" by pamphleteering ministers such as William Barlow and William Leigh.[13] Third, the play anachronistically constructs an image of treason as symbolically Catholic, echoing the contemporary propaganda on the crime. The traitors take the sacrament and associate treason with religious doctrine (see 1.1.485–87; and 3.2.135).

Dramatizing the precise moment in 63 B.C. when Cicero saved the Senate from treasonous attack, *Catiline* is frequently read as an explicit celebration of Cicero's virtuous triumph and an implicit celebration of King James's victory over the Gunpowder traitors.[14] This reading makes historical sense: as noted above, Jonson, who converted back to Anglicanism the year before *Catiline*'s production, had assisted the state in its post-plot investigations while continuing to compose royal masques for James and Queen Anne. Despite the historical attraction of this argument on Jonson's support for the state's victory, the playwright nevertheless eludes such political flag waving.[15] The play's "political dynamics," as Julie Sanders notes, "are not so clear" as to support either royalism or republicanism. Instead, the play explores "alternative political opinions without necessarily opting for one way over another."[16] Such compromise is troubling, however, since it is not based on consensus. Instead, as this chapter will argue, *Catiline* reproduces and refuses to reconcile the political divisions splitting both Republican Rome and post-plot England. Struggling to fight a treasonous threat, the hero Cicero must troublingly invoke discretionary power to execute the traitors. If such extralegal maneuvers seem necessary, Cicero's exercise of such power nevertheless contributes to the later downfall of the Republic. As a result, this compromised hero frustrates audience sympathy and exposes the dangerous connection of treason and tyranny.

Specifically, Jonson's dramatic contribution to the post–Gunpowder Plot controversy engages with the original, and radical, question of whether use of extralegal power can ever be justified. Rather than critique or celebrate James's *motives* in exercising discretionary power after 1605, as his contemporaries did, Jonson's play imaginatively provides the most favorable conditions for support of extralegal powers. Catiline's treason legitimates Cicero's use of emergency prerogative, and the play ends with the consul's triumph over the traitors. Indeed, as Philip J. Ayres writes, Jonson supports the Roman senate "literally to the hilt with regard to its right to invoke the *senatus consultum ultimum*," a power that Jonson views as "correctly employed."[17] Jonson mars this satisfying narrative, however, by highlighting not only the necessity but also the dangers of Cicero's extralegal actions. Even as Jonson offers short-term justification of discretionary power, his play nevertheless fails to endorse even this one exception to a model of law-based rule, demonstrating instead how the use of extralegal power, as much as treasonous plotting, threatens the state.[18]

Silent leges inter arma; or, "The laws are silent in war"

Even constitutional theorists concede that the king may exercise absolute power in one area: defending the state in case of emergency. Henry of Bracton and John Fortescue both repeatedly emphasize that the king is constitutionally bound to common law; yet each theorist distinguishes between the king's royal and political powers or the "laws and arms" of kingship.[19] The king, as Fortescue writes, should be both "guarded with arms" and "armed with laws.[20] In *De Republica Anglorum,* Thomas Smith elaborates on the distinction between civil and martial kingship, writing that "in warre time and in the field the prince hath also absolute power, so that his worde is law; he may put to death, or to other bodilie punishment whom he shall think so to deserve, without process of law or form of judgment."[21] Here a king's power in extraordinary circumstances may include extralegal measures that help preserve the common good.

The notion of martial or royal power as temporary also appears in William Lambarde's 1591 *Archion, or A Commentary upon the High Courts of Justice in England.* Here the king relies on discretionary power in emergency situations; he argues: "sundry things doe fall out both in Peace and Warre, that doe require an extraordinary helpe, and cannot awaite the usuall cure of common rule and settled Justice." Such matters must, he writes, be "left to the aide of absolute Power, and irregular Authoritie."[22] Even Sir Edward Coke articulates a defense of the king's absolute power in the case of war, claiming that "there is prerogative indisputable and prerogative disputable. Prerogative indisputable, is that the king hath to make war; disputable prerogative is tied to the laws of England."[23] Following Glenn Burgess, we can interpret this distinction between absolute and ordinary power in these texts as a sign of the duplex powers of kingship, namely, "the old distinction between the king's ordinary legal prerogatives (in the plural) and his emergency prerogative."[24] John Guy, concurring, writes that the "royal prerogative was a supplement to common law and not an alternative; hence it is anachronistic to posit the existence of two conflicting ideologies before 1625."[25]

The consensus in English legal theory on civil and martial power falters after 1605, however, as subjects deemed James's crisis measures innovative and extraordinary, not merely conventional. First, as discussed in the previous chapter, in 1606 James introduced his controversial oath of allegiance. The oath policy, James would argue in his later polemics, was a necessary response to a state emergency: the crisis of treason required the king to bolster his temporal authority against the papacy's alleged deposing power.[26] James's sweeping new recusant legislation also strengthened the state against its enemies. These new policies sparked heavy debate, however, evident in the controversy surrounding the oath, addressed in the last chapter. The recusant legislation equally prompted disagreement and underwent heavy revision in committees, as with the "Bill for the preservation of the king's majesties subjects in their due obedience," which was reported as "brought in from the committee by Sir H. Hubbard with amendments, alterations, additions. Which were twice read. Many exceptions made to this bill, and upon several questions moved, it was thought fit to be recommitted to the former committee."[27]

These "exceptions" stalled passage of the bill in part because certain members of Parliament lobbied for even more severe legislation. James protested that these policies should fall under his discretion, brushing aside the House of Commons petition on recusancy by claiming that "it is a matter merely belonging unto himself; and that it shall be needless to press him in it."[28] But the commons balked at the king's refusal, saying that "it was not only against, but a great wound to, the gravity and liberty of the house to deny it."[29] While the king viewed the recusancy legislation as a matter "belonging unto himself," that is, as part of his own prerogative, the commons insisted on their own liberties instead, successfully causing James to relent and read their petition. Here

James claims discretion in order to reign in the more vociferous anti-Catholic forces in Parliament, but his claim to singularity only excited further division and caused the king to concede.

Some members of Parliament also protested the king's perceived expansion of his prerogative in relation to issues seemingly disconnected from the threat of treason, such as his policy on taxation, known as impositions, and the union with Scotland. As James Daly notes about the Bates case concerning impositions: "Instead of an absolute discretion within specified classes of powers (e.g., coinage, war and peace) there was an absolute discretion of a larger and less defined nature."[30] These exercises of discretionary power provoked parliamentary debates in which subjects questioned the application of wartime powers in post-plot England. In the 1610 Parliament, Thomas Hedley claims that "this [common] lawe holds allwayes except in tyme of warre, and then *inter arma silent leges*," but he goes on to argue that "in peace, the common law is to lymitt the prerogative of the King."[31] Hedley reasons that, in the current time of peace, the king's policies cannot fall under the discretionary power. Similarly, Thomas Crew argues of the king's innovative policy on impositions that "the King of England in some cases hathe an absolute power, as in tyme of warre, which being grounded upon necessity is become legall . . . [but he finds] the word imposition a stranger and an alien: no ground in our lawe, no mencion of this imposition."[32]

Although conceding that the king has emergency power in time of war, Crew and Hedley challenge James's attempt to exercise such power after the Gunpowder Plot, as he strives to do with innovative policies such as impositions and the union with Scotland, introduced in the 1606 and 1610 parliaments. In contrast, Francis Bacon voiced his favor for the king's extraordinary power in 1608, writing:

> in time of wars . . . *silent leges inter arma*. And yet the sovereignty and imperial power of the king is so far from being then extinguished or suspended, as contrariwise it is raised and made more absolute; for then he may proceed by his supreme authority, and martial law, without observing formalities of the laws of his kingdom. . . . For Bracton, out of Justinian, doth truly define the crown to consist of laws and arms, power civil and martial. With the latter whereof the law doth not intermeddle.[33]

Bacon's argument rehearses precisely the distinction evident in the legal theory of Bracton, Fortescue, and Smith between the crown's duplex powers. Yet if Crew and Hedley acknowledge, with Bacon, the familiar theory of wartime prerogative, these men dispute James's application of it after the Gunpowder Plot. This dispute is particularly acute in 1610, when Hedley and Crew offer their alternate interpretations of discretionary power. At this point, the goodwill felt toward the recently saved king was less immediate than in 1606 and, as Derek Hirst argues, "although James's practical policies were essentially conciliatory, a thread of suspicion of the monarch's discretionary power runs through the sessions of this long parliament."[34] Viewed through post–Gunpowder Plot debates in Parliament, the distinction between royal and politic power appears, as Francis Oakley argues, not simply "two parallel or coordinate powers each confined by law to its own proper sphere" but, instead, "two powers, one of which was in essence superior to the other, and which in time of necessity or for reason of state could transcend the other and encroach its domain."[35]

Both Bacon and Hedley, while offering opposite arguments on the king's discretionary powers, cite Cicero's famous phrase: "Silent leges inter arma"; or, "The laws are silent in war." This phrase originates from Cicero's argument in favor of the use of discretionary power in his *Oratione pro Milone*, justifying the suspension of law in times of war. Here he writes, "if our life be in danger from plots, or from open violence, or from the weapons of robbers or enemies, every means of securing our safety is honorable. For laws are silent when arms are raised."[36] A state facing a treasonous threat, Cicero argues, has the right to defend itself by whatever means necessary. Cicero's defense of discretionary power may seem surprising, since, for Jonson's audience, he would be more familiar as the orator who sanctioned rule of law in texts such as *De Legibus* and *De Officiis*. Philip Melancthon's influential 1534 edition of *De Officiis*, for example, encourages study of his works as the grounds for establishing a civil society based in rule of law: "As it is right for Christians to develop and foster a civil society, so this doctrine of civic morals and duties [i.e., *De Officiis*] must be studied. For it is not godly to live like the Cyclops, without a legal order or an ethical doctrine."[37] Like *De Officiis*, *De Legibus*—which similarly insists on laws as the bedrock of the healthy commonwealth—established Cicero as an advocate of "legal order" and "civil society," to use Melancthon's phrases. Indeed, Cicero is what Peter Miller terms "the philosophically inclined defender . . . [of] the rule of law."[38] There was, he elaborates, "no greater exemplar of patriotic statesmanship." Richard Tuck also notes how Ciceronian humanism, with its emphasis on rule of law and the *vita activa,* was frequently read against Tacitean skepticism based in self-interest.[39]

Nowhere is the dual role of Cicero as the magistrate who both rules by law and invokes necessity to transgress such law more evident than in his dealings with the Catilinian conspirators. In order to prosecute the conspirators, Cicero had been granted the *senatus consultum ultimum* ("ultimate decree of the senate").[40] This decree, referred to as the s.c.u., enabled the consul to protect the Republic by whatever means necessary. Cicero used this discretionary power to argue in favor of executing the traitors, despite the fact that Roman law prescribed exile, not execution, for its citizens. He garnered the Senate's support through a series of famous speeches in 63 B.C. Nevertheless, as Consul governing under the s.c.u., he assumed full responsibility for transgressing Roman laws, and thus suffered exile three years later, when an opponent pressed for a senate bill condemning those leaders who had executed Roman citizens.[41]

At stake in the figure of Cicero is the tension surrounding a statesperson who maintains and upholds his county's laws while occasionally bending those laws in the name of protecting the state. Constitutional theorists sanction precisely this type of leader, one who governs under the law except in the case of emergency. Cicero's conflict, familiar to English legal theory as the need to exercise discretionary power within a context of support for law-based rule, makes him an apt figure for Bacon and Hedley to cite in post–Gunpowder Plot debates. Yet the citation of Cicero's phrase in Parliament is not without historical irony, given his later exile. Furthermore, the opposing use of Cicero's phrase by Bacon and Hedley suggests the interpretive conflict surrounding the Roman consul's legacy: how does one define a crisis or wartime? When can a ruler exercise discretionary power, and how effective is its use? Grappling with Cicero's legacy on the issue of extralegal prerogative in post–Gunpowder Plot England requires a turn to the era's fullest examination of Cicero's fight against treason: Jonson's *Catiline.*

Jonson's Catiline

Jonson's play proved a box office flop.[42] Despite this sensational topic, even Samuel Pepys complained that the play "doth appear the worst upon the stage, I mean the least diverting, that ever I saw."[43] In the preface to the printed edition, Jonson discusses the play's poor reception. Addressing the reader, he claims:

> you commend the two first acts with the people, because they are the worst; and dislike the oration of Cicero, in regard you read some pieces of it at school, and understand them not yet.[44]

The play, as Jonson's preface suggests, is split in two halves. The first half centers around Catiline's plot against the state, and the second half depicts Cicero's struggle to prosecute the criminals. The first of these narratives is sensational, the second somber; the first action-packed, the second oration-dominated. The audience commended the first half: here the play moves swiftly as the conspirators energetically plot. In the unpopular second half, Cicero's orations before the senate slow down the pace. These scenes force the audience to consider the risks of the state's fight against crime: what are the implications of exiling Catiline, as required by law? Or the consequences of executing him, thereby transgressing Roman law?

Before we reach such heady questions, Jonson entertains us with Catiline's bloody and treasonous plotting. The play opens with the ghost of the traitor Sylla watching Catiline in his study, urging him to meditate on fiendish crimes. Sylla commands, "Let the long-hid seeds / Of treason in thee now shoot forth in deeds / Ranker than horror" (1.2.25–27). Hidden within the heart of the criminal, treasonous desire matures into action, destroying innocent rulers and subjects. Such deeds include "incests, murders, rapes" of Vestal nuns, daughters, and mothers (30). Juxtaposing demonic traitors and innocent nuns, Jonson's tableau evokes, in nearly parodic form, 1606 texts such as "A True and Perfect Relation" and "Picture of a Papist," discussed in chapter 5. Jonson reinforces such sensationalism by depicting these traitors as animals, not men. In "their windings," their "subtle turnings," and "their snaky ways," Catiline's followers "creep upon their breasts" through "woods of darkness" on "paths ne'er trod by men, but wolves and panthers" (3.2.182–86). Forsaking the path of humanity, the traitor becomes the satanic snake that creeps in darkness on its belly.

Catiline's followers, the audience learns, seek wealth and power: Lentulus participates out of inflated ambition for his family name; Cethegus, out of lust for war; Lentulus and Curius, out of revenge for their fallen fortunes. Other participants join because of their debts, their lost hopes, or their former crimes. Appealing to base desires, Catiline gathers a crew of traitors who revel in the chaos they will create. They seek to return to the earlier period of Sylla's rule, when "the free sword took leave / To act all that it would!" (1.1.230–31). During this time, Cethegus claims:

> Slaughter bestrid the streets and stretch'd himself
> To seem more huge, whilst to his stained thighs
> The gore he drew flow'd up and carried down
> Whole heaps of limbs and bodies through his arch.
> No age was spar'd, no sex . . .
> Not infants in the porch of life were free.
> The sick, the old, that could but hope a day
> Longer by nature's bounty, not let stay.
> Virgins and widows, matrons, pregnant wives
> All died.
>
> (1.1.235–43)

Addressing this horror, Catiline cries, "this shall be again, and more and more" (254). Jonson distorts the Roman triumphal arch, which celebrates the empire's military prowess, into an arch of "Slaughter" through which "limbs and bodies" rather than victorious armies parade. Romans themselves are the victims, as "Slaughter" gorges on "infants," "the sick, the old," and "virgins and widows, matrons, pregnant wives." This list reveals how Rome destroys her own reproductive potential, killing those women and infants that help the city renew itself. Cethegus's unnatural portrait of an empty city "stained" with "gore" betrays the ignorance of these traitors who revel in the destruction of the very treasures they seek to control.

Nature responds with horror to Catiline's treason. When Catiline first meets with the conspirators, Lentulus describes with enthusiasm the sky as having "all the weights of sleep and death hung at it. / She is not rosy-finger'd, but swoll'n black. / Her face is like a water turn'd to blood" (1.1.193–95). This haunting description of the stormy sky exposes the twisted aesthetic and moral sensibilities of the traitors, who revel in the unnatural bruising of the sky "swoll'n black." They welcome "sleep" and "death" just as Shakespeare's Macbeths had done before them. Rather than celebrate divine transformation—water into wine—these men revel in the demonic inverse—water into blood. The sky represents the twisted sacrament that these men then plan to drink as the scene continues. Once the men take the mixture of blood and wine, darkness unnaturally descends on them during the day. Longinus claims "A strange, unwonted horror doth invade me; / I know not what it is," followed by the stage direction *A darkness comes over the place* and then *A groan of many people is heard underground* (311–14). Jonson symbolizes in the most conventional terms possible the dark violence of the deadly plot, as compared to the "rosy" sunshine of Rome itself. Were his contemporary audience inclined to find treason against the state material for comedy, Jonson's very exaggerations could signal a parodic reading of the opening act.

Certainly the play's opening scene presents a highly propagandistic portrait of treason. This portrait resonates with the opposition of demonic traitor and vulnerable state familiar to Jonson's audience from contemporary propaganda. But the play presses on the stark opposition of victim and traitor so far as to make it seem laughable. These men have no political purpose; they merely seek to cover gambling debts by killing the old "that could but hope a day / longer." Planning to attack nuns, virgins, pregnant women, and nonagenarians, these traitors have fantasies based in adolescent desire, not organized political principles. Even if the audience takes the first scenes straight, Jonson's commitment to this section of the play seems ambivalent. He describes it as "the worst," and condemns his audience for liking it. Contrasting the first portion of the play with the more laudable second half, Jonson implies that the play's opening serves as a preface for or contrast to his main argument in later acts.

Catiline does, of course, justify his plot on more stable political grounds than rape and murder. He claims to undertake treason, his "great and goodliest action" (338), in the name of liberty: "we do redeem ourselves to liberty / And break the iron yoke forg'd for our necks" (344–45). He understands treason as salvation, from slavery toward freedom, from state-imposed submission to the natural state of liberty. These lines in Jonson radically condense their source in Sallust. Sallust's Catiline laments (in Heywood's 1608 translation),

> Courage my Companions: Loe, that, that Liberty, which so long you
> have expected, and so often implored, now calleth on your valours. And
> not it alone, for besides, you have wealth, a just cause, and honor on

your sides. These are your Trophies of victory . . . unless your spirits bee so basely dejected, that you had rather live in subjection, then commaund with Honour.[45]

Here Sallust's word for the subservient men is *obnoxii*, resonating with Donne's word condemning Barlow as discussed in chapter 5. When someone is obnoxious, Sallust's Catiline suggests, he suffers from a base condition that naturally prompts revolt. Further, Sallust links freedom, liberty, and progress: "it is incredible to report, in howe short a time, the Citty, having obtained this forme of Liberty in Government, increased and prospered."[46] Of course, Sallust's Catiline, like Jonson's after him, longs for "awe" rather than equity. Jonson's Catiline appears even more starkly a figure of self-serving desire, and his two lines on liberty are buried under multiple speeches celebrating greed and violence. Tragically, the category of liberty seems to have little currency in a state where "decrees are bought, and laws are sold, / Honors and offices for gold" (579–80).

Jonson's Cicero

Any hope for the state's salvation lies in Cicero. At the start of act 3 he is depicted as a ruler who has "no urns" or "dusty monuments" (3.1.14). He is instead "a new man" (19), a Roman who is, in opposition to Catiline and his followers, a civil servant eager to protect the state. Evoking Jonson's own status as a non-noble, new man, Cicero earns his title through his merit rather than birthright. Sempronia's phrase for Cicero, evocative of Shakespeare as much as Jonson, introduces his character; she terms him "a mere upstart / That has no pedigree, no house, no coat, / No ensigns of a family" (2.1.119–21). While Sempronia's snobbery might replicate Jonson's own, nevertheless her comments, in the context of the play, expose her corruption. She is short-sided, placing greater value on social status than pursuit of the common good. In this she is not alone.

Fellow senators resent Cicero's climb to prominence, manifesting their suspicions of the new consul by questioning his fight against Catiline. When, in his first speech in the play, Cicero informs the senate that there are "some turbulent practices / Already on foot, and rumors of moe dangers," Crassus murmurs in an aside, "Or you will make them, if there be none" (3.1.51–53). Crassus implies that the new senator fabricates the crime in order to earn political glory by uncovering it. As he tells Catulus and Caesar later in the scene, "Treasons and guilty men are made in states / Too oft to dignify the magistrates" (102–3). This suspicious equation, that "new men" fake treason to dignify themselves, resonates with 1605 accusations against Robert Cecil, who helped James to discover the Gunpowder Plot. It is a familiar charge, to blame the state for unrest that plagues it. Ironically, Crassus's line could apply to himself as a magistrate who "makes" treason to serve his own ambition: the two senators who vigorously mock Cicero, Crassus and Caesar, are themselves participants in Catiline's plot. Jonson thus depicts two Romes: the Rome of Cicero, who fights a treasonous threat, and the Rome of other senators such as Crassus and Cicero, who participate in it.

Cicero recognizes the danger he faces in accusing Catiline, "Especially in such an envious state / That sooner will accuse the magistrate / Than the delinquent " (3.2.252–54). As a result of this political danger and the feigned cynicism of the guilty senators, Cicero initially fails to warn the Senate of treason because no one believes his allegations about Catiline. As he claims, "so incredible / Their plots have seem'd, or I so vain to make / These things for mine own glory and false greatness, / As hath been given out" (4.2.18–20). Encountering resistance from corrupt senators, Cicero's election at least comforts virtuous citizens and the chorus. The chorus to the second act, for example, prays for the election of a principled consul, saying, "put it in the public voice / To make a free and worthy choice" (2.1.372–73). Furthermore, they ask, "let whom we name / . . . study conscience above fame" (375–78). Cicero's election appears to fulfill the chorus's prayer, particularly because he echoes their language of "conscience."

Cicero employs the language of conscience throughout the play. In fighting the traitors, for example, he claims to turn to "the unbated strengths / Of a firm conscience, which shall arm each step / Taken for the state" (3.4.29–31). The notion of the conscience as a weapon employed against evil resonates with Donne's hope, in *Pseudo-Martyr*, that this faculty helps the subject navigate the murky waters of contemporary controversy. When Cicero praises Fulvia for helping expose Catiline's treason, he again invokes the value of the conscience, and, in doing so, offers her comfort that equally applies to his own efforts. If Rome should prove ungrateful to her, he says, her virtuous efforts are "paid / In conscience of the fact: so much good deeds / Reward themselves" (3.2.63–65). Cicero tallies his actions through conscience, not reward, an argument that echoes with Donne's praise of conscience over material comforts discussed in the previous chapter. Finally, Cicero's closing lines echo the Chorus's speech directly: celebrating his success in fighting treason, he claims that if the memory of this triumphant day lives on, it "shall much affect my conscience, / Which I must always study before fame" (5.9.95–96). In closing the play with these lines, Jonson gestures toward Cicero's role as a pure, principled ruler who upholds the values so crucial to Rome's chorus.

Cicero's orations further reinforce his role as the virtuous consul striving to protect Rome. Surrounded by corrupt and ambitious countrymen, he delivers a series of orations that uphold the common good and consensual decision making over personal, oligarchical rule. Jonson translates these famous orations directly into his play, and thus, unlike Sallust, he allows the consul to speak for himself. If Sallust's famous rivalry with Cicero may prevent him from openly celebrating the consul's successes, Jonson has no such reservation. His first oration in the Senate, for example, reveals how he defers to the wishes of other senators over his own. Although he wants to use the decree of the s.c.u., which has been "let dull and rust" (4.2.146), to execute Catiline, he waits: "while there is one that dares defend thee," he tells Catiline, "live" (169).

Cicero reiterates this claim in the fourth oration. Here he tells the Senate that he is "not readier to obey, than to defend / Whatever you shall act" (5.6.91–92). His gesture toward the Senate's will establishes his role as a servant of the state rather than as a self-promoting, ambitious statesman. His repeated reference to Rome's glorious past, while echoing similar gestures by Catiline's followers, further establish the consul's concern for the state: Rome is a "glorious city" and a "light of all the earth" (5.4.156–57), he claims, evoking a shared pride and memory among the senators. He upholds a model of the consensus-driven state at odds with the Senate's current configuration: Catiline, Crassus, and Caesar, participants in the treason, all sit in this same body. But Cicero's deference to the will of the state's "fathers" establishes his desire for such a community even if fictional or utopian in Rome's current state. Cicero's motives in fighting Catiline remain, as Katharine Eisaman Maus illuminates, "morally impeccable."[47]

Yet in fighting Catiline's traitors, on the one side, and corrupt Roman oligarchs, on the other, Jonson's Cicero charts a delicate political path in protecting the state. He attempts to uphold the Republican form of government while maneuvering around Catiline's followers who corrupt the senate's workings. Here is a moment of crisis, and this crisis poses crucial political questions about the priorities of the state: Is the state one that upholds the law or bends it for necessity? Is it one that honors its form of government in a crisis or that alters it? Answers become clear as Cicero's attempt to maneuver between law and necessity proves non-navigable: despite his virtue, Cicero must resort to devious and corrupt methods in order to protect the state. Such methods, following Blair Worden's analysis, are clearly pragmatic. Jonson distinguishes, Worden argues, between "political means, which are morally autonomous, and political ends, which must be virtuous."[48] Cicero thus deploys the reason of state arguments familiar from Machiavelli. By distinguishing between Jonson and Cicero, however, we can open another layer of the play's argumentation: if Cicero appears, following Worden, as a Machiavellian-style ruler, one who offers an end-based justification for action rather than a principled one, in Cicero's limited success Jonson highlights his reservations about such Machiavellian pragmatism: danger lies in compromising political principles even for virtuous ends.

Cicero's corruption emerges slowly. First, he simply employs Curius as his spy. In doing so, however, he persuades Curius to break his sacrament and betray his fellow conspirators; as Cicero tells him, anachronistically, "no religion binds men to be traitors" (3.2.135), a phrase that links the play to the post-plot association of treason and religion. Cicero's line might appear sympathetic—a good magistrate attempts to free Curius from a corrupt sacrament. This line could equally be read as glib; if a sacrament is a contract, how can Curius break this "bind" at his convenience? Cicero's goals in rooting out treason elicit audience sympathy but his methods increasingly do not. After counseling Curius to break his oath, the consul then wants him to continue meeting with the conspirators in order to learn "what new ones they draw in" (188). Rather than expose the treason immediately, Cicero plans to wait and thereby entrap more men lured into the treasonous plot, a move in sharp contrast to Jonson's source; in Cicero's first oration itself, the consul wishes to expose Catiline's vulnerable political position in order to dissuade other senators from becoming involved in the plot.

Employing this spy, Jonson's Cicero attempts to maintain his high moral ground by condemning the very followers who assist his cause. He mocks Curius and the courtesan Fulvia, both of whom gather information for him, as "geese and harlots," further deeming Fulvia "a common strumpet, worthless to be named" (3.2.230, 217). The play mirrors Cicero's haughty condemnation of his helpers in Catiline's own attitude toward his fellow traitors. In a parallel soliloquy at the end of the next scene, Catiline exclaims, "What ministers men must for practice use!" (3.3.225), characterizing his own followers as "the dregs of mankind" (227). If figures like Fulvia, Curius, Lentulus, and Cethegus are the dregs of the Roman state, nevertheless Cicero and Catiline both appear hypocritical in their attempt to condemn the very figures they rely on to support their opposing causes. Cicero's dismissal of Fulvia is especially unattractive. As a "new man" without "urns or monuments," Cicero mocks Fulvia in precisely the same terms with which Sempronia derides him. Cicero's coupling of name with wealth, and the dismissal of commonness as worthlessness, is based in the same prejudice that fuels the traitors. No wonder Roman citizens are greedy, we might think, if even virtuous magistrates link wealth to political recognition.

Another layer to Cicero's corruption emerges when he manipulates evidence in order to convince the Senate of the conspirators' guilt. When he learns that Catiline seeks allies in the foreign army of the Allobroges, he approaches their Roman patron and demands his help in entrapping the traitors. According to Cicero's plan, Sanga will ask Catiline to supply him with a written request to join in the plot. Cicero will then pretend to capture the Allobrogian troops and seize these incriminating letters, securing proof of the treason while saving Sanga from the appearance of betraying Catiline. With this plan, as Cicero claims, "ill deeds are well turn'd back upon their authors, / And 'gainst an injurer the revenge is just" (4.5.101–2). When Cicero later expresses false surprise as his fellow countrymen open the letters on the Senate floor, the play stages the way in which state authorities invent evidence to prove their otherwise insupportable charges of treason.

Having manipulated evidence, Cicero then refuses to risk his political position by fighting Caesar, who is implicated in the treason. Cicero learns of Caesar's complicity through his spy, Curius, yet he dismisses evidence about Caesar's guilt. Ignoring the advice of fellow senator Cato who justly insists that all the conspirators should be punished, Cicero instead convinces Cato to overlook Caesar's participation, allegedly in the interest of political stability: "Caesar and Crassus, if they be ill men, / Are mighty ones," Cicero claims, adding "I'll make / Myself no enemies, nor the state no traitors" (4.2.471–78). Although he justifies his action in the name of the state, Cicero also betrays his cowardice. As a newly elected consul unpopular among other senators, Cicero occupies a weak political position. He refuses to "make himself enemies" or to further threaten his position as consul. Yet, in so doing, he protects Caesar more than Rome.

The play's final scene stages the encounter of Cato and Cicero with Caesar as they debate the punishment of the traitors. Jonson's portrait of the Concord House scene proves a striking contrast to Sallust, suggesting the ways in which Jonson pushes his critique of Roman oligarchy further than the classical historian. While Sallust celebrated Caesar as the proponent of law, Jonson highlights Caesar's corruption, thereby offering a bleaker reading of Rome's future. In the debate between Syllanus, Cato, and Caesar on the legal precedents for executing traitors, Caesar's argument, convincing in Sallust, is compromised by the senator's obvious guilt in Jonson. When Caesar argues "I think it fit to stay where our laws do" (5.6.43), suggesting that to a citizen of Rome "our laws give exile and not death" (62), senators initially agree with him, ignorant of Caesar's complicity in the crime. Yet the audience recognizes that Caesar wishes to "stay where [the] laws do" not out of respect for his country's constitution but out of his interest in protecting his fellow conspirators. Placing Caesar's famous speech in a context that undermines its argument, Jonson suggests that even corrupt leaders might argue in favor of following the laws; such speeches should not, however, mask their pretensions to absolute power, evident in Caesar's later rise. The irony of the senator defending the Republican constitution seems to elude Sallust, historically Caesar's supporter, but the irony fuels Jonson's scene.

Jonson completes his portrait of the compromised Cicero in representing the Senate's vote on execution. Cicero had claimed in his oration to put the Senate's consensus before his own will. Yet, in the final scene, he manipulates the outcome, both through his ally Cato and his timely use of evidence. Cicero's view in favor of execution is voiced by Cato, allowing Cicero to preserve his role as moderator of debate while ensuring that his opinion receives a hearing. Against Caesar's speech, Cato advocates using the discretionary powers, allowed by the s.c.u., to execute the traitors; as he claims, "to spare these men were to commit / A greater wickedness than you would revenge" (5.6.140–41). Banishing Catiline, Cato argues, would only allow him to build up foreign support for his attack on Rome; rather than punish treason, the senators would help to fuel it, a potentially desirable outcome for the treasonous Caesar. Cicero himself expresses such a view throughout the play and uses Cato as his "counsel" arguing in favor of the powers of the s.c.u.

Cicero further directs the scene by discreetly introducing evidence against Caesar in an effort to force him into submission. When the Senate sides in favor of Cato, Caesar refuses to compromise, saying, "I am not yet chang'd in my sentence, Fathers" (152). To this, Cato claims "no matter," and immediately private letters, presumably concerning the plot, appear for Caesar. Eager to have the letters read, Cato declares, "I crave to have 'em read for the Republic" (156), to which Caesar answers that it is a private letter, and "though you hate me, / Do not discover it" (158–59). This potentially compromising evidence of the senator's involvement with Catiline forces Caesar's consent for the executions. When confronted with evidence of his own complicity, Caesar grudgingly concedes to Cicero in order that the letters remain unread, while also warning, "You'll repent / this rashness, Cicero" (160–61). Taking the rash measures he considers necessary for the common good, Cicero contradicts his earlier orations on consensual politics. As a result, he endangers the Republic by transgressing its laws, fabricating evidence, and manufacturing consent. By constructing evidence to prove the treason, and by saving Caesar from exposure as an accomplice, Cicero manipulates the responses of the senators in order to produce his desired outcome. The unified vote for execution is not the product of consensus but, instead, of Cicero's coercion of his opposition.

Cicero's suspension of law and the manipulation of consensus reveal a ruler that ignores the state's own form of governance. Indeed, as Jonathan Goldberg terms it, "Cicero's is a familiar form, the mask of republicanism covering absolutism."[49] The resulting consolidation of power, although exercised only temporarily, introduces a form of government that will emerge as fully fledged tyranny under the empire. Rather than respect the Republican model of government, Cicero anticipates this form of absolute power, albeit in the interest of protecting the state from its enemies. The play thus ends with the clear implication of treason to come. The Republic remains, as Anne Barton notes, "doomed to succumb to Caesar," a historical truth that would have been familiar to Jonson's audience.[50]

Tragically, in Jonson's play, moments of crisis strain virtue. Even the best ruler with the best intentions may be forced to make dangerous compromises. Jonson depicts Cicero's unrivaled virtue as he attempts to restore political order to Rome. Cicero's motives are beyond reproach, and his honorable ends are based in protecting the common good. In representing Cicero's struggle against treason, however, Jonson reveals precisely how treason can be productive of tyranny, altering a moderate, virtuous ruler into one who sidesteps law, albeit momentarily. Such suspension of law in the name of necessity has long-term consequences: moments of crisis come to define the state since here the state defines its priorities most clearly. Rather than view the treason as an exceptional moment, then, Jonson represents Catiline's conspiracy as an event that exposes the latent conflicts in Rome, conflicts that will eventually prove to be the state's downfall.

Even if Cicero's goals are impossible to fault, his methods depend on the servitude rather than the liberty of citizens. Quentin Skinner helps to elucidate this point: even if the Republic upholds the liberty of its citizens on principle, nevertheless "public servitude can arise," Skinner writes in his analysis of the neo-Roman theory of free states, "when the internal constitution of a state allows for the exercise of any discretionary or prerogative powers on the part of those governing it."[51] With the ability to suspend law comes the subjection of citizens to the will of the ruler, leading a writer like Milton to explore, as Skinner notes, how "discretionary powers invariably serve to reduce free nations to the status of slaves."[52] Regardless of the justification for taking such measures, the mere existence of extralegal power threatens the liberty of subjects. This stark political wisdom exposes the difficulties facing Jonson's Cicero: he wishes to obey his conscience, a practice beyond reproach and celebrated by the Chorus, but, in doing so against the opinions of other senators, he enforces his will on the citizens of Rome. Acting in good conscience, Cicero nevertheless exercises the powers of a tyrant.

Unable to sustain a straightforward portrait of Cicero as the play's heroic ruler who battles demonic traitors, Jonson not surprisingly divided the response of his audience. He prevents his viewers from collapsing solely into identification with Cicero by refusing to replicate the most simplistic opposition of ruler and traitor. Consequently Jonson forces his audience to think through the issues of law, conscience, and necessity at stake in the treasonous events surrounding them in 1611. The tension in Cicero, between his rhetorical gestures toward community and consensus, and his political machinations evocative of oligarchy, resonate with King James's own exercise of power in the years prior to 1611. Like Jonson's Cicero, James insists on his pacific, moderate rule, a point he stresses in his oath of allegiance polemics in 1606 and 1609. His policies secured nonetheless a degree of unprecedented absolute authority against his Catholic subjects. Jonson engages with the resulting questions on authority and extralegal power, so central to the oath of allegiance debate, through the lens of Roman history; like Hayward, Savile, and Grenewey before him, Jonson turns to classical representations of Rome in order to analyze models of liberty and sovereignty without obviously entangling contemporary personalities. Viewing the tensions in Stuart England from a distance allows Jonson to develop a nuanced theory on the relationship of treason and tyranny. Jonson thereby uses Sallust's critique of monarchy as the backbone of his history, just as Hayward had invoked Tacitus's exposure of imperial abuses. Thus each writer adapts his source material to contemporary concerns on the nature of resistance, tyranny, and good governance.

Treason and Tyranny

Studying the responses of Jonson and Donne to post–Gunpowder Plot controversies reveals the delicate position of middle-ground Protestants who supported the king without subscribing to theories of absolute or divine-right sovereignty. If the post-plot propaganda asserted James's rule as divine and condemned English Catholics as traitors, the contributions of Jonson and Donne to the debate on treason challenged such sensationalist polemics. While Donne recognized the split loyalties of English Catholics and encouraged his readers to foster their conscience over blind obedience, Jonson also addressed, and challenged, post–Gunpowder Plot sensationalism, undermining the simplistic association of Catholicism and treason. The opening of Jonson's play initially confirms royal fears of demonic Catholic traitors and thus appears to support the contemporary model of treason as an unnatural crime against a virtuous ruler, as asserted in the post-plot propaganda. In the second half of the play, however, Jonson exposes how Cicero's attempt to protect the common good undermines the state instead by consolidating power in the figure of the consul. Turning to his conscience, the faculty Donne so vigorously defends, allows Cicero to uphold his own judgment and exercise his will over his fellow senators.

In their representations of threats to the state, both Jonson and Donne expose the dialectical relation between treason and tyranny. Violent attacks against a ruler, when unsuccessful, can result in an exercise of absolute power that has the potential to permanently alter the workings of the state. In invoking extralegal power, a ruler undermines the liberty necessary for subjects to live outside a condition of subjection. Thus Jonson and Donne expand notions of tyranny beyond its association with the brutal exercise of power. The despot is not simply the ruler who enforces his own will over the common good. Undermining this simplistic dichotomy between the ruler's will and the good of the nation, these writers suggest instead that tyranny emerges through a particular style of exercising power over the conscience and will of subjects: invoking discretionary power to rule over the law, even for the good of the state, spells tyranny. This form of government can emerge, therefore, under a ruler who exercises his own will in *defense* of the common good rather than just over it. By defining tyranny away from a pejorative judgment against a ruler's character— no longer associating it with bad intentions or decadent personal desires—these writers make room for a discussion of despotic activities independent of critiques of a particular king.

The examples of Donne and Jonson further suggest how, during the years following one of the most dramatic attempts at treason ever witnessed by the English state, the nation was not unified in its condemnation of treason. Instead, the polemics between and among Protestants and Catholics attest to the burgeoning public debate on the legal and political parameters of treason. This debate challenges the fiction of political consensus by exposing the ideological stakes at issue in the conflict; questions of law, common good, and absolute power were not merely invoked before a continental audience but appeared as well in parliamentary debates, domestic polemic, and dramatic texts. Recognizing this debate also challenges the overemphasis on the absolutist nature of James's monarchy. Although the king asserted such power through his post-1605 legislation, he faced significant challenges not only from the expected audience of radical Jesuits and monarchomachs but also from the political middle-grounders. As moderate subjects weighed into the debate, they wrested the discussion of tyranny and treason away from radical resistance theorists while nevertheless challenging James's absolutist claims in the oath of allegiance controversy. Treason threatens the state, but so, too, does the momentary exercise of absolute power, and the resulting dialectic between treason and tyranny erodes virtuous government based in protection of the common good. In exposing this dialectic, post–Gunpowder Plot writers articulate, even in supporting the king's post-plot policies, the rights of the subject to freedom of conscience and the primacy of law. With this articulation of rights, we find the emergence of what may be called an early modern public sphere: subjects ranging from royal absolutists and monarchomachs to moderate loyalists weighed into the political controversies surrounding them and increasingly debated the rules governing relations.

Afterword

It is neither desirable nor remotely likely that civil liberty will occupy as favored a position in wartime as it does in peacetime. But it is both desirable and likely that more careful attention will be paid by the courts to the basis for the government's claims of necessity as a basis for curtailing civil liberty. The laws will thus not be silent in time of war, but they will speak in a somewhat different voice.

William H. Rehnquist, *All the Laws but One: Civil Liberties in Wartime*

The question of whether laws should fall silent in war is an urgent one. States tend to define or redefine themselves in moments of crisis, when wartime leaders may invoke discretionary powers to suspend certain laws and liberties. In the name of necessity and the common good, such leaders may temporarily violate constitutional principles or common law traditions. But emergency actions produce long-term effects. In distinguishing between principles fundamental to the survival of the state and contingent practices that can be deferred temporarily, leaders face a thorny question: what laws and liberties can be revoked in an effort to preserve the state before the state itself is irrevocably altered?

Legal theorists have long sanctioned the temporary, emergency powers by which leaders silence the laws or, as the late chief justice William H. Rehnquist asserts in the epigraph to this closing chapter, mold them to "speak in a somewhat different voice." Yet the confidence with which Rehnquist counterposes liberty and wartime power belies the historical irony of the Ciceronian adage he evokes: "Laws are silent in war."[1] This irony, discussed in chapter 7, lies in Cicero's own fate: having used emergency power to fight Catiline's treason in 63 B.C., he was exiled three years later for this sidestepping of Roman law.

Cicero's fate poses a pressing question for jurists such as Rehnquist. Although legal theorists might concur that the laws are silent in wartime, leaders and subjects less easily agree on the two critical and seemingly straightforward terms "war" and "law." The eventual exile of Cicero demonstrates shifting understandings of what constitutes a crisis and an appropriate response. A time of treasonous activity brings this question to the fore especially starkly since, unlike the case of two warring states, a treasonous threat can be from within or without, and can be posed by an individual or a group. A time of treason, therefore, cannot easily be categorized. It is neither a time of war nor of peace and, indeed, troubles the clear delineation between the two categories. In fighting treason, the state simply has a scale of higher and lower alerts, ranging from green to red. This sliding scale of danger reinforces how treason's rainbow hovers over but will never disappear from our cultural landscape.

When a period of crisis has no foreseeable end, the exercise of emergency powers propounded by both Cicero and Rehnquist becomes acutely problematic. Even if the exercise of power is in the name of the common good, how long will subjects or citizens live in the condition of emergency before opposing the state's invocation of autocratic authority in the name of necessity? This book, particularly in its look at the oath of allegiance crisis, highlights the emergence of dissent out of concerns about excessive application of state power in time of treason. Perhaps willing to grant temporary license at first, subjects increasingly draw negative attention to innovative government practices which threaten to shift to the realm of permanency. Put another way, however much the fight against treason requires the suspension or expansion of law in the name of necessity, subjects and citizens nevertheless can and do respond to this crisis by invoking the suspended rights of law, conscience, and property. An oppositional relationship thus exists between, on the one hand, constrictions of rights and interpretations in the fight against treason and, on the other, the emerging voices of dissent against the state's assertion of sovereignty.

The state might attempt to forestall such opposition by turning to the other broad term in Cicero's equation, namely, "law." Cicero's formula juxtaposes law and peacetime with war and emergency, positioning law in opposition to temporary chaos, necessity, and absolute authority. If the laws speak in wartime, Cicero implies, then the state acts customarily and not temporarily—it acts in accordance with its own established practices. Yet law is not merely the guarantor of civil liberties or consensual rule. Laws, after all, can be changed, customs altered, and borders sealed. Practices that were formerly legal suddenly become condemned by new laws; in wartime, some laws are silent while others speak freshly and loudly. Innovative laws, like the legislation on treason by words, appear as part of a new regime to enforce the increasing prerogative of the state.

Fighting treason involves a twofold process: on one side, suspending law in a time of crisis in order to fight the temporary threat, and, on the other, passing new legislation to help deal in the longer term with this treasonous emergency. Law is the instrument at once protecting rights and encroaching upon them. Recognizing this dual role of law helps to expose how law and treason exist not in opposition to each other—just as law and emergency are not conflicting, despite Cicero's adage—but instead in a relationship of mutual dependence. Law both defines treason and uses the threat of treason in order to expand. This exposition highlights the danger law itself poses as a mechanism for increasing state authority in a time of emergency. This is not to discount the seriousness of a treasonous threat nor the necessity of the state's fight against its violent opponents. Exposing this dynamic helps instead to draw attention to the familiar historical question haunting apparently temporary practices: at what point does the restriction of movement, expression, interpretation, or religion irrevocably compromise the very state one is fighting to save?

If the crisis is always defined as the unexpected strike, the demonic opponent, then fighting treason becomes an activity situated outside the bounds of government itself—it is what "we" are not. Treason is not simply, although it can be, a foreign emergency or a violent, oppositional force. Rather, by viewing treason as a threat defined in and through law, one that expands and contracts, and is both dangerous to the state and at times self-serving, we are then better able to analyze the interdependence of sovereignty and treason law.[2]

When a state is struggling against a real (or even imagined) present danger, however, it is almost structurally impossible to perceive the relationship of treason to sovereignty, that is, to approach treason both as a legal concept and as an action. This kind of meditative and analytical response to crisis rarely emerges from state magistrates, as this book has attempted to show, but it frequently typifies the work of literary writers. Fictional texts offer one of the few loci for the sustained yet imaginative consideration of treason as a conceptual, linguistic, and representational issue. In depicting treason at a remove—either temporally or spatially—literature forces a pause in the inevitable dynamic charted above between terror and law, emergency and prerogative. This caesura, the pause of the imagination, becomes a way of thinking about the stakes in treason in a manner less hysterical, momentary, or incendiary than the current crisis. The representational issues embedded in the treasonous threat come to the fore: if the state represents the interests of the common good, how does the definition of common good shift in crisis and whom does such a shift serve and represent?

Even if the state, in its claim of necessity, can bury these questions of representation until the practices established in a time of crisis become more permanent prerogatives of the state, the literary text frequently does not. Here we might recall the literature explored in this book: Hayward's *Henry IV,* Shakespeare's *Richard II* and *Macbeth,* and Jonson's *Catiline* each use the lens of history to explore questions of rulership and public defense in a time of crisis. In the galvanizing and fracturing of political opinion that characterizes treason, such imaginative representations can help negotiate the crisis not solely by offering answers but also by highlighting the deeper questions at stake in the state's response. In the tangled emergency of treason, sovereignty, and law, literature thus is able to speak with what we might call a somewhat different voice.

Notes

1. Sovereignty, Treason Law, and the Political Imagination in Early Modern England

For their comments on this chapter I am grateful to Marilynn Desmond, Jared Farmer, Heather James, David Román, and Bruce Smith.

1. "A History of the Gunpowder Treason, collected from Approved Authors as well Popish as Protestant" (London: Richard Chiswel, 1678), sig. C1r., p. 17. The letter, which I discuss in chapter 5, is preserved in the Public Record Office, *State Papers, Domestic, James I* 14 / 216, no. 2. Hereafter cited as *SPD*.

2. For a rehearsal of the debates surrounding the letter, see Antonia Fraser, *The Gunpowder Plot: Terror and Faith in 1605* (London: Mandarin, 1997), 152–55.

3. Frances E. Dolan, *Dangerous Familiars: Representations of Domestic Crime in England, 1550–1700* (Ithaca, N.Y.: Cornell University Press, 1994). Dolan's careful unpacking of the overlapping loyalties at stake in domestic crime is apt for my own reading of treason, a crime that implicates competing models of allegiance (to crown and faith) as I discuss in chapter 7. See also Frances E. Dolan, *Whores of Babylon: Catholicism, Gender, and Seventeenth-Century Print Culture* (Ithaca, N.Y.: Cornell University Press, 1999), 2, where she writes that, with treason, reports and narrations themselves are "what 'really happened.'"

4. We can cement this point about the replaying of treason by remembering the continuing tradition of "exorcising" the plot through the burning of the Guy scarecrow every November 5 in certain British towns (most notably in Lewes, according to Antonia Fraser [*The Gunpowder Plot*, 293–94]).

5. 26 Hen.8 c.13 in *Statutes of the Realm*, vol. 3 (London: G. Eyre and A. Strahan, 1817), 508.

6. Although I argue, in the following pages, that language does not constitute action—its work lies in its vital mediation of imagination and action—nevertheless it is interesting to consider how the Tudor statute itself anticipates speech-act theory in understanding language as a form of action. See J. L. Austin, *How to Do Things with Words* (Oxford: Clarendon, 1962); Rosalind Coward and John Ellis, *Language and Materialism* (New York: Routledge, 1977); J. Hillis Miller, *Speech Acts in Literature* (Stanford: Stanford University Press, 2001); John R. Searle, *Speech Acts: An Essay in the Philosophy of Language* (Cambridge: Cambridge University Press, 1969); and idem, *Expression and Meaning: Studies in the Theory of Speech Acts* (Cambridge: Cambridge University Press, 1979).

7. The model of spectacular treason is explored most famously in the analysis of execution in Michel Foucault, *Discipline and Punish: The Birth of the Prison,* trans. Alan Sheridan (New York: Vintage Books, 1995 [1978]). Here Foucault contrasts the phenomenon of internalizing punishment, characteristic of modern prison culture, with the early modern practice of spectacular torture and the execution of traitors. While his brief analysis of early modern execution as spectacular obscures the interpretive work necessary to comprehend and prosecute treason, Foucault's incisive analysis of the constitutive role of discourse in *The History of Sexuality,* trans. Robert Hurley, vol. 1, *An Introduction* (New York: Random House, 1980), helps to illuminate precisely this point about treason: the political crime, like the criminalized sexual practices Foucault discusses, exists in the languages surrounding it, creating it, and controlling it.

8. John Barrell, *Imagining the King's Death: Figurative Treason, Fantasies of Regicide, 1793–1796* (Oxford: Oxford University Press, 2000), chap. 2, esp. 129–35; Karen Cunningham, *Imaginary Betrayals: Subjectivity and the Discourses of Treason in Early Modern England* (Philadelphia: University of Pennsylvania Press, 2002).

9. See *Cobbett's Complete Collection of State Trials and Proceedings for High Treason and Other Crimes and Misdemeanors from the Earliest Period to the Present Time,* ed. John Cobbett and William Howell, vol. 2 (1603–1627) of 21 vols. (London: T. C. Hansard, 1816), 182. For an analysis of this passage, see Fraser, *Gunpowder Plot,* 2:143.

10. In other words, these writers recognize, with Thomas Hobbes, that authority, not truth, makes treason law. See Thomas Hobbes, *Leviathan* (Oxford: Oxford University Press, 1996), part 2, chap. 18, "The Rights of Sovereigns by Institution," 119. Victoria Kahn, "Hamlet or Hecuba: Carl Schmitt's Decision," *Representations* 83 (summer 2003): 67–96, 70, helped me to realize Hobbes's aptness for my argument. Specifically Kahn draws attention to the contractual nature of sovereign authority in Hobbes, an authority "predicated on the consent of the individual to the political contract and to the mechanisms of political representation" (78). In doing so, Kahn wrests Hobbes away from Carl Schmitt, who interprets Hobbes first as a "hero of decisionism" and then as "a tarnished figure" who "unwittingly inaugurated the protoliberal, technological vitiation of politics" (80). Kahn's distinction is especially useful to my argument about how writers, in a time of treasonous crisis, rather than capitulating to a Schmittian decisionist sovereign instead stage the representational underpinnings of sovereignty.

11. Kahn, "Hamlet or Hecuba," 86. Here Kahn refers to Hamlet's speech on the players as part of her larger argument on Carl Schmitt's misreading of Shakespeare and Hobbes.

12. Ben Jonson, *Catiline*, ed. W. F. Bolton and Jane F. Gardner, Regents Renaissance Drama series (London: Edward Arnold, 1972), 3.1.102–3. The speaker is Crassus.

13. Tracing this shift in Tudor law, this book resonates with work by Alan Orr and Lisa Steffen on the ways that England, in the late Stuart period, defined itself through its treason laws. While both Orr and Steffen concentrate on the execution of Charles I as the central case for their arguments, this book examines how earlier in the sixteenth century, during a time devoid of king killing, the law nevertheless anticipates this political shift toward defending the dignity of the state as much as the king's body. See D. Alan Orr, *Treason and the State: Law, Politics and Ideology in the English Civil War* (Cambridge: Cambridge University Press, 2002); and Lisa Steffen, *Defining a British State: Treason and National Identity, 1608–1820* (Basingstoke, U.K.: Palgrave, 2001).

14. 25 Edw.3 c.2 in *Statutes of the Realm*, vol. 1 (1810), 20.

15. Ibid.

16. John Bellamy, *The Tudor Law of Treason* (London: Routledge, Kegan and Paul, 1979), 10.

17. This 1352 statute proved at times more adaptable than the 1534 treason legislation, however, because it did not require two witnesses. Tudor monarchs would thus invoke the earlier statute in cases where they did not have the witnesses necessary to secure a conviction under the 1534 law. See Bellamy, *The Tudor Law of Treason*, 50.

18. *Cobbett's Complete Collection of State Trials*, vol. 1 (1163–1600), 889–90.

19. On the relationship between compass, imagine, and action, Sir Matthew Hale offers a helpful explication of judicial constructions. He writes of the phrase compassing and imagining the death of the king that "compassing by bare words is not an overt act, as appears by many temporary statutes against it: 26 H8 c.13; 1 EI c.6; 12 EI c.1; 14 EI c.1, and etc. but the same set down by him in writing is an overt act" (*Pleas of the Crown; or, A Methodical Summary of the Principal Matters Relating to That Subject* [London, 1678], 13).

20. With constructive treason, judges exercised wide latitude in interpreting the law, and thus included activities not clearly covered in the 1352 statute (such as speech). On constructive treason, see Bellamy, *The Law of Treason in England;* idem, *The Tudor Law of Treason;* Samuel Rezneck, "Constructive Treason by Words in the Fifteenth Century," *American Historical Review* 33.3 (April 1928): 544–52; and Steffen, *Defining a British State,* 14–18, 24–27. On constructive treason in the early modern period in relation to literature, see Barrell, *Imagining the King's Death,* chap. 2, esp. 129–35; Cunningham, *Imaginary Betrayals;* and Luke Wilson, *Theatres of Intention: Drama and the Law in Early Modern England* (Stanford: Stanford University Press, 2000), 44.

21. *Cobbett's Complete Collection of State Trials*, 1:1003.

22. Ibid., 1:1042.

23. To "judge the mind" by the "outward facts" is not, however, a straight-

forward process. What does such a construction mean? Luke Wilson helps unpack this connection of mind and "outward fact" in *Theatres of Intention*. The word "intention," which describes the relationship between thought and action, hinges on a structural or temporal delay; in this delay Wilson posits dramatic action, both criminal and fictional.

24. Cunningham, *Imaginary Betrayals*, 11.

25. Barrell, *Imagining the King's Death*, 33.

26. This act represented the culmination of three years' worth of efforts to revise the treason law. Initially these changes were not meant to be substantive and were particularly aimed at those subjects with dual allegiances to England and Rome, a problem specifically born of Henry's break with the pope. Increasingly, however, Henry and Cromwell recognized the need for a law to control protest surrounding Henry's marriages and his break with Rome beyond the First Act of Succession, which controlled writing but not spoken words. See Bellamy, *The Tudor Law of Treason*, 31; G. R. Elton, *Policy and Police: The Enforcement of the Reformation in the Age of Thomas Cromwell* (Cambridge: Cambridge University Press, 1972), 269–70.

27. 26 Hen.8 c.13 in *Statutes of the Realm*, vol. 3, 508. On Thomas Cromwell's and Thomas Audley's process of drafting the treason legislation between 1531 and 1534, see Elton, *Policy and Police*, 265–92; see also Samuel Rezneck, "The Trial of Treason in Tudor England," *Essays in History and Political Theory in Honour of C. H. McIlwain*, ed. Carl Frederick Wittke, 258–88 (Cambridge, Mass.: Harvard University Press, 1936).

28. The charge of treason by words had common law precedent in the fifteenth century, when the crown attempted to prosecute subjects who derogated the royal authority. On the precedents in common law, see Bellamy, *The Law of Treason in England*; Rezneck, "Constructive Treason by Words"; and Isobel D. Thornley, "Treason by Words in the Fifteenth Century," *English Historical Review* 32.128 (October 1917): 556–61. See also G. R. Elton who argues that "treason by words was not so unprecedented or outrageous as indignant opinion, then and since, has liked to maintain" even as he acknowledges that the 1534 treason act "contained the first major redefinition of treason since 1352 and its import was wide" (*Policy and Police*, 289, 286).

29. Bellamy, *The Tudor Law of Treason*, 14. See PRO SP 1/93 fo.52 in J. S. Brewer, J. Gairdner, and R. H. Brodie, eds., *Calendar of Letters and Papers, Foreign and Domestic Henry VIII* (1862–1932), viii, no. 856.

30. 1 Edw.6 c.12 in *Statutes of the Realm*, vol. 4 (1819), 18. Protector Somerset instituted this act, perhaps in an attempt to gain popularity and support from Edward VI's subjects.

31. *Cobbett's Complete Collection of State Trials*, 1:896.

32. 13 Elizabeth c.1. in *Statutes of the Realm*, vol. 4 (1819), 526. See also John Rastell, "A Collection in English, of the Statutes now in force, continued from the beginning of the Magna Charta . . . until the end of the session of Parliament holden in the 23rd yeere of the Reigne of our gratious Queen Elizabeth" (London: Christopher Barker, printer to the Queenes Majestie, 1583).

33. In 1628, in Pine's case, the judges ruled that "there is no treason at this

day but by the statute 25 Edw.3 c.2 for imagining the death of the king, etc,
and the indictment must be framed upon one of the points in that statute:
and the words spoken here can be but evidence to discover the corrupt heart
of him that spake them; but of themselves they are not treason, neither can
any indictment be framed upon them" (*Cobbett's Complete Collection of State
Trials*, vol. 3 (1627–1640), 368). For a discussion of treasonous words that invokes this ruling, see Thornley, "Treason by Words," 556.

34. Bellamy, *The Law of Treason in England*; idem, *The Tudor Law of Treason*, esp.
10–15; Elton, *Policy and Police*, 282–9; Lacey Baldwin Smith, *Treason in Tudor England: Politics and Paranoia* (Princeton, N.J.: Princeton University Press, 1986),
136–41; Rezneck, "Constructive Treason"; Thornley, "Treason by Words."

35. Elton, *Policy and Police*, 391.

36. Bellamy, *The Tudor Law of Treason*, 242.

37. Constance Jordan, *Shakespeare's Monarchies: Ruler and Subject in the Romances* (Ithaca, N.Y.: Cornell University Press, 1997), 7.

38. Richard II notoriously practiced against his enemies through the expansion of treason law, as I discuss in chapter 3, and Henry VIII similarly
employed the treason charge as a weapon in his administration of the Reformation, discussed briefly above.

39. Pierre Nora, "The Return of the Event," in *Histories: French Constructions
of the Past*, ed. Jacques Revel and Lynn Hunt, trans. Arthur Goldhammer
(New York: New Press, 1996), 427–36. On the notion of the event in the early
modern period, see Jacques Lezra, *Unspeakable Subjects: The Genealogy of the
Event in Early Modern Europe* (Stanford: Stanford University Press, 1997).

40. See Mervyn James, "At the Crossroads of the Political Culture: The Essex
Revolt, 1601," in idem, *Society, Politics, and Culture: Studies in Early Modern England* (Cambridge: Cambridge University Press, 1986), 417–32; Wallace Mac-
Caffrey, *Elizabeth I* (New York: Edward Arnold, 1993); and idem, *Elizabeth I: War
and Politics, 1588–1603* (Princeton, N.J.: Princeton University Press, 1992).

41. Notably, however, in an abstract of treason charges compiled against the
earl in 1600, he is indeed accused of plotting with Philip II of Spain, despite
the fact that Essex had spent his military career fighting against the Spanish
(see *SPD* 12/275, no. 33). Nevertheless, historians repeatedly point to Essex
as a Protestant hawk at court. John Guy notes how he "pursued ideology as
much as patronage. He assumed the militant Protestant mantle of Leicester,
Walsingham, and the Sidneys" (*Tudor England* [Oxford: Oxford University
Press, 1988] 440). For the most comprehensive discussion of Essex and
faction, see Paul E. J. Hammer, *The Polarisation of Elizabethan Politics: The Political Career of Robert Devereux, 2nd Earl of Essex, 1585–1597* (Cambridge:
Cambridge University Press, 1999).

42. On the Gunpowder Plot, see Paul Durst, *Intended Treason: What Really
Happened in the Gunpowder Plot* (London: W. H. Allen, 1970); Fraser, *The Gunpowder Plot*; Alan Haynes, *The Gunpowder Plot: Faith in Rebellion* (Dover, U.K.:
Alan Sutton, 1994); and Mark Nicholls, *Investigating Gunpowder Plot* (Manchester, U.K.: Manchester University Press, 1991).

43. Hammer, *Polarisation*, 161.

44. Ibid., 174.

45. Ibid., 174–75.

46. Johann P. Sommerville, *Politics and Ideology in England 1603–1640* (New York: Longman, 1986), 115. On the influence of absolutist and divine right discourses on literature of the 1590s, see Christopher Pye, *The Regal Phantasm: Shakespeare and the Politics of Spectacle* (London: Routledge, 1990); Leonard Tennenhouse, *Power on Display: The Politics of Shakespeare's Genres* (New York: Methuen, 1986).

47. Cyndia Susan Clegg, *Press Censorship in Elizabethan England* (Cambridge: Cambridge University Press, 1997). On early modern censorship, see also Richard Burt, *Licensed by Authority: Ben Jonson and the Discourses of Censorship* (Ithaca, N.Y.: Cornell University Press, 1993); Janet Clare, *Art Made Tongue-Tied by Authority: Elizabethan and Jacobean Dramatic Censorship*, 2nd ed. (Manchester, U.K.: Manchester University Press, 1999); Richard Dutton, *Licensing, Censorship, and Authority in Early Modern England: Buggeswords* (London: Palgrave/Macmillan, 2001); and Annabel Patterson, *Censorship and Interpretation: The Conditions of Writing and Reading in Early Modern Europe* (Madison: University of Wisconsin, 1984). My thinking on censorship has also been influenced by Richard Meyer, *Outlaw Representation: Censorship and Homosexuality in Twentieth-Century American Art* (Oxford: Oxford University Press, 2002).

48. On Bodin and Machiavelli in England, see Quentin Skinner, *The Foundations of Modern Political Thought*, vol. 1, *The Renaissance* (Cambridge: Cambridge University Press, 1978), 194–228, 251–62; and Richard Tuck, *Philosophy and Government, 1572–1651* (Cambridge: Cambridge University Press, 1993), 104–19.

49. My thinking on republicanism has been influenced by Norbrook, *Writing the English Republic*; Skinner, *Foundations*; Blair Worden, *Republicanism, Liberty, and Commercial Society, 1649–1776*, ed. David Wootton (Stanford: Stanford University Press, 1994), 45–196. For my understanding of constitutionalism in this period, I draw on the work of J. G. A. Pocock, *The Ancient Constitution and the Feudal Law: A Study of English Historical Thought in the Seventeenth Century* (Cambridge: Cambridge University Press, 1957); and Corinne Comstock Weston and Janelle Renfrow Greenberg, *Subjects and Sovereigns: The Grand Controversy over Legal Sovereignty in Stuart England* (Cambridge: Cambridge University Press, 1981).

50. I am indebted to the studies of nonelite theater audiences by Stephen Mullaney, *The Place of the Stage: License, Play, and Power in Renaissance England* (Ann Arbor: University of Michigan Press, 1995); and Jean E. Howard, *The Stage and Social Struggle in Early Modern England* (London: Routledge, 1994).

51. Glen Burgess, *Absolute Monarchy and the Stuart Constitution* (New Haven: Yale University Press, 1996), 101. Nicholas Henshall also challenges the theory of the rise of absolutism (*The Myth of Absolutism* [London: Longman, 1992]).

52. Texts such as Anon. [possibly de Mornay], *Vindicae Contra Tyrannos* (1579) and George Buchanan, *De jure regni apud Scotos* (1579) proved especially substantial contributions to this growing body of resistance theory.

53. Peter Lake, with Michael Questier, *The Anti-Christ's Lewd Hat: Protestants,*

Papists, and Players in Post-Reformation England (New Haven: Yale University Press, 2002), 208.

54. Jürgen Habermas, *The Structural Transformation of the Public Sphere: An Inquiry into a Category of Bourgeois Society,* trans. Thomas Burger, with the assistance of Frederick Lawrence (London: Polity, 1989), 27.

55. Sharon Achienstein, *Milton and the Revolutionary Reader* (Princeton, N.J.: Princeton University Press, 1994), 9; Norbrook, *Writing the English Republic,* 13; Nigel Smith, *Literature and Revolution in England, 1640–1660* (New Haven: Yale University Press, 1994); David Zaret, "Religion, Science, and Printing in the Public Spheres in Seventeenth-Century England," in *Habermas and the Public Sphere,* ed. Craig Calhoun, 212–35 (Cambridge, Mass.: MIT Press, 1992), 213.

56. NACBS pre-circulated paper, Philadelphia, Pa., October 30, 2004.

57. On the concept of an early modern public sphere, see Richard Burt, ed., *The Administration of Aesthetics: Censorship, Political Criticism, and the Public Sphere* (Minneapolis: University of Minnesota Press, 1994); Timothy Dykstal, *The Luxury of Skepticism: Politics, Philosophy, and Dialogue in the English Public Sphere, 1660–1740* (Charlottesville: University Press of Virginia, 2001); Alexandra Halask, *The Marketplace of Print: Pamphlets and the Public Sphere in Early Modern England* (Cambridge: Cambridge University Press, 1999); Lake and Questier, *The Anti-Christ's Lewd Hat;* Joad Raymond, *The Invention of the Newspaper: English Newsbooks, 1641–9* (Oxford: Oxford University Press, 1996); idem, ed., *News, Newspapers, and Society in Early Modern Britain* (Portland, Ore.: Frank Cass, 1999); idem, *Pamphlets and Pamphleteering in Early Modern Britain* (Cambridge: Cambridge University Press, 2003); and David Zaret, *Origins of Democratic Culture: Printing, Petitions and the Public Sphere in Early Modern England* (Princeton, N.J.: Princeton University Press, 2000).

58. Katharine Eisaman Maus, *Inwardness and Theater in the English Renaissance* (Chicago: University of Chicago Press, 1995), 107.

59. Joan B. Landes, "The Public and the Private Sphere: A Feminist Reconsideration," in *Feminists Read Habermas: Gendering the Subject of Discourse,* ed. Johanna Meehan, 91–116 (New York: Routledge, 1995), 98.

2. The Treason of Hayward's *Henry IV*

1. John Hayward, *The Lives of the III Normans, Kings of England* (London, 1613), 1.

2. *State Papers, Domestic, Elizabeth* 12/278, no. 78: the examination of Gelly Merick. See also *SPD* 12/278, no. 85: the examination of Augustine Phillips, which mentions the playing of "the deposing and killing of King Richard the second." The debates surrounding this performance are by now well known; the references in both depositions have led scholars to believe that the play is Shakespeare's, although no precise title or author is mentioned. Shakespeare's is the only extant play on the killing of Richard, and the company was his. Hayward's *Henry IV* depicts the deposition and killing of Richard II, but no performance of this prose history has ever been recorded.

3. Examination of John Wolfe, *SPD* 12 / 275, no. 28 (July 1600).

4. Scholars who discuss his Jacobean writings also ignore his earlier prose history. See Glenn Burgess, *Absolute Monarchy and the Stuart Constitution* (New Haven: Yale University Press, 1996), 7–10, 72–78; Richard Helgerson, *Forms of Nationhood* (Chicago: University of Chicago Press, 1992), 76; and Constance Jordan, *Shakespeare's Monarchies* (Ithaca, N.Y.: Cornell University Press, 1997), 118.

5. See Robert P. Adams, "Despotism, Censorship and Mirrors of Power Politics in Late Elizabethan Times," in *Sixteenth Century Journal* 10.3 (fall 1979): 5–16. See also Evelyn May Albright, "Shakespeare's *Richard II* and the Essex Conspiracy," *PMLA* 42 (1927): 686–720; and R. Heffner, "Shakespeare, Hayward and Essex," *PMLA* 45 (1930): 754–80.

6. On Hayward as a politic historian, see S. L. Goldberg, "Sir John Hayward, 'Politic' Historian," *Review of English Studies*, n.s., 6.23 (1955): 233–44; F. J. Levy, "Hayward, Daniel, and the Beginnings of Politic History in England," *Huntington Library Quarterly* 50.1 (winter 1987): 1–37. See also the more brief analyses of Hayward in A. R. Braunmiller, "King John and Historiography," *English Literary History* 55.2 (1988): 309–32; Mervyn James, *Society, Politics and Culture: Studies in Early Modern England* (Cambridge: Cambridge University Press, 1986), 417–32; Annabel Patterson, "'Roman Cast Similitude:' Ben Jonson and the English Use of Roman History," in *Rome in the Renaissance*, ed. Paul A. Ramsey (Binghamton, N.Y.: Medieval and Renaissance Texts and Studies, 1982), 381–94; Malcolm Smuts, "Court Centered Politics and the Uses of Roman Historians, c. 1590–1630," *Culture and Politics in Early Stuart England*, ed. Kevin Sharpe and Peter Lake (New York: Macmillan, 1994), 21–43; Blair Worden, "Ben Jonson among the Historians," *Culture and Politics in Early Stuart England*, 67–89.

7. See Arthur Kinney, "Essex and Shakespeare versus Hayward," *Shakespeare Quarterly* 44.4 (1993): 464–66, 466; Leeds Barroll, "A New History for Shakespeare and His Time," *Shakespeare Quarterly* 39.4 (1988): 441–64, 453; and John Guy, *Tudor England*, 447. See also James R. Siemon who analyzes Coke's response to Hayward in "'Word Itself against the Word:' Close Reading after Voloshinov," *Shakespeare Reread: The Texts in New Contexts*, ed. Russ McDonald (Ithaca, N.Y.: Cornell University Press, 1993), 226–58, 235–38.

8. Blair Worden, "Which Play Was Performed at the Globe Theatre on 7 February 1601?" *London Review of Books* 25.13 (July 10, 2003), 22–23. On the issue of which play may have appeared the night before the Essex uprising, see also Leeds Barroll, "A New History," and Charles R. Forker, ed., *King Richard II* by William Shakespeare, Arden Shakespeare (London: Thompson Learning, 2002), 1–55.

9. F. J. Levy, *Tudor Historical Thought* (San Marino, Calif.: Huntington Library, 1967), 259; and Cyndia Susan Clegg, *Press Censorship in Elizabethan England* (Cambridge: Cambridge University Press, 1997), 217. For an analysis of Hayward in terms of Elizabethan press licensing and censorship, see also Adams, "Despotism"; and Richard Dutton, "Buggeswords: Samuel Harsnett and the Licensing, Suppression and Afterlife of Dr. John Hayward's *The First Part of*

the Life and Reign of King Henry IV," *Criticism* 35.3 (summer 1993): 305–39. On the arrest of Hayward for his association with Essex, see also W. W. Greg, "Samuel Harsnett and Hayward's Henry IV," *The Library,* 5th series, 9.1 (March 1956): 1–10; J. J. Manning's excellent introduction to his edition of John Hayward's *The First and Second Parts of the Life and Raigne of King Henrie IIII* (London: Royal Historical Society, 1991), 1–57; Annabel Patterson, *Censorship and Interpretation* (Madison: University of Wisconsin Press, 1984), 54–55.

10. D. R. Woolf, *The Idea of History in Early Stuart England* (Toronto: University of Toronto Press, 1990), 107; and Clegg, *Press Censorship in Elizabethan England,* 202.

11. Notable exceptions include J. J. Manning, introduction to Hayward, *The Life and Raigne of King Henrie IIII;* and Lisa Richardson, "Sir John Hayward and Early Stuart Historiography" (Ph.D. diss., University of Cambridge, 1999).

12. I use the term "royalist," following Johann P. Sommerville, to designate a subject who supports royal authority against the crown's opponents. I do not use "royalist" as a synonym for royal absolutist. For a useful discussion of the term, see Sommerville, "Absolutism and Royalism," in *The Cambridge History of Political Thought, 1450–1700,* ed. J. H. Burns, with the assistance of Mark Goldie (Cambridge: Cambridge University Press, 1991), 348–49.

13. John Hayward, *Henry IV,* ed. Manning, 62. All further citations will be to this edition and will be given in the text. For clarity, I have chosen to use the spelling *Henry IV* for Hayward's title in the text, although the original, full title, which J. J. Manning uses for his edition of the work, is *The Life and Raigne of King Henrie IIII.*

14. Coke to Hayward, *SPD* 12/275, no. 25 (July 11, 1601).

15. *SPD* 12/278, no. 17. The practice of inventing speeches had been employed by humanist historiographers, including Holinshed and Hall, on whom Hayward drew. For Hayward's justification of the practice, see Margaret Dowling, "Sir John Hayward's Troubles over His Life of Henry IV," *The Library,* 4th ser., 9 (1931): 212–24; S. L. Goldberg, "Sir John Hayward, 'Politic' Historian."

16. *SPD* 12/274, no. 58. These notes are unsigned but recorded as Chief Justice Popham's in the *Calendar of State Papers,* Domestic series.

17. *SPD* 12/278, no. 17.

18. See Hayward, *The Life and Raigne of King Henrie IIII,* ed. J. J. Manning (London: Royal Historical Society, 1991). Manning argues that Hayward's title, *The First and Second Parts of the Raigne of King Henrie IIII,* perfectly represents the material contained in his history when we consider both the first and second parts of *Life and Raigne* together (17–42).

19. *SPD* 12/275, no. 28.

20. *SPD* 12/275, no. 31.

21. Ibid. On Harsnett, see Richard Dutton's "Buggeswords"; and W. W. Greg, "Samuel Harsnett."

22. *SPD* 12/275, no. 33. This document, from July 1600, lists evidence of treason against the earl the month after the York House proceedings, which supposedly cleared him from suspicion of wrongdoing in Ireland. I am grateful to Cyndia Susan Clegg for help in deciphering the chronology of events surrounding Hayward's interrogations and the York House trial. In untangling these mixed references to the "treasonable book" at which the earl was "so often present at the playing thereof," Evelyn May Albright argues that "Shakespeare depended on Hayward for matter of fact or for motivation" ("Shakespeare's *Richard II* and the Essex Conspiracy," *PMLA* 42 [1927]: 686–720, quote at 706); Leeds Barroll contends that the entangled reference from the abstract suggests that the Essex play was thought to be a "dramatization of Hayward's book" ("A New History for Shakespeare and His Time," *Shakespeare Quarterly* 39 [1988], 453); and Peter Ure claims that the "playing" refers to a "dramatic show based on Hayward, and full of pointed political analogies" (introduction to William Shakespeare, *King Richard II*, Arden Shakespeare, ed. Peter Ure [London and New York: Methuen, 1956; repr. 1984], lxi).

23. Stephanus Junius Brutus, the Celt (anonymous, attributed to Philippe Duplessis Mornay), *Vindiciae, contra tyrannos or, concerning the legitimate power of a prince over the people, and of the people over a prince* (1579), ed. and trans. George Garnett (Cambridge: Cambridge University Press, 1994), 75; John Bale, "Faithful Admonition of a Certain True Pastor" (1554); and John Ponet, "A Short Treatise of Politic Power" (1556). See also Robert M. Kingdon, "Calvinism and Resistance Theory, 1550–1580," in Burns, with Goldie, *The Cambridge History of Political Thought, 1450–1700*, 193–218.

24. R. Doleman [Robert Persons], *A Conference about the Next Succession to the Crown of England* (1594), part 1, 73. Published under the pseudonym R. Doleman, *A Conference* is conventionally attributed to Father Robert Persons although the *Dictionary of Anonymous and Pseudonymous Publications in the English Language*, ed. John Horden, Samuel Halkett, and John Laing, 3rd ed. (New York: Longman, 1980) places Cardinal William Allen as the primary author. I follow the conventional practice in listing Persons as the author.

25. On the issue of the coronation oath, see J. H. Salmon, "Catholic Resistance Theory, Ultramonanism, and the Royalist Response, 1580–1620," in Burns, with Goldie, *The Cambridge History of Political Thought, 1450–1700*, 219–53; Percy Ernst Schramm, *A History of the English Coronation*, trans. Leopold G. Wickham Legg (Oxford: Clarendon, 1937); Sommerville, "Absolutism and Royalism"; and idem, *Politics and Ideology in England*. On the coronation oath of Richard II as a contract binding the king to rule under the laws, see Gillespie, "Richard II," 115–38; and Saul, *Richard II*, 24–27.

26. N. D. (Father Robert Persons), "A Temperate Ward-word, to the turbulant and seditious Watch-Word of Sir Francis Hastings knight, who indevoreth to slaunder the whole Catholique cause" (Imprinted with licence, 1599), 34.

27. P. J. Holmes, *Resistance and Compromise: The Political Thought of the Elizabethan Catholics* (Cambridge: Cambridge University Press, 1982), 150. For Catholic resistance theory, see Doleman [Persons], *A Conference*; Cardinal William Allen, *A True, sincere and modest defence of English Catholics* (1584), ed. R. M. Kingdon (Ithaca, N.Y.: Cornell University Press, 1965), 171. See also

T. H. Clancy, *Papist Pamphleteers: The Allen-Persons Party and the Political Thought of the Counter-Reformation, 1572–1615* (Chicago: Loyola University Press, 1964); Peter Milward, *Religious Controversies of the Elizabethan Age: A Survey of Printed Sources* (Lincoln: University of Nebraska Press, 1977), 114–15; J. H. M. Salmon, "Catholic Resistance Theory, Ultramonanism and the Royalist Response, 1580–1620," in Burns, with Goldie, *The Cambridge History of Political Thought,* 219–53.

28. *SPD* 12/274, no. 58.

29. *SPD* 12/275, no. 25.

30. "Sir Francis Bacon's Theory of Civil History-Writing," *ELH* 8.3 (1941): 168. See also F. J. Levy, "Hayward, Daniel, and the Beginnings of Politic History in England," *Huntington Library Quarterly* (winter 1987): 1–37; and A. R. Braunmiller, "King John and Historiography."

31. Paul E. J. Hammer, *The Polarisation of Elizabethan Politics,* 129.

32. Cyndia Susan Clegg, "Censorship and the Problems with History in Shakespeare's England," in *A Companion to Shakespeare's Works,* Vol. 2, *The Histories,* ed. Richard Dutton and Jean E. Howard (London: Blackwell, 2003), 48–69. I am grateful to Professor Clegg for sharing a longer version of her essay with me as well.

33. July 1600, *SPD* 12/275, no. 28. On Wolfe's testimony, see Harry R. Hoppe, "John Wolfe, Printer and Publisher, 1579–1601," *The Library,* 4th ser., 14 (1933): 241–89.

34. Alberico Gentili, *De Jure Belli commentatio prima* (London: John Wolfe, 1588): "Armor et belli artib. praestantiss. Litteris et pacis itidem artib. ornatiss."

35. Roger Williams, *A Brief Discourse of War* (London: Thomas Orwin, 1590), A2v.

36. Williams writes, if only the army had "sailed streight to Lisborne, as the Earle of Essex did, neither Soldier nor Captain can deny, but the towne had been ours" (*A Brief Discourse of War,* 9).

37. George Chapman, *Seven Bookes of the Iliades of Homer* (London: John Windet, 1598), A3r, A4r-5v.

38. Katharine Eisamann Maus, in *The Norton Shakespeare,* ed. Stephen Greenblatt, Walter Cohen, Jean E. Howard, and Katharine Eisaman Maus (New York: W. W. Norton, 1997), 1445.

39. Stephen Orgel, "Making Greatness Familiar," in *The Power of Forms in the English Renaissance,* ed. Stephen Greenblatt (Norman, Okla.: Pilgrim Books, 1982), 44. My use of the term "chivalric" is meant to complement the historiographical emphasis on the earl's militarism. See Hammer, "Patronage at Court, Faction and the Earl of Essex," in *The Reign of Elizabeth,* ed. John Guy (Cambridge: Cambridge University Press, 1995), 65–86; and idem, *Polarisation.* See also MacCaffrey's *Elizabeth I: War and Politics* and James's "At the Crossroads of the Political Culture" in which the earl is presented as an aggressive advocate of a militaristic foreign policy. For a compelling reading of Essex's chivalric behavior as "a homosocial escape route from the power of his monarch," see Eric S. Mallin, *Inscribing the Time: Shakespeare and the*

End of Elizabethan England (Berkeley: University of California Press, 1995), 25–61.

40. Richard C. McCoy, "'A Dangerous Image': The Earl of Essex and Elizabethan Chivalry," *Journal of Medieval and Renaissance Studies* 13.2 (1983): 313–29, 313.

41. The scholarship on Tacitus in the Renaissance, with the exception of Richard Tuck's *Philosophy and Government* (Cambridge: Cambridge University Press, 1993), 104–9, frequently overlooks his influence in 1590s England and focuses instead on the English interest in Tacitus in the seventeenth century. As Kenneth C. Schellhase writes "James' predecessor, Queen Elizabeth, for one, remained ignorant of Tacitus until late in her reign, and through the entire sixteenth century only few historians, etiquette writers, and grammarians were much better informed" (*Tacitus in Renaissance Political Thought* [Chicago: Chicago University Press, 1976], 157). Ronald Mellor concurs: "It was only with the accession of the learned James VI of Scotland as James I of England that Tacitus was much read and cited in English intellectual circles" (*Tacitus* [New York and London: Routledge, 1993], 149). See also the collection of essays by Dorey Luce, T. J. Woodman, and A. J. Woodman, eds., *Tacitus and the Tacitean Tradition* (Princeton, N.J.: Princeton University Press, 1993), on the continental interest in Tacitus in the sixteenth century and the English interest in him in the seventeenth and eighteenth centuries.

42. Henry Savile, *Fower Bookes of the Histories of Cornelius Tacitus* (London, 1591). Savile's translation features a section of his own devising, *The Ende of Nero and the Beginning of Galba*. This ambitious supplement completes the lost portion of the *Annals* and the *Histories*, thereby linking the whole of Tacitus's canon into a continuous narrative extending from the end of Tacitus's *Annals*, on the death of Nero, to the beginning of his *Histories*, in which Galba has succeeded to the position of emperor. Ben Jonson praises this addition in "Epigram XCV: To Sir Henry Savile," in *The Complete Poems*, ed. George Parfitt (London: Penguin Books, 1975; repr. 1996), 66. On Savile at Eton, where he became provost in 1596, see H. C. Maxwell Lyte, *A History of Eton College, 1440–1875* (London, 1877), 188–91.

43. Tacitus, *Annales*, trans. Richard Grenewey (London, 1598).

44. "A.B. to the Reader," *The Ende of Nero and Beginning of Galba: Fower Bookes of the Histories of Cornelius Tacitus*, 2nd ed. (London: Arn. Hatfield, 1598). On Essex as author, see Ben Jonson who writes that "Essex wrote that epistle or preface before the translation of the last part of Tacitus, which is A.B." ("Conversations with Drummond," in *Ben Jonson: Works*, ed. C. H. Hereford, Percy Simpson, and Evelyn Simpson, 11 vols. [Oxford: Clarendon, 1925–52], vol. 1 [1950], 142). On Essex's identity as author, see also Alan T. Bradford, "Stuart Absolutism and the 'Utility' of Tacitus," *Huntington Library Quarterly* 46.2 (spring 1983): 132; and Lisa Jardine and Alan Stewart, *Hostage to Fortune: The Troubled Life of Francis Bacon, 1561–1626* (London: Victor Gollancz, 1998).

45. On the utility of politic history, see F. J. Levy, "Francis Bacon and the Style of Politics," in *Renaissance Historicism: Selections from English Literary Renais-*

sance, ed. Arthur F. Kinney and Dan S. Collins (Amherst: University of Massachusetts Press, 1987); Leonard F. Dean, "Sir Francis Bacon's Theory of Civil History Writing"; Malcolm Smuts, "Court Centered Politics and the Uses of Romans Historians, c. 1590–1630."

46. Savile also stresses, in the section he authored, how the Roman army had no limitations in terms of expense, a position that contrasts with the constricted position of England's forces under Elizabeth. In a 1595 letter to Lord Burgleigh, Savile again emphasizes the resources of the Roman Empire when compared to the Elizabethan regime. See Henry Savile, "Report of the Wages paid to the ancient Roman Soldiers, their Vittayling, and Apparrell. In a Letter to Lord Burleigh (1595)," British Library 184.a.14.

47. "Dedication," *The Ende of Nero*.

48. For Elizabeth's writings, see the recent editions of *Elizabeth I: Collected Works*, ed. Leah S. Marcus, Janel Mueller, and Mary Beth Rose (Chicago: University of Chicago Press, 2000); and *Elizabeth I: Autograph Compositions and Foreign Language Originals*, ed. Janel Mueller and Leah S. Marcus (Chicago: University of Chicago Press, 2003).

49. Paul E. J. Hammer, "The Uses of Scholarship: the Secretariat of Robert Devereux, Second Earl of Essex, c. 1585–1601," *English Historical Review* (February 1994): 26–51, 43.

50. BL Mss. RP 6340 (iv), 1r: "Letter from the Earl of Essex to the Earl of Rutland," undated. Although Hammer does not note this copy of Essex's letter, he does address questions about the authorship and circulation of Essex's letters to Rutland in "The Earl of Essex, Fulke Greville, and the Employment of Scholars," *Studies in Philology* 91 (1994): 167–80, 171–72.

51. BL Egerton Mss. 2262 (f4r): "Sir H. Savile Advice to the Earl of Rutland," attributed to the Earl of Essex, 1596.

52. Essex also stresses a loyalist context for reading Tacitus in his preface to Savile's translation. He notes how Savile's portraits of Nero and Galba should elicit gratitude from Elizabeth's subjects, since the portrait of Roman tyranny contrasts with "our owne happie government." By studying another state in Tacitus, namely, imperial despotism, readers can better understand the "peace," and "benefits" they enjoy in Elizabeth's England ("A.B. to the Reader," *The Ende of Nero*).

53. Lisa Richardson charts on a line-by-line basis the connections between Hayward and Tacitus in "Sir John Hayward and Early Stuart Historiography." See, especially, volume 2, which documents the sources for Hayward's texts.

54. Hayward's interest in Tacitus recalls that of Bodin. See Jean Bodin, *Methodus ad facilem historiarum cognitionem*, in *Oeuvres philosophiques de Jean Bodin*, ed. Pierre Mesnard (Paris, 1951) (*Method for the Easy Comprehension of History*, trans. Beatrice Reynolds [New York: Columbia University Press, 1945]). On Bodin's use of Tacitus, see Julian H. Franklin, "Sovereignty and the Mixed Constitution: Bodin and His Critics," in Burns, with Goldie, *The Cambridge History of Political Thought*, 298–328, 305.

55. Brian P. Levack, "Law and Ideology: The Civil Law and Theories of Absolutism in Elizabethan and Jacobean England," in *The Historical Renaissance*, ed. Heather Dubrow and Richard Strier, 220–41 (Chicago: University of Chicago Press, 1988), 226.

56. Jean Bodin, *On Sovereignty: Four Chapters from the Six Books of the Commonwealth,* ed. and trans. Julian H. Franklin (Cambridge: Cambridge University Press, 1992) 115. For the source of Carlisle's speech in Bodin, see Edwin B. Benjamin, "Sir John Hayward and Tacitus," *Review of English Studies,* n.s., 8 (1957): 275–76; and Braunmiller, "King John," 323.

57. Edward John Long Scott, ed., *Letter-booke of Gabriel Harvey* (London: Camden Society, 1884), 79, cited in Sommerville, *Politics and Ideology in England,* 39.

58. *SPD* 12/275, no. 25.

59. See Brian P. Levack's invaluable collective bibliography of civilians in *The Civil Lawyers in England: 1603–1641: A Political Study* (Oxford: Clarendon, 1973). On royalism and civil law, in addition to Levack see J. W. Allen, *History of Political Thought in the Sixteenth Century* (London: Methuen, 1928), 281.

60. Francis Bacon, *Sir Francis Bacon His Apologie in certaine imputations concerning the late Earle of Essex* (1604), in *The Works of Francis Bacon,* ed. James Spedding, Robert Leslie Ellis, and Douglas Denon Heath, vol. 10 (London: Longmans, Green, Reader and Dyer, 1868), 150.

61. On Bacon's familiarity with the civil law, see Paul H. Kocher, "Francis Bacon and the Science of Jurisprudence," *Journal of the History of Ideas* 18 (1957): 3–26; reprinted in *Essential Articles for the Study of Francis Bacon,* ed. Brian Vickers (London: Sidgwick and Jackson, 1968), 167–94.

62. Justinian, *Institutes,* trans. and intro. Peter Kirks and Grant McLeod; Latin text edited by Paul Krueger (Ithaca, N.Y.: Cornell University Press, 1987), 1.2.6, 36.

63. Levack, *Civil Lawyers,* 89.

64. *An Answer to a Conference concerning Succession* (London, 1603). For Hayward's royalist colleagues, see John Cowell, *The Interpreter: or book containing the signification of words* (Cambridge, 1607); and Matthew Sutcliffe, Dean of Exeter, "An Answer to a certain calumnious letter published by John Throckmorton" (London, 1594); "A Brief Replie to a certain odious and slanderous libel" (1600); and "A New Challenge made to N.D." (1600). Sutcliffe became, under James, the founder of the King's College at Chelsea, established with the mission of studying and writing "polemical divinity." John Hayward was one of the two historians appointed to Chelsea, although the college lacked adequate funding and closed under Charles I. See Levack, *Civil Lawyers,* 4; and Thomas Faulkner, *An Historical and Topographical Description of Chelsea and Its Environs,* vol. 2 of 2 vols. (Chelsea, 1829), 218–34.

65. J. Bruce, ed., introduction to *Annals of the first four years of the reign of Queen Elizabeth* (London: Publications of the Camden Society VII, 1840), xv.

66. *An Answer,* Dedication: A2r.

67. Ibid., K1v.

68. Ibid.

69. Manning, *Life and Raigne,* 4. Printed for the first time in 1991, the newly titled *The Second Part of the Life and Raigne of King Henrie IIII* offers a critique of the king in terms that echo those of *An Answer.*

70. *An Answer*, L1v.

71. Clegg, *Press Censorship in Elizabethan England*, 202–10.

72. Levack, *Civil Lawyers*, 1.

73. "Apology concerning the Earl of Essex," 150. Another version of this story lies in Bacon's "Apophthegms." Here he writes, "The book of the deposing of Richard the second and the coming in of Henry the fourth, supposed to be written by Dr. Hayward, who was committed to the Tower for it, had much incensed queen Elizabeth. And she asked Mr. Bacon, being then of her learned counsel; Whether there were no treason contained in it? Mr. Bacon intending to do him a pleasure, and to take off the Queen's bitterness with a jest, answered; No, madam, for treason I cannot deliver opinion that there is any, but very much felony. The Queen, apprehending it gladly, asked: How and wherein? Mr Bacon answered; Because he had stolen many of his sentences and conceits out of Cornelius Tacitus" (Francis Bacon, *Works* [London, 1859], 7:133).

74. Bacon's initially successful defense of Hayward is complicated in two ways, however. First, Hayward was interrogated for a second time, in January 1601, suggesting that Bacon did not fully persuade Elizabeth. Second, and more complex, Bacon himself used Hayward's text as evidentiary fodder against Essex in the York House proceedings of June 1600. He did so at the Queen's request, as I discuss in "Trying Treason," doctoral dissertation (University of Wisconsin, Madison, 2000).

75. *SPD* 12/275, no. 33.

76. William Camden, *The History of the Most Renowned and Victorious Princess Elizabeth, Late Queen of England*, 4th ed. (London, 1688), 610. I am grateful to Paul Hammer for directing me to this reference.

77. BL Add. 40838: "Copy of a letter written by the Earl of Essex to the Earl of Southampton, March 1600," 9r.

78. MacCaffrey, *Elizabeth I: War and Politics*, 530–31.

79. John Nichols, *The Progresses and Public Processions of Queen Elizabeth*, vol. 3 (London: John Nichols and Son, 1783; repr. 1823), 552. Elizabeth spoke this line several months after Essex's death, in a conversation with her adviser, William Lambarde, on August 4, 1601, a fact that severely undermines direct association of the quote with the performance of *Richard II* the year before. For excellent discussions of circumstances surrounding the quote, see Barroll, "A New History," 441–64, 447; and Cyndia Susan Clegg, "Archival Poetics and the Politics of Literature: Essex and Hayward Revisited," *Studies in the Literary Imagination* 32, no.1 (spring 1999): 115–32, 119.

3. Shakespeare's Anatomy of Resistance in *Richard II*

1. *SPD* 12/278, no. 78.

2. For accounts of the Essex Rebellion, see Guy, *Tudor England*, 449–52; Hammer, "Patronage at Court," 65–86; and idem, *Polarisation*, which does not address the rebellion but is invaluable in understanding the Essex faction; Mervyn James, *Society, Politics and Culture: Studies in Early Modern England*

(Cambridge: Cambridge University Press, 1986); MacCaffrey, *Elizabeth I*; and idem, *Elizabeth I: War and Politics.*

3. Barroll, "A New History"; and Margaret Shewring, *King Richard II* (Manchester, U.K.: Manchester University Press, 1996), 27.

4. On the dating of Shakespeare's play, Forker suggests that the first performance probably occurred in the autumn of 1595 (introduction to *King Richard II*, 111–20). The first quarto of the play appeared in 1597, after its initial run by the Chamberlain's Men.

5. Donna B. Hamilton, "The State of the Law in *Richard II*," *Shakespeare Quarterly* 34 (1983): 5–17. Hamilton offers an extended discussion of Fortescue and Bracton in relation to law-centered kingship in the play; on political theory in relation to Shakespeare more generally, I also am informed by Constance Jordan, *Shakespeare's Monarchies.*

6. The deposition scene is absent from the three quarto editions of Shakespeare's *Tragedy of Richard II* printed during Elizabeth's lifetime, but debate continues as to whether this omission results from some form of censorship or simply indicates the scene's later composition. The fullest examination remains Cyndia Susan Clegg, "*Richard II* and Elizabethan Press Censorship," *Shakespeare Quarterly* 48 (1997): 432–48; and her introduction to *A Peaceable and prosperous regiment of blessed Queen Elizabeth: A facsimile from Holinshed's Chronicles (1587)*, ed. Cyndia Susan Clegg (San Marino, Calif.: Huntington Library Press, 2005), 1–18, which establishes that the deposition scene was not, in fact, censored. For arguments supporting the censorship or suppression of the scene, see J. J. Manning, introduction to Hayward, *The Life and Raigne of King Henrie IIII*, 21; as well as Janet Clare, "The Censorship of the Deposition Scene in *Richard II*," *Review of English Studies*, n.s., 41 (February 1990): 89–94; C. A. Greer, "The Deposition Scene of *Richard II*," *Notes and Queries* (November 8, 1952): 492–93; idem, "More about the Deposition Scene of *Richard II*," *Notes and Queries* (February, 1953): 49–50; Ure, introduction to *King Richard II*, xiii–lxxxiii, quote at xiv; and Forker, introduction to *King Richard II*, 111–22. For the argument that the scene may have been a later addition to the play, and thus was not censored, see Barroll, "A New History," 453; David Bergeron, "The Deposition Scene in *Richard II*," *Renaissance Papers* (1974): 31–37; and Worden, "Which Play?"

7. "Omagium et sacramentum ligiantiae potius sunt et vehementius ligant ratione coronae quam personae regis," in *English Constitutional Documents: 1307–1485*, ed. Eleanor C. Lodge and Gladys A. Thornton (Cambridge: Cambridge University Press, 1935), 11.

8. Bertie Wilkinson, *Constitutional History of Medieval England, 1216–1399*, 3 vols. (London and New York: Longmans, Green, 1952), 3:80.

9. Richard Firth Green, *A Crisis of Truth: Literature and Law in Richardian England* (Philadelphia: University of Pennsylvania Press, 2002).

10. Bertie Wilkinson, *Constitutional History of Medieval England, 1216–1399*, 2:130.

11. John Bellamy, *The Law of Treason in England in the Later Middle Ages* (Cambridge: Cambridge University Press, 1970), 137.

12. J. Neville Figgis, *The Theory of the Divine Right of Kings* (Cambridge: Cambridge University Press, 1896), 81. On Richard's reign, see Nigel Saul, *Richard II* (New Haven: Yale University Press, 1997), as well as *The Age of Richard II*, ed. James L. Gillespie, 51–69 (New York: St. Martin's, 1997). For an argument against the king's alleged tyranny, see Caroline Barron, *Politics and Crisis in Fourteenth-Century England* (London: Alan Sutton, 1990), 132–49.

13. Figgs, *Divine Right*, 81. On the issue of the ancient constitution, see Glenn Burgess, *The Politics of the Ancient Constitution* (University Park: Pennsylvania State University Press, 1992), 79–106; and idem, *Absolute Monarchy and the Stuart Constitution* (New Haven: Yale University Press, 1996), 42.

14. *The Mirror for Magistrates*, ed. Lily B. Campbell (Cambridge: Cambridge University Press, 1938), 111–18, ll. 4, 32; Raphael Holinshed, *Chronicles on England, Scotland and Ireland (1587)*, vol. 3 (London, 1587), 496.

15. *Mirror for Magistrates*, l. 33; Holinshed, *Chronicles*, 496.

16. Dermot Cavanagh, "The Language of Treason in *Richard II*," *Shakespeare Studies* 27, ed. Leeds Barroll (London: Associated University Presses, 1999), 137; and idem, *Language and Politics in the Sixteenth-Century History Play* (Basingstoke, U.K.: Palgrave Macmillan, 2003), 106.

17. Annabel Patterson, *Reading Holinshed's Chronicles* (Chicago: University of Chicago Press, 1994), 159.

18. Phyllis Rackin, *Stages of History: Shakespeare's English Chronicles* (Ithaca, N.Y.: Cornell University Press, 1990), 118.

19. Here I concur with my generous former teacher, the late Ronald R. MacDonald, who notes "in banishing Mowbray, Richard attempts to take refuge in the notion of the king's magical and ritual power" ("Uneasy Lies: Language and History in Shakespeare's Lancastrian Tetralogy," *Shakespeare Quarterly* 35 [1984]: 22–39, 25).

20. Cavanagh, *Language and Politics*, 104.

21. Bellamy examines in detail the king's expanding prerogative and abuse of treason law in this incident in his *Law of Treason*, 109–15.

22. The writings of John Fortescue reinforce the ways in which the Justinianic maxim ("the prince's pleasure has the force of law") was uncustomary in medieval England.

23. Charles R. Forker, "'Edward II' and Its Shakespearean Relatives," in *Shakespeare's English Histories: A Quest for Form and Genre*, ed. John W. Velz (Binghamton, N.Y.: Medieval and Renaissance Texts and Studies, 1996), 83.

24. Naomi Conn Liebler, "The Mockery King of Snow: *Richard II* and the Sacrifice of Ritual," in *True Rites and Maimed Rites: Ritual and Anti-Ritual in Shakespeare and His Age*, ed. Linda Woodbridge and Edward Berry (Urbana: University of Illinois Press, 1992), 220–39, 221.

25. Harry Berger Jr. insightfully notes, given that in the first two acts Richard "cheerfully demonstrates his lawlessness, his appeals to the rhetoric of divinely ordained kingship in acts 3 and 4 can hardly be accepted at face value" (*Imaginary Audition: Shakespeare on Stage and Page* [Berkeley: University of California, 1989], 51). See also his "*Richard II* 3.2: An Exercise in Imaginary Audition," *ELH* 55.4 (winter 1988): 755–96. See also S. K. Heninger Jr., "The

Sun-King Analogy in *Richard II*," *Shakespeare Quarterly* 11 (1960): 324. For an opposite reading, stressing the play's vindication of royal absolutism, see Jack Gohn Benoit, "*Richard II*: Shakespeare's Legal Brief on the Royal Prerogative and the Succession to the Throne," *Georgetown Law Journal* 70 (1982): 943–73.

26. Christopher Highley, *Shakespeare, Spenser, and the Crisis in Ireland* (Cambridge: Cambridge University Press, 1997), 66.

27. In thinking about Gaunt's death, I am influenced by Harry Berger Jr., "*Ars Moriendi* in Progress, or John of Gaunt and the Practice of Strategic Dying," *Yale Journal of Criticism: Interpretation in the Humanities* 1.1 (1987): 39–67.

28. For the association of "prick" with issues of sexuality and reproduction, see the *Oxford English Dictionary* definition of "prick" as a verb with "various pregnant uses," as in the case of Stephen Gosson's *Schoole of Abuse*, where he refers to plays which "effeminate the mind, as pricking unto vice." See also the entry noting the "course use" of "prick" familiar from slang, dating from a 1592 citation in R.D.'s *Hypnerotomachio*.

29. Norbrook, "'A Liberal Tongue,'" 37–51, 43–44.

30. Peter Ure, *King Richard II*, 62, note to 2.1.202–4. While phrases such as "letters patents" and "sue his livery" may be unfamiliar to modern ears, an early modern audience would be accustomed to these legal terms. Legal language was not so specialized a professional discourse as to be reserved only for lawyers. Not only would Shakespeare's audience members have represented themselves in court but the gentry also protected the legal interests of their estates themselves; given the prevalence of property disputes, a sixteenth-century audience would likely be familiar with this terminology, as Heather Dubrow suggests in *Shakespeare and Domestic Loss* (Cambridge: Cambridge University Press, 1999). Even among the non-landholding audience, legal transactions that involved inheritance were among the most common, since those with any worldly goods would be interested in protecting their estate as it transferred from one generation to the next.

31. William O. Scott, "Landholding, Leasing, and Inheritance in *Richard II*," *SEL: Studies in English Literature 1500–1900* 42.2 (2002): 275–92.

32. Treason was distinguished from other crimes by the severity of its punishment, which included disinheritance. In several cases in the fourteenth century where a subject had not been convicted in court as a traitor, the king could, for example, seize the estates of subjects as a "forfeiture of war," thereby avoiding the problems of a trial. Alternately, in the case of the traitor who had been convicted in court and yet fled abroad to escape execution, the crown could nevertheless capture his remaining property. In both these cases, the crown would seize the subject's estate in keeping with the punishment for treason, regardless of whether the crown had secured a conviction in court. See Bellamy, *Law of Treason*, 80.

33. Northumberland has already begun plotting Bolingbroke's return before the seizing of Gaunt's property. Yet the shape of act 2, scene 1, highlights the causal relation between Richard's abuse of the law and the increasing ranks of traitors.

34. On the issue of reproduction and succession, see Graham Holderness, "'A Woman's War': A Feminist Reading of *Richard II*," *Shakespeare Left and Right*, ed. Ivo Kamps (New York: Routledge, 1991), 167–83, who analyzes the play's minor female roles in terms of the exclusion of women from the patriarchal, chivalric society of Richard's England; Coppélia Kahn, "'The Shadow of the Male': Masculine Identity in the History Plays," *Man's Estate: Masculine Identity in Shakespeare* (Berkeley: University of California Press, 1981), 47–81, who reads Richard as the play's maternal figure while Bolingbroke represents the masculine principle of succession (67); and Meredith Skura, "Marlowe's *Edward II*: Penetrating Language in Shakespeare's *Richard II*," *Shakespeare Survey* 50, ed. Stanley Wells (Cambridge: Cambridge University Press, 1997): 41–56, 49. I am grateful to David Ruiter for directing me to Skura's persuasive article.

35. Sir John Fortescue, *On the Laws and Governance of England*, ed. Shelley Lockwood, *Cambridge Texts in the History of Political Thought* (Cambridge: Cambridge University Press, 1997), 53. The contemporary translation by Robert Mulcaster reads, "That king which is not hable to performe [his duty of protecting his people], must of necessitie be judged impotent and weake. But if he be so overcome of hys own affections and lusts or so oppressed wyth povertie, that hee can not withhold his hands from the pilling of his subjects whereby himself improverisheth them and suffreth them not to live and to be sustained upon their own substaunces, how muche more weake or feble is he in this respect to be judged then if he were not hable to defende them agaynst the injuries of others" (Fortescue, *A Learned Commendation*, fol. 87, sig. Lviiir–v).

36. I am grateful to John King for bringing these character dynamics to my attention (Huntington Renaissance Seminar).

37. Henry of Bracton, *On the Laws and Customs of England* [*De legibus et consuetudinibus angliae*], ed. George E. Woodbine, trans. Samuel E. Thorne (Cambridge, Mass.: Belknap Press of Harvard University Press, 1968), 33. Bracton's theory of sovereignty would be familiar to Shakespeare's audience, as discussed in chapter 1 of this volume, and in Hamilton, "The State of the Law in *Richard II*." Michael Mendle notes that "Bracton's judgement that the king had no peer among men but was 'under the law, because the law makes the king,' became a seventeenth-century commonplace" ("Parliamentary Sovereignty: A Very English Absolutism," in *Political Discourse in Early Modern Britain*, ed. Nicholas Phillipson and Quentin Skinner, 97–119 [Cambridge: Cambridge University Press, 1993], 102 n. 12).

38. On the "hollow womb," see Clayton G. MacKenzie, "Paradise and Paradise Lost in *Richard II*," *Shakespeare Quarterly* 37 (1986): 318–39; and Robert N. Watson, "Kinship and Kingship: Ambition in Shakespeare's Major Tragedies," *Shakespeare and the Hazards of Ambition* (Cambridge, Mass.: Harvard University Press, 1984), 14–82, who persuasively analyzes Richard's meditations in Pomfret as an unsuccessful attempt to breed a new identity, while generating only stillbirths.

39. Lars Engle, *Shakespearean Pragmatism: Market of His Time* (Chicago: University of Chicago Press, 1993), 127. See also Nina Levine, "Extending Credit in the Henry IV Plays," *Shakespeare Quarterly* 51.4 (winter 2000): 403–31, 420.

40. H. R. Coursen, *The Leasing Out of England: Shakespeare's Second Henriad* (Washington, D.C.: University Press of America, 1982), 109.

41. Richard's exceptionalism recalls the analysis of Giorgio Agamben, *Homo Sacer: Sovereign Power and Bare Life,* trans. Daniel Heller-Roazen (Stanford: Stanford University Press, 1998). The dialectic relationship between the sovereign and bare life, both based in exile—or exceptionalism—marks Richard's wild swings between his role as god's minister and as an impoverished palmer as well.

42. Christopher Pye, *The Regal Phantasm: Shakespeare and the Politics of Spectacle* (New York: Routledge, 1990), 85.

4. Scaffolds of Treason in Shakespeare's *Macbeth*

1. This reading appears, for example, in texts loosely linked to Essex such as Samuel Daniel's *Philotas* and Ben Jonson's *Sejanus*—although I follow Philip Ayres in reading the latter text as a commentary more on the treason of Raleigh than Essex (introduction to *Sejanus: His Fall* [Manchester, U.K.: Manchester University Press, 1990], 1–46).

2. G. M. [Gervaise Markham], "Honour in His Perfection" (London, 1624), 26.

3. BL Mss. Add. 4155, "State Papers: An Account of Essex's Execution." See also, among numerous manuscript copies of this speech, Huntington Mss. 46714, Hunt. Mss. 41952, BL Mss. 2194, and BL Harleian Mss. 5202.

4. Huntington Mss. 46714, 24v: "The Arraignment and Execution of the Earl of Essex." See also Hunt. Mss. 41952 and BL Mss. Add. 4155 for similar accounts.

5. PRO, *Privy Council Registers*, vol. 32 (1600–1601), 161.

6. Ibid., 218.

7. Ibid., 258–59.

8. Ibid., vol. 31 (1600–1601), 194. By the end of Elizabeth's reign, Catesby's estate had been nearly depleted because of recusancy fines leveled against his father, who was imprisoned frequently. Forced to sell his estate of Castleton to pay his fine for the Essex Rebellion, he then lived with his widowed mother at Ashby St. Legers.

9. Barlow, "A True and Perfect Relation," E1r. According to Mark Nicholls, Catesby and Tresham may have sent Anthony Dutton rather than Wright into Spain, but they offered the latter's name to the crown, because, while Dutton was still alive, Wright had died in the skirmish after the Gunpowder Plot (*Investigating the Gunpowder Plot,* 57).

10. H.M.C. Salisbury Mss., xvii.512 (26 November 1605), in Albert Joseph Loomie, *Guy Fawkes in Spain: The "Spanish Treason" in Spanish Documents* (London: Bulletin of the Institute of Historical Research, Special Supplement No. 9, November 1971). Speed's account varies slightly. He writes how "Henry Garnet the Superiour of the Jesuites, Catesby and others sent Thomas Winter into Spaine to negotiate with King Philip in the name of the English

Catholikes . . . to grant some pensions unto sundry persons devoted to his service in England" and to "give advertisement of the discontents that the young Gentlemen and Souldiers had conceived upon the death of Essex, whereby a most fit occasion was then offered to forward the common cause" (John Speed, *The Historie of Great Britaine under the conquests of ye Romans, Saxons, Danes and Normans*, vol. 2 [London, 1611], 889).

11. BL Add. 40838, 11v: "The Copy of a letter to Mr. Antony Bacon concerning reports of the Earl of Essex's confession," and Hunt. Mss. 46714, 6v.

12. Hunt. Mss. 46714, 6r. I am grateful to Paul Hammer for sharing his insights on Essex's relationship to James. According to Jardine, this black bag containing papers about the Gunpowder Plot was alleged to be among Coke's papers when he was fired in 1618 (*Narrative*, x).

13. Henry Garnet to Robert Persons, in Philip Caraman, *Henry Garnet 1555–1606 and the Gunpowder Plot* (London: Longmans, 1964), 304.

14. *Father John Gerard's Narrative of the Gunpowder Plot*, ed. John Morris (London: Longmans and Green, 1871), 20–25.

15. Derek Hirst, *Authority and Conflict: England, 1603–1658* (Cambridge, Mass.: Harvard University Press, 1986), 98.

16. 25 June 1604: execution of statute laws against recusants in *The Journals of the House of Commons*, vol. 1 (November 8, 1547–March 2, 1628) (reprinted by order of House of Commons, 1803), 245. James expanded this legislation in the aftermath of the Main and Bye plots engineered by Raleigh and Cobham. Hirst writes of this period, "the spring of 1605 brought over 5,000 convictions and fines" (*Authority and Conflict*, 106).

17. *A Jacobean Journal*, ed. G. B. Harrison (London: George Routledge, 1941), May 4, 1603 [perhaps February 10, 1605], 186.

18. *Les Reportes del Cases in Camera Stellata, 1593–1609*, from the original ms. of John Hawarde, ed. William Paley Baildon (privately printed, 1894), 188.

19. Ibid.

20. Huntington Mss. EL 1221.

21. The connection between James's treatment of Catholic recusants and the Gunpowder Plot remains the subject of historiographical debate. On the one hand, many historians, including Nicholls (*Investigating the Gunpowder Plot*), stress how James strove to protect his Catholic subjects against more reactionary members of Parliament; the plot stemmed not from James's domestic policies but instead from the radical plotting of Jesuits. On the other hand, the conjunction of two Jacobean policies, namely, recusancy legislation and the peace with Spain, proved prompting enough for alienated English Catholics to contemplate treason once again.

22. Scholars continue to debate the occasion of the first performance. See Gary Wills, *Witches and Jesuits: Shakespeare's Macbeth* (Oxford: Oxford University Press, 1995), for the most comprehensive recent discussion of the issue. Other helpful assessments include Kenneth Muir, introduction to *Macbeth*, The Arden Shakespeare, ed. idem (London: Methuen, 1964; repr. 1984), xv–xxv; and Henry Paul, *The Royal Play of Macbeth* (New York: Macmillan, 1950), 15–24.

23. As a central figure in the English Catholic community and a proponent of equivocation, Garnet was one of the crown's most important prisoners, even though he played only a minor role in the Gunpowder Plot itself. See Henry Garnet, "A Treatise of Equivocation," also published as "A Treatise against Lying and Fraudulent Dissimulation," Bodleian, Laud MS., misc. 655; also edited by David Jardine (London: Longman, Brown, Green, and Longmans, 1851). Scholars cite the equivocation jokes within the Porter scene as topical references to Father Garnet's infamous equivocation when questioned about his role in the Gunpowder Plot. See Caraman, *Henry Garnet*; Alan Haynes, *Gunpowder Plot: Faith in Rebellion* (Dover: Alan Sutton, 1994), 133; Frank L. Huntley, "*Macbeth* and the Background of Jesuitical Equivocation," *PMLA* 79 (1964): 390–400; Muir, "Introduction to *Macbeth*," xx–xxii; and Wills, *Witches and Jesuits*.

24. Leonard Tennenhouse, *Power on Display: The Politics of Shakespeare's Genres* (London: Methuen, 1986), 130. See also Antonia Fraser, who writes that the play "is a work redolent with outrage at the monstrous upsetting of the natural order, which is brought about when subjects kill their lawful sovereign" (*Faith in Treason: The Story of the Gunpowder Plot* [New York: Doubleday, 1996], 280); and Alvin Kernan's forceful argument that Shakespeare transformed Holinshed "to fit his patron's political myth," creating a story that conveys "a sacred event in the history of divine right legitimacy" (*Shakespeare, the King's Playwright: Theater in the Stuart Court, 1603–1613* [New Haven: Yale University Press, 1995], 78).

25. Marjorie Garber, "*Macbeth*: The Male Medusa," *Shakespeare's Ghost Writers: Literature as Uncanny Causality* (New York: Methuen, 1987), 88–123; 114; repr. in Susanne L. Wofford, ed., *Shakespeare's Late Tragedies: A Collection of Critical Essays* (Upper Saddle River, N.J.: Prentice Hall, 1996), 74–103; 98.

26. William Shakespeare, *Macbeth*, The Arden Shakespeare, ed. Kenneth Muir (London: Metheun, 1964; repr. 1984). All citations from the play are to this edition.

27. The speeches appear individually in contemporary manuscripts and printed matter, and are also catalogued in *Cobbett's Complete Collection of State Trials*, vols. 1 and 2. For other editions containing primary materials on execution, see C. G. L. Du Cann, *English Treason Trials* (London: Frederick Muller, 1964); Joseph H. Marshburn and Alan R. Velie, *Blood and Knavery: A Collection of English Renaissance Pamphlets and Ballads of Crime and Sin* (Rutherford, N.J.: Fairleigh Dickinson University Press, 1973); Donald Thomas, ed., *State Trials: Treason and Libel*, vol. 1 (London: Routledge and Kegan Paul, 1972).

28. Foucault, *Discipline and Punish*; J. A. Sharpe, "Last Dying Speeches: Religion, Ideology, and Public Execution in Seventeenth-Century England," *Past and Present* 107 (1985): 144–67; Lacey Baldwin Smith, "English Treason Trials and Confessions in the Sixteenth Century," *Journal of the History of Ideas* 15 (1954): 471–98; and Smith, *Treason in Tudor England*. The analyses of Sharpe and Smith, while not directly engaging with the work of Michel Foucault, nevertheless corroborate his argument that execution practices staged an invincible display of state force. Foucault, however, goes on to analyze how the tension of the ceremony occasionally worked against the sovereign; particularly toward the end of the sixteenth century, the audience increasingly rioted at the scaffold spectacle (*Discipline and Punish*, 59–69). On continental execution, see Lisa Silverman, *Tortured Subjects: Pain, Truth and the Body in Early Modern France* (Chicago: University of Chicago Press, 2001), esp. chap. 6; and Pieter Spierenburg, *The Spectacle of Suffering* (Cambridge: Cambridge University Press, 1984). For a discussion of conversion right before scaffold speeches, see M. C. Questier, *Conversion, Politics and Religion in England, 1580–1625* (Cambridge: Cambridge University Press, 1996).

29. Philip Sidney, "The Defence of Poesy," in *Sir Philip Sidney: Selected Prose and Poetry*, ed. Robert Kimbrough, 102–58 (Madison: University of Wisconsin Press, 1983), 129. George Puttenham shares Sidney's view of tragedy as educative, writing how "the bad and illawdable parts of all estates and degrees were taxed by the Poets in one sort or an other and those of great Princes by Tradedie in especial, and not till after their deaths . . . to th'intent that such exemplifying (as it were) of their blames and adversities, being now dead, might worke for a secret reprehension to others that were alive, living in the same or like abuses (*The Arte of English Poesie* (London, 1589), 36; D2v.

30. See also Janet Adelman, who offers a powerful reading of Duncan's corpse as a Medusa figure in "Escaping the Matrix: The Construction of Masculinity in *Macbeth* and *Coriolanus*," in idem, *Suffocating Mothers: Fantasies of Maternal Origin in Shakespeare's Plays, Hamlet to The Tempest* (New York: Routledge, 1992), 133.

31. Wilbur Sanders, *The Dramatist and the Received Idea* (Cambridge: Cambridge University Press, 1968), 258; David Scott Kastan, *Shakespeare and the Shapes of Time* (London: Macmillan, 1982), 79–101, quote at 95.

32. Adelman, *Suffocating Mothers*, 146; Peter Stallybrass, "*Macbeth* and Witchcraft," in *Focus on Macbeth*, John Russell Brown (London: Routledge, 1982), 189–209, esp. 200–202. For further analysis of the play's gendered outcome, see Frances E. Dolan, *Dangerous Familiars: Representations of Domestic Crime in England, 1550–1700* (Ithaca, N.Y.: Cornell University Press, 1994), 224–230, esp. 229; Carol Thomas Neely, "'Documents in Madness': Reading Madness and Gender in Shakespeare's Tragedies and Early Modern Culture," in *Shakespearean Tragedy and Gender*, ed. Shirley Nelson Garner and Madelon Sprengnether (Bloomington: Indiana University Press, 1996).

33. Alan Sinfield, *Faultlines: Cultural Materialism and the Politics of Dissident Reading* (Berkeley: University of California Press, 1992), 103.

34. "A True Relation of all such things as passed at the Execution of M. Garnet, the third of May, anno 1606," in "A True and Perfect Relation of the Whole Proceedings against the late most barbarous traitors" (London: Robert Barker, 1606), sig. Fff2r-v.

35. Peter Lake, with Michael Questier, *The Anti-Christ's Lewd Hat* (New Haven: Yale University Press, 2003), 230.

36. See, for example, the speeches of prisoners associated with the Northern Rebellion, the Babington Plot and the Essex Rebellion, including those of Christopher Norton, Thomas Salisbury, and Robert Devereux, the second earl of Essex, in "The several Confessions of Thomas Norton and Christopher Norton, two of the Northern Rebels, who suffered at Tyburn" (London: William How for Richard Jones); and *Cobbett's Complete Collection of State Trials*, 1:1085, 1158–59, 1412–14; "Account of the Execution of the Earl of Essex," *State Papers Domestic, Elizabeth I:* 12 / 278, no. 12 (February 25, 1601). See also the account of his execution in SPD 12 / 278, nos. 113, 114.

37. Dolan, "'Gentlemen, I Have One Thing More to Say': Women on Scaffolds in England, 1563–1680," *Modern Philology* 92.2 (November 1994): 157–79, quote at 157; and Thomas W. Laqueur, "Crowns, Carnival and the State in English Executions, 1604–1868," *The First Modern Society: Essays in English History in Honour of Lawrence Stone*, ed. A. L. Beier, David Cannadine, and James M. Rosenheim (Cambridge: Cambridge University Press, 1989), 305–55. Dolan's argument bears out in the case of Robert Keyes, one of the Gunpowder conspirators who was alternately reported to have died devoutly or, according to another source, to have died "like a desperate villain, using little speech, with small or no shew of repentance" (*Harleian Miscellany*, ed. William Oldys, vol. 3 [London, 1808–13], 134).

38. "A True Declaration of the Happy Conversion, Contrition and Christian Preparation of Francis Robinson, Gentleman, who for Counterfeiting the Great Seale of England was Drawen, Hang'd and Quartered at Charing Crosse, on Friday Last, being the Thirteenth Day of November, 1618" (London, 1618), sig. A4r. For a mention of Francis Robinson, see Sharpe, "Last Dying Speeches," 150.

39. Edward III had defined treason and its punishment in 1352 in a statute that served as the basis for early modern statutes on treason, as discussed in chapter 1. See 25 Edw. III st.5 c.2, cited in *Statutes of the Realm*, vol. 1 (Record Commission, 1810–28), 319–20. On treason law, see Bellamy, *The Tudor Law of Treason*.

40. "The Araignment and Execution of the late Traytors" (London: Jeffrey Chorlton, 1606), sig. C3r.

41. Ibid., ""sig. B4r.

42. The form of his spiritual contrition, however, could break convention and provoke the audience, as in the case of Catholic prisoners who uttered prayers while making the sign of the cross. The Catholic prayers of Gunpowder plotter Sir Everard Digby were condemned by the pamphleteer who recorded the incident as "vain and superstitious crossing." See James F. Larkin and Paul L. Hughes, eds., "The Arraignment and Execution of the Late Traitors," in *Stuart Royal Proclamations*, vol. 1 of 2 vols. (Oxford: Clarendon, 1973–80), 128.

43. Thomas Beacon, *The Sicke Mans Salve* (London: John Daye, 1582), 229. On the *ars moriendi*, see Nancy Lee Beaty, *The Craft of Dying: A Study in the Literary Tradition of the Ars Moriendi in England* (New Haven: Yale University Press, 1970); Sister Mary Catharine O'Conner, *The Art of Dying Well: The Development of the Ars Moriendi* (New York: Columbia University Press, 1942). For readings of the *ars moriendi* in Shakespeare, see Harry Berger Jr., "Ars Moriendi in Progress, or John of Gaunt and the Practice of Strategic Dying," *Yale Journal of Criticism: Interpretation in the Humanities* 1.1 (1987): 39–67; Duncan Harris, "Tombs, Guidebooks and Shakespearean Drama: Death in the Renaissance," *Mosaic* 15.1 (1982): 23.

44. "A True and Perfect Relation of the Whole Proceedings against the late most barbarous Traitors" (London: Robert Barker, 1606), sig. K2v.

45. "Araignement and Execution," sig. B4v.

46. *Cobbett's Complete Collection of State Trials*, 1:1413.

47. Ibid.

48. "Araignement and Execution," sig. B2v. Subsequent references are included parenthetically in the text.

49. Steven Mullaney, *The Place of the Stage*, 112–13. Although Mullaney argues that the liberty of the theater to comment on dominant cultures diminishes as it becomes a more permanent feature of the London landscape, his chapter on *Macbeth* nevertheless demonstrates the play's oppositional potential. My analysis of the play is indebted both to his *Place of the Stage* and "Lying Like Truth: Riddle, Representation, and Treason in Renaissance England," *English Literary History* 47 (1980): 32–47, 41; repr. in Wofford, *Shakespeare's Late Tragedies*, 61–73.

50. Early modern law condemned the prophecy of a sovereign's death as treason since, according to 25 Edw. III, st.5 c.2 and 13 Eliz. I, c.1, it was to "imagine . . . bodily harme to the King or Queene or heires apparent" or "deprive them of the dignity, title, or name of their royal estates." Cited in *Statutes of the Realm*, vol. 1 (Record Commission, 1810–28), 319–20; and in "An Exposition of Certain Difficult and obscure words and terms of the Lawes of this Realme" (London, 1592), 461–62.

51. Coddon, "'Unreal Mockery,'" 494. See also her analysis of scaffold speeches in "'Suche Strange Desygns': Madness, Subjectivity, and Treason in *Hamlet* and Elizabethan Culture," in *Case Studies in Contemporary Literature: Hamlet*, ed. Susanne L. Wofford (Boston: Bedford Books of St. Martin's Press, 1994), 380–402. On Cawdor's speech, see also Henry N. Paul, *Royal Play*, 233, who briefly compares the dying speech of Cawdor to that of Robert Devereux, the second earl of Essex.

52. Kenneth Muir, "Image and Symbol in *Macbeth*," *Shakespeare Survey* 19 (1966): 45–54. Also see Roy Walker, *The Time Is Free: A Study of Macbeth* (London: Andrew Dakers, 1949), 23, who compares the phrase "the dearest thing" to the phrase "eternal jewel" from act 3, scene 1, line 67.

53. "His Majesties Speech in this Parliament, together with a discourse of the manner of the discovery of this late intended treason" [*King's Book*] (London: Robert Barker, 1605), E3r. For brief discussions of the *King's Book*, see Paul Durst, *Intended Treason: What Really Happened in the Gunpowder Plot* (London: W. H. Allen, 1970), 97; Nicholls, *Investigating Gunpowder Plot*, 29; and Pye, *Regal Phantasm*, 134.

54. William Barlow, "The Sermon preached at Paules Cross, the tenth day of November, being the next Sunday after the discovery of this late horrible treason" (London: Mathew Law, 1606), E2r–E3r.

55. The example of William Parry's attempted treason against Elizabeth helps to verify the association of monarchical authority with exposing "the mind in the face," further suggesting Duncan's inadequacy. Parry had conspired with Mary, queen of Scotland, to assassinate Elizabeth in 1585, yet, finding himself alone with the queen, instead of murdering her as he had planned, he confessed his plot, perhaps under the mistaken assumption that he might receive a reward. See Raphael Holinshed, *Chronicles of England, Scotland and Ireland*, vol. 4 (London: J. Johnson, 1807–8) 561–63; Guy, *Tudor England*, 332, 444; MacCaffrey, *Elizabeth I*, 344.

56. Harry Berger Jr., "The Early Scenes of *Macbeth:* Preface to a New Interpretation," *ELH* 47 (1980): 1–31, quote at 4. See also idem, "Text against Performance in Shakespeare: The Example of *Macbeth*," in Greenblatt, *Power of Forms*, 49–79.

57. Jonathan Goldberg, "*Macbeth* and Source," in *Shakespeare Reproduced: The Text in History and Ideology*, ed. Jean E. Howard and Marion F. O'Connor (London: Methuen, 1987), 242–64, quote at 249. On Duncan's faults, see Michael Hawkins, "History, Politics and *Macbeth*," in Brown, *Focus on Macbeth*, 155–87, who notes that "many of the attributes ascribed to Duncan have a questionable double edge in a king" (173); and David Norbrook, "*Macbeth* and the Politics of Historiography," in *Politics of Discourse: The Literature and History of Seventeenth-Century England*, ed. Kevin Sharpe and Steven N. Zwicker (Berkeley: University of California Press, 1987), 78–116, who writes that "Duncan is no very impressive judge of character" (94). Subsequent references are included parenthetically in the text.

58. Peter Lake and Michael Questier offer an especially rich discussion of the gallows-speech pamphleteers in *Anti-Christ's Lewd Hat*, chap. 7, 229–80.

59. *SPD* 14/216, no. 12. The original letter has been removed from the State Papers and replaced with this later copy.

60. "A History of the Gunpowder Treason, collected from Approved Authors as well Popish as Protestant" (London: Richard Chiswel, 1678), sig. C1r.

61. *King's Book*, F3r. The *King's Book* was printed only a month after the plot and presents the official version of events. It is a composite publication containing "His Majesties Speech in this Last Session of Parliament . . . Together with a discourse of the maner of the discovery of this late intended Treason joyned with an Examination of some of the prisoners" (London, 1605).

62. "A History of the Gunpowder Treason," sig. C1r.

63. Ibid.

64. On the relationship between Shakespeare's play and historical accounts such as Holinshed's *Chronicles* and George Buchanan's *De jure regni apud Scotos; Or, A dialogue, concerning the due priviledge of government in the kingdom of Scotland* (1579), see, for example, the illuminating analyses of Norbrook, "*Macbeth* and the Politics of Historiography"; and Arthur F. Kinney, "Scottish History, The Union of the Crowns, and the Issue of Right Rule: The Case of Shakespeare's *Macbeth*," in *Renaissance Culture in Context*, ed. Jean R. Brink and William F. Gentrup (Aldershot: Scolar, 1993), 21.

65. Hawkins, "History," 177. See also David Scott Kastan's insightful reading of the play in his *Shakespeare after Theory* (London: Routledge, 1999), which notes the doubling of the Norwegian rebellion that opens the play and Malcolm's rebellion in the final act (177).

66. King James VI and I, "The Trew Law of Free Monarchies," 79.

67. Adelman, *Suffocating Mothers,* 144–46.

68. While the scene with Macduff has been characterized as a perfunctory paraphrase from Holinshed, Marvin Rosenberg has reminded us of the theatrical success of this suspenseful scene, particularly for spectators who do not know the outcome in advance; see Rosenberg, *The Masks of Macbeth* (Berkeley: University of California Press, 1978), 543. On the relationship between the texts of Shakespeare and Holinshed, see also Goldberg, "*Macbeth* and Source"; Hawkins, "History"; and Norbrook, "*Macbeth* and the Politics of Historiography."

69. Susanne L. Wofford, "The Body Unseamed: Shakespeare's Late Tragedies," in idem, *Shakespeare's Late Tragedies,* 3.

70. At least, that is, as long as Shakespeare leaves Mary, queen of Scotland, out of the line.

5. Donne's *Pseudo-Martyr* and Post–Gunpowder Plot Law

1. "Nicolò Molin, Venetian Ambassador to England, to the Doge and the Senate (November 9, 1605)," vol. 10 (1603–7), *Calendar of State Papers relating to Venice,* ed. Horatio F. Brown (London: Her Majesty's Stationary Office, 1900), 285.

2. The Archbishop of Canterbury introduced a successful motion into The House of Lords on January 21, 1606, that "a Committee might be appointed, to consider how the Laws are already in Force, that tend to the Preservation of Religion, His Majesty, the State, and Common-wealth; and what Defects are in the Execution of them, or what New Laws may be thought needful." See *Journals of the House of Lords* (1578–1614), vol. 2 (London: Her Majesty's Stationary Office), 360. The House of Commons also drafted a petition, on June 16, 1607, "to consider the better execution of lawes in force against recusants." See *Journals of the House of Commons,* vol. 1, November 8, 1547–March 2, 1628 (reprinted by order of House of Commons, 1803), 384.

3. *Journals of the House of Lords,* 364, 371, 399.

4. The oath of allegiance statute (3 & 4 Jac. I, c.4) was passed in the second session of James's first parliament. See *Statutes of the Realm,* 4:1071–77; and "Anno Regni Jacobi . . . 3rd. At the second session of the Parliament" (London: Robert Barker, 1606), sig. C4a-b. On the oath of allegiance, see M. C. Questier, "Loyalty, Religion and State Power in Early Modern England: English Romanism and the Jacobean Oath of Allegiance," *Historical Journal* 40.2 (June 1997): 311–29; Clarence J. Ryan, "The Jacobean Oath of Allegiance and English Lay Catholics," *Catholic Historical Review* 28.2 (1942): 159–83; Johann P. Sommerville, "Jacobean Political Thought and the Controversy over the Oath of Allegiance" (Ph.D. diss., University of Cambridge, 1981).

5. *Statutes of the Realm,* iv, 1074.

6. 3 James I, c.4 and 5; *Statutes of the Realm,* iv, 1071–82. Praemunire signified the offense of appealing to or obeying a foreign dignitary (namely, the pope), thus challenging the supremacy of the monarch and thereby committing treason. In December 1530 the clergy had been accused of praemunire as part of Henry VIII's attack on the Catholic Church. Henry's 1534 Succession Act, on one level, anticipates the Jacobean oath of allegiance, since the act required subjects to take an oath supporting the king's second marriage and effectively asserted the English state's supremacy over the Catholic Church. With notable exceptions such as Thomas More and his fellow prisoners, Bishop Fisher and Nicholas Watson, however, most subjects swore to the oath even if they later fought against the separation from Rome, charting a via media between their loyalty to the English state and their Catholic faith. In 1606 this route of compromise no longer existed, since the pope threatened excommunication for anyone taking the oath, while the king declared that anyone who refused it was a traitor. A subject of James could thus find him- or herself executed for treason not for defending or protecting papal rights but merely for refusing to suffer excommunication. See G. R. Elton, *Reform and Reformation: England, 1509–1558* (Cambridge, Mass.: Harvard University Press, 1977), 185; A. G. Dickens, *The English Reformation,* 2nd ed. (University Park: Pennsylvania State University Press, 1989 [1964]).

7. Stefania Tutino, "Notes on Machiavelli and Ignatius Loyola in John Donne's *Ignatius His Conclave* and *Pseudo-Martyr,*" *English Historical Review* (November 2004): 1–14; 13.

8. Hirst, *Authority and Conflict,* 107.

9. Alan Haynes, *The Gunpowder Plot: Faith in Rebellion* (Dover, N.H.: Alan Sutton, 1994), 120.

10. David Wooton, *Divine Right and Democracy: An Anthology of Political Writing in Stuart England* (London: Penguin Books, 1986), 30; J. Neville Figgis, *The Theory of the Divine Right of Kings* (Cambridge: Cambridge University Press, 1896), 135. Since James's succession to the English throne challenged English law (namely, the will of Henry VIII and the Act of 1584), the king would undermine his claim to the throne if he upheld English law over royal sovereignty, a point both Wooton and Figgis make.

11. Questier, "Loyalty, Religion and State Power," 311.

12. Ibid., 321.

13. Johann P. Sommerville, *Politics and Ideology in England, 1603–1640* (New York: Longman, 1986), 117. See also the second edition, *Royalists and Patriots: Politics and Ideology in England, 1603–1640* (London: Longman, 1999). See also Corinne Comstock Weston and Janelle Renfrow Greenberg, *Subjects and Sovereigns: The Grand Controversy over Legal Sovereignty in Stuart England* (Cambridge: Cambridge University Press, 1981), 17, who sup-port more broadly an argument on Jacobean absolute sovereignty through the order theory of kingship, which "placed the king in a position of undoubted superiority in the years before 1642."

14. Roger Lockyer, *The Early Stuarts: A Political History of England, 1603–1642*

(London: Longman, 1989), 286. See also Nicholas Henshall, *The Myth of Absolutism: Change and Continuity in Early Modern European Monarchy* (London: Longman, 1992), esp. 134–45.

15. Nicholls, *Investigating the Gunpowder Plot,* 48. See also Antonia Fraser, *The Gunpowder Plot: Terror and Faith in 1605* (London: Mandarin, 1997), 283; Haynes, *The Gunpowder Plot,* 119–20. Both Fraser and Haynes stress the king's clemency toward his Catholic subjects, even in the years after the plot.

16. Glenn Burgess, *Absolute Monarchy and the Stuart Constitution* (New Haven: Yale University Press, 1996), 101.

17. Charles Howard McIlwain, ed., *The Political Works of James I* (New York: Russell and Russell, 1965), lvii.

18. Questier, "Loyalty, Religion and State Power," 312, 317.

19. Habermas, *Structural Transformation of the Public Sphere,* 27.

20. On Donne's absolutism, see John Carey, *John Donne: Life, Mind and Art* (London: Faber and Faber, 1981; repr. 1990), 17; Jonathan Goldberg, *James I and the Politics of Literature: Jonson, Shakespeare, Donne, and Their Contemporaries* (Stanford: Stanford University Press, 1983; repr. 1989), 219; Debora Kuller Shuger, *Habits of Thought in the English Renaissance: Religion, Politics, and the Dominant Culture* (Berkeley: University of California Press, 1990), 183.

21. See Lowell Gallagher, *Medusa's Gaze: Casuistry and Conscience in the Renaissance* (Stanford: Stanford University Press, 1991), esp. chap. 2.

22. William Barlow, "The Sermon preached at Paules Crosse, the tenth day of November, being the next Sunday after the Discovery of this late Horrible Treason" (London: Mathew Law, 1606); Ormerod, "The Picture of a Papist, or a relation of the damnable heresies, detestable qualities, and diabolicall practices of sundry hereticks in former ages, and of the papists in this age" (London: Nathaniel Fosbrooke, 1606); "The Arraignment and Execution of the late Traytors" (London: Jeffrey Chorlton, 1606). See also Richard Montague, later chaplain to James I, in his "Meditation upon occasion of our much admired deliverance from the more than popish designe of the 5th November, 1605" (Huntington Library MS 1733, fol.9r).

23. Barlow, "The Sermon preached at Paules Crosse," E2v. On the connection between James and David, see Linda Levy Peck, *The Mental World of the Jacobean Court* (Cambridge: Cambridge University Press, 1991), 8; Kevin Sharpe, "The King's Writ: Authors and Royal Authority in Early Modern England," in *Culture and Politics in Early Stuart England,* ed. Kevin Sharpe and Peter Lake (Stanford: Stanford University Press, 1993), 117–38, 124–25. To James, the model of David challenges the claims of resistance theorists, since David refused to challenge Saul, despite that he no longer held God's spirit because he disobeyed a divine commandment. As Saul later tells Samuel, "I have sinned, for I have transgressed the commandment of the Lord, and thy words, because I feared the people, and obeyed their voice" in *The Book of Samuel, The Authorised King James Version,* Pocket Canon series (Edinburgh: Canongate, 1999), 1.15.24. This reading of the David story conflicts, however, with earlier readings of the biblical precedent, as J. H. Burns discusses: "though chosen by God and anointed by Samuel, [David's] right was only

ad regnum, not yet in regno—a right to exercise royal power could come only from his acceptance by the people" ("Scholasticism: Survival and Revival," in Burns, with Goldie, *The Cambridge History of Political Thought,* 145). Furthermore, James clashes with Robert Bellarmine and the Cardinal Perron over the interpretation of Saul; James argues that Perron misreads the Saul story: the withdrawal of divine sanction did not suggest that the king could be deposed by his subjects, as Perron falsely believes. See James VI and I, "A Remonstrance for the Right of Kings (1615)," in *The Political Works of James I,* 169–268; 213.

24. [Robert Cecil, Marquis of Salisbury], "An Answere to Certaine Scandalous Papers, scattered abroad under colour of a Catholicke Admonition" (London: Robert Barker, 1606), D3r-v.

25. "His Majesties speach in this last session of Parliament, as neere his very words as could be gathered at the instant. Together with a discourse of the maner of the discovery of this late intended Treason, joyned with the Examination of some of the prisoners" (London: Robert Barker, 1605), B1r.

26. James VI and I, "The King Majesties Speach (March 21, 1609)," (London: Robert Barker, 1609), A4v-B1r.

27. James VI and I, "A Premonition to all most mighty monarchies, kings, free princes, and states of Christendome," in *The Political Works of James I,* 151; "Remonstrance," 234.

28. James VI and I, "Remonstrance," 227.

29. Ibid., 235.

30. "The Arraignment and Execution of the late Traytors" (London: Jeffrey Chorlton, 1606), D2r.

31. Robert Persons, "A Discussion of the Answer of M. William Barlow to the book entitled 'Judgement of a Catholic Englishman living in banishment for his Religion" (no location, 1612), 15.

32. Ibid.

33. "Catholicis Anglis Paulus PP Quintus," in *SPD* 14/23, no. 15. I am using the translation "Pope Paulus the fift, to the English Catholickes," in *King James VI and I, Political Writings,* ed. Johann P. Sommerville (Cambridge: Cambridge University Press, 1994), 89–90. For a contemporary copy in Latin, see Huntington Library MS 2179/2180.

34. "Pope Paulus the fift," 90.

35. On the issue of Catholic indefectibility, see Thomas H. Clancy, *Papist Pamphleteers: The Allen-Persons Party and the Political Thought of the Counter-Reformation in England, 1572–1615* (Chicago: Loyola University Press, 1964), 89.

36. "Master Blackwels Letter to the Romish Catholikes in England," in "A Large Examination taken at Lambeth" (Robert Barker, 1607), V3r.

37. *CSP, Venice* (September 13, 1606), 401.

38. Cardinal Robert Bellarmine, "To the Very Reverend Mr. George Blackwell, Arch-priest of the English," in "Triplici Nodo, Triplici Ceneus, or An Apologie for the Oath of Allegiance" (London: Robert Barker, 1607), C3r-v. This text was published in February 1607 [i.e., 1608].

39. Ibid., C4r.

40. Ibid., C2r.

41. Ibid.

42. "Mr. George Blackwel . . . his Answers" (London: Robert Barker, 1607), A3v.

43. Ibid., B1v.

44. "Mr Blackwels answer to Cardinal Bellarmine's Letter," published as an appendix to "Triplici Nodo," E2v.

45. "The Examination of George Blackwell, January 20, 1607 [1608]" (London, 1607), 4–6.

46. "Catholicis Anglis Paulus PP Quintus," in *SPD* 14 / 23, no. 15. Translation in *Political Writings,* 97.

47. James VI and I, "Triplici Nodo," in *Political Writings,* 86. All further citations will be to this text. On contemporary arguments in favor of the oath of allegiance, see also Huntington Library MS 2187, a "discourse proving lawfulness of oath of allegiance by John Goode," and Huntington Library MS 2188–91.

48. James VI and I, "A Premonition," 157.

49. Ibid., 118.

50. Ibid., 157.

51. James VI and I, "Triplici Nodo," 87.

52. James I, "His Majesties Speach in this last session of Parliament" (London: Robert Barker, 1605), C2r.

53. James VI and I, "A Premonition," 155.

54. Pierre Du Moulin, Minister in the Church of Paris, "The Accomplishment of the Prophecies; or the Third Booke in defense of the Catholicke faith . . . Against the allegations of R. Bellarmine; and F. N. Coëffeteau and other Doctors of the Romish Church," trans. J. Heath, Fellow of New College, Oxford (Oxford: Joseph Barnes, 1613), A2v.

55. Johann P. Sommerville, "James I and the Divine Right of Kings: English Politics and Continental Theory," in *The Mental World of the Jacobean Court,* ed. Linda Levy Peck (Cambridge: Cambridge University Press, 1991), 55–70, quote at 59.

56. James VI and I, "A Premonition," 117.

57. James VI and I, "Triplici Nodo," 128

58. Ibid., 118; James VI and I, "Remonstrance," 234.

59. James VI and I, "Triplici Nodo," 120.

60. James VI and I, "A Premonition," 121.

61. Huntington Library, Ellemsere MS 6240 (May 1608 at Whitehall), 1r.

62. James VI and I, "A Premonition," 113.

63. "Zorzi Giustinian, Venetian Ambassador in England, to the Doge and Senate (February 24 1606)," *CSP, Venice,* vol. 10, 321–22.

64. "F.R.G. upon the oath of allegiance, an. 1603 [sic]," British Library Add. MS 28252.

65. BL Mss. Add. 14030, Yelverton Papers: "Letter by Robert Persons on oath of allegiance, 1606." See also "A Discourse against taking the Oathe in En-

gland, written by F. Persons," (Stonyhurst MS., Collectanea P, 161–74; and "Letter to Father Henry Garnet," August 26, 1606 (British Library, Add. 14, 140, no. 30, fol. 87).

66. Lake and Questier, *The Anti-Christ's Lewd Hat*, xxvi.

67. Evelyn M. Simpson also calls it, "without a doubt, the least interesting of Donne's early works" (*A Study of the Prose Works of John Donne*, 2nd ed. [Oxford: Clarendon, 1948], 179; in *John Donne: Selected Prose*, ed. Evelyn Simpson [Oxford: Clarendon, 1967], 43). Contrast Simpson's characterization with Richard Strier's more accurate description of *Pseudo-Martyr* as Donne's "most sober, important, and public piece of writing," in "Radical Donne: 'Satire III,'" *ELH* 60.2 (1993): 283–322, quote at 284. See also Richard Strier, "John Donne and the Politics of Devotion," *Religion, Literature, and Politics in Post-Reformation England, 1540–1688*, ed. Donna B. Hamilton and Richard Strier (Cambridge: Cambridge University Press, 1996), 93–114.

68. Isaac Walton, *Lives of Doctor John Donne, Henry Wotton, Richard Hooker, and George Herbert* (London, 1670), 33.

69. John Donne, "To the High and Mightie Prince James," *Pseudo-Martyr, wherein out of Certain Propositions and Gradations, this Conclusion is evicted, that those which are of the Romane Religion in this Kingdome may and ought to take the Oath of Allegiance* (London, 1610), ed. Anthony Raspa (Montreal: McGill-Queen's University Press, 1993), 3. All future citations will be in the text and to this edition. On the issue of royal commissioning, see R. C. Bald, *John Donne: A Life* (Oxford: Clarendon, 1970; repr. 1986), 220; and Simpson, *Prose Works of John Donne*.

70. Bald, *John Donne*, 201–2; and Carey, *John Donne*, 17.

71. Annabel Patterson, *Censorship and Interpretation: The Conditions of Writing and Reading in Early Modern Europe* (Madison: University of Wisconsin Press, 1984), 103. On Donne's absolutism, see Carey, *John Donne*; Goldberg, *James I*; and Shuger, *Habits of Thought*. Patterson's comment on Pseudo-Martyr contrasts with her more general analysis of Donne in the period after 1606, according to which he "was never so simply the king's man," in "Quod Oportet Versus Quod Convenit: John Donne, Kingsman?" in *Critical Essays on John Donne*, ed. Arthur Marotti (New York: G. K. Hall, 1994), 141–79, quote at 144.

72. James VI and I, "Triplici Nodo," 86.

73. Condemning such death as suicide in *Pseudo-Martyr*, Donne's work bears an interesting relation to the prose work composed, although not published, immediately before: *Biathanatos*. In this earlier work Donne argues in support of suicide, whereas here he rehearses the spiritual arguments against self-inflicted death.

74. I am grateful to Sandra McPherson for comments leading me to clarify this point on the distinction between obedience and submission.

75. On Donne's critical relationship to authority, see Arthur Marotti, *John Donne, Coterie Poet* (Madison: University of Wisconsin Press, 1986); David Norbrook, "The Monarchy of Wit and the Republic of Letters: Donne's Politics," in *Soliciting Interpretation: Literary Theory and Seventeenth-Century En-*

glish Poetry, ed. Elizabeth D. Harvey and Katharine Eisaman Maus (Chicago: University of Chicago Press, 1990), 3–36.

76. Shuger, *Habits of Thought*, 197.

77. "The Sunne Rising," in *The Complete English Poems of John Donne*, ed. C. A. Patrides (London: Everyman, 1985), 53.

78. "The Defence of Poesy," in *Sir Philip Sidney: Selected Prose and Poetry*, ed. Robert Kimbrough (Madison: University of Wisconsin Press, 1983), 109.

79. Meg Lota Brown, *Donne and the Politics of Conscience in Early Modern England* (Lieden: E. J. Brill, 1995), 84–85.

80. Douglas Trevor, "John Donne's *Pseudo-Martyr* and the Oath of Allegiance Controversy," *Reformation*, vol. 5 (2000): 103–37. Trevor cites Burgess, *Absolute Monarchy*, 12.

81. For an analysis of Donne, Barlow, and Fitzherbert, see Trevor, "John Donne's *Pseudo-Martyr*."

82. John Donne, "To his honorable friend, Sir H[enry] G[oodyer]," in *Life and Letters of John Donne*, ed. Edmund Gosse, vol. 1 (London: William Heinemann, 1899), 221–23, 222.

83. Ibid.

84. Quentin Skinner, *Liberty before Liberalism* (Cambridge: Cambridge University Press, 1998), 42–44.

85. On the issue of textual scholarship in Donne and the oath of allegiance controversy more broadly, see Trevor, "John Donne's *Pseudo-Martyr*."

86. John Donne, *Life and Letters*, 1:221.

87. Anthony Raspa, "Time, History and Typology in John Donne's *Pseudo-Martyr*," *Renaissance and Reformation*, n.s., 11.1 (1987): 182.

88. Strier, "Radical Donne," 285.

89. Donne's use of the conscience in *Pseudo-Martyr* anticipates his January 1615 preface to *Essays in Divinity*. In the preface Donne expresses admiration for the conscience as a site of independent thought and reason, implying that reason is not a universal faculty as we might expect but, instead, is contingent, contextual, and various. I am grateful to Janel Mueller for drawing my attention to this preface.

6. Treason and Emergency Power in Jonson's *Catiline*

1. Ben Jonson, "Ben Jonson's Conversations with William Drummond of Hawthornden," in *Ben Jonson*, ed. C. H. Hereford and Percy Simpson, vol. 1 (Oxford: Clarendon, 1925), 139 (ll. 250–51).

2. On the dinner in the Strand, see Alan Haynes, *Gunpowder Plot: Faith in Rebellion* (Bridgend, U.K.: Sutton, 1994), 45; and Nicolls, *Investigating Gunpowder Plot*, 39.

3. Jonson, "Conversations," 141 (l. 327). For an analysis of *Sejanus*, see Blair Worden, "Ben Jonson among the Historians," in Sharpe and Lake, *Culture and Politics in Early Stuart England*, 67–89.

4. Hereford and Simpson, *Ben Jonson*, 203.

5. Ibid.

6. David Riggs, *Ben Jonson: A Life* (Cambridge, Mass.: Harvard University Press, 1989), 127. Jonson's editors, Hereford and Simpson, claim that Jonson "was not in their [the conspirators'] secrets; their cause was in no sense his" in Hereford and Simpson, *Ben Jonson*, 40.

7. Jonson, "Conversations," vol. 2, ll. 313–15.

8. Kay, *A Literary Life*, 77.

9. Riggs, *Ben Jonson*, 176.

10. Omerod, "Picture of a Papist" (London: Nathaniel Fosbrooke, 1606), V4r; "A Discourse of the Maner of the Discovery of this late intended treason" (London: Robert Barker, 1605), E4v.

11. Barbara N. De Luna, *Jonson's Romish Plot: A Study of "Catiline" and Its Historical Context* (Oxford: Clarendon, 1967).

12. Ben Jonson, *Catiline*, ed. W. F. Bolton and Jane F. Gardner, Regents Renaissance Drama series (London: Edward Arnold, 1972). All references are to this edition unless otherwise noted.

13. Elaborating, Catiline claims, "The horrors that do strike the world should come / Loud and unlook'd for: till they strike, be dumb" (1.1.528–29; see also 1.1.5; 3.3.74; 4.2.373–74; and 5.4.159). See Barlow's sermon on the Gunpowder Plot, where he deems the treason "a deadly blow" (B2v), as does William Leigh, "Great Britaines, great deliverance, from the great danger of the popish powder" (173).

14. For a comprehensive defense of Cicero, see Blair Worden, "Politics in *Catiline:* Jonson and His Sources," *Re-Presenting Ben Jonson: Text, History, Performance,* ed. Martin Butler (London: Macmillan, 1999), 152–73, esp. 158–64.

15. I am indebted to these notable exceptions to the consensus on Cicero's virtuous triumph: John Michael Archer, *Sovereignty and Intelligence: Spying and Court Culture in the English Renaissance* (Stanford: Stanford University Press, 1993), 95–120; Jonathan Goldberg, *James I and the Politics of Literature* (Stanford: Stanford University Press, 1989), 196–203; Julie Sanders, *Ben Jonson's Theatrical Republics* (London: Macmillan, 1998), chap. 2, esp. 16–26; William W. E. Slights, *Ben Jonson and the Art of Secrecy* (Ontario: University of Toronto Press, 1994), chap. 6, 130–44.

16. Sanders, *Ben Jonson's Theatrical Republics*, esp. 11–33.

17. Philip J. Ayres, "The Nature of Jonson's Roman History," *English Literary Renaissance* 16.1 (1986): 166–181, quote at 174.

18. Scholars more frequently turn to *Sejanus* to analyze how Jonson employed Roman settings for contemporary political ends. For a fascinating case study of how one reader, Sir William Drake, approached Jonson's *Sejanus,* see Kevin Sharpe, *Reading Revolutions: The Politics of Reading in Early Modern England* (New Haven: Yale University Press, 2000). Here Sharpe writes, "The commonplace books of Sir William Drake (with, we recall, extensive notes from *Sejanus*) . . . provide clear evidence that, away from the stage, other readers of the classics brought their 'integrity,' their self and mo-

ment, to those texts and reread them as a commentary on their own society and state" (288).

19. Henry Bracton, *De Legibus et Consuetudinibus Angliae, or On the Laws and Customs of England,* trans. Samuel E. Thorne, vol. 2 (Cambridge, Mass.: Belknap Press of Harvard University Press, 1968); Latin text, ed. George E. Woodbine (New Haven: Yale University Press, 1922), libr. 1, cap. 8, p. 19, 33. As a treatise upholding practices of law-based rule, *De Legibus* states, in an often-cited phrase, that "the king must not be under man but under God and under the law." Some scholars interpret this phrase to suggest the king's legal and political supremacy over his subjects even as he rules beneath the law. See C. H. McIlwain, *Constitutionalism Ancient and Modern* (Ithaca, N.Y.: Cornell University Press, 1940), 69–90, who makes the controversial distinction between "jurisdictio" and "gubernaculum" in Bracton, for example.

20. Maister Fortescue, knight, *A Learned commendation of the politique lawes of England,* trans. Robert Mulcaster (London: Richarde Tottell, 1573).

21. Sir Thomas Smith, *De Republica Anglorum* (London, 1583), 44.

22. William Lambard, *Archion, or Commentary upon the High Courts of Justice in England* (London, 1591; repr. 1635), 88–89.

23. *The Parliamentary History of England from the Earliest Period to the Year 1803,* vol. 1 (1066–1626) (London, 1806), col. 1193; cited in Glenn Burgess, *The Politics of the Ancient Constitution* (University Park: Pennsylvania State University Press, 1992), 158.

24. Burgess, *Politics,* 167.

25. John Guy, "The 'Imperial Crown' and the Liberty of the Subject: The English Constitution from Magna Carta to the Bill of Rights," *Court, Country and Culture: Essays on Early Modern British History in Honor of Perez Zagorin,* ed. B. Kunze and D. Brautigam (Rochester: University of Rochester Press, 1992), 75.

26. As James argues in his responses to the resulting controversy, the oath simply separated loyal subjects from those who, as he puts it, are "caried away with the like fanaticall zeale that the Powder-Traitors were" (*Triplici Nodo,* 86). For a discussion of the oath controversy, see chapter 5.

27. *Commons Journals* (March 25, 1606): 288–89.

28. *Commons Journals* (June 16, 1607): 384.

29. Ibid.

30. James Daly, "The Idea of Absolute Monarchy," *Historical Journal* 21.2 (1978): 227–50, quote at 232.

31. Thomas Hedley, "Speech in Parliament (June 28)," *Parliamentary Debates 1610,* ed. Samuel Rawson Gardiner (London: Camden Society, 1862), 72.

32. Thomas Crew, "Speech in Parliament (June 29)," *Parliamentary Debates 1610,* 93.

33. Francis Bacon argued before the Exchequer Chamber in association with Calvin's Case (*Case of the Post-Nati [1608],* in *The Works of Francis Bacon,* ed. James Spedding, Robert Leslie Ellis, Douglas Denon Heath, vol. 15 [London: Longmans, Green, Reader, and Dyer, 1868], 229).

34. Hirst, *Authority and Conflict,* 112.

35. Francis Oakley, "Jacobean Political Theology: The Absolute and Ordinary Powers of the King," *Journal of the History of Ideas* 29.3 (1968): 323–46, quote at 343.

36. Cicero, *The Orations*, trans. C. D. Yonge, vol. 3 (London: Bell and Daldy, 1872), 4.11: "*si vita nostra in aliquas insidias, si in vim et in tela aut latronum aut inimicorum incidisset, omnis honesta ratio esset expediendae salutis. Silent enim leges inter arma.*"

37. Philip Melancthon, *Werke* (Gutersloh, 1961), 3.86. Cited and translated in Richard Tuck, *Philosophy and Government* (Cambridge: Cambridge University Press, 1993), 18. Cicero, *De Officiis*, trans. Walter Miller (Loeb Classical Library, 1913). See, esp., sections 1.11, 3.25, and 3.28.

38. Peter N. Miller, *Defining the Common Good: Empire, Religion, and Philosophy in Eighteenth-Century Britain* (Cambridge: Cambridge University Press, 1994), 5; on Cicero, see, esp., 5–51. Cicero's actions in the case of Catiline appear to justify, as Miller argues earlier, however, "the legitimacy of extra-legal measures, including violence, in pursuit of the security and well-being of the community" (24), and yet his Renaissance legacy celebrates the magistrate's emphasis on rule of law.

39. Tuck, *Philosophy and Government*, 40, 53, 63; on Cicero, see, esp., 12–39.

40. For Cicero's discussion of this decree, see "In Catilinam I," in *Orations*, trans. C. Macdonald, vol. 10 (Cambridge, Mass.: Harvard University Press, 1977; repr. 2001), 34–37.

41. F. R. Cowell, *Cicero and the Roman Republic* (London: Penguin Books, 1948); T. N. Mitchell, *Cicero: The Ascending Years* (New Haven: Yale University Press, 1979); *Cicero: The Senior Statesman* (New Haven: Yale University Press, 1991). On Cicero, in addition to the above, see also Markku Peltonen, *Classical Humanism and Republicanism in English Political Thought, 1570–1640* (Cambridge: Cambridge University Press, 1995), esp. 134–77; *The Oxford Classical Dictionary*, ed. Simon Hornblower and Antony Spawforth, 3rd ed. (Oxford: Oxford University Press, 1999).

42. The play became popular in the Restoration, under Charles II. See Anne Barton, *Ben Jonson, Dramatist* (Cambridge: Cambridge University Press, 1984), 154. Despite its unpopularity in 1611, however, the play's obscured charms should at least excite the perverse tastes of literary scholars. Yet *Catiline* has attracted only a fraction of the critical attention devoted to its partner play, *Sejanus*, rarely warranting more than a section of a chapter in monographs solely on Jonsonian drama (the notable exception is De Luna's *Jonson's Romish Plot*).

43. *The Diary of Samuel Pepys*, ed. Robert Latham and William Matthews, vol. 9 (1668–69) (London, 1970–83), 395.

44. Ben Jonson, *Catiline*, ed. W. F. Bolton and Jane F. Gardner, Regents Renaissance Drama series (London: Edward Arnold, 1972).

45. Sallust, *The Conspiracy of Catiline*, trans. Thomas Heywood (London: Constable, 1924), 75.

46. Ibid., 61–62. On the term "obnoxius," see Quentin Skinner, *Liberty before Liberalism* (Cambridge: Cambridge University Press, 1998), 42.

47. Katharine Eisaman Maus, *Ben Jonson and the Roman Frame of Mind* (Princeton, N.J.: Princeton University Press, 1984), 75. See also Joseph Allen Bryant Jr., "*Catiline* and the Nature of Jonson's Tragic Fable," in *Ben Jonson: A Collection of Critical Essays,* ed. Jonas A. Barish (Upper Saddle River, N.J.: Prentice Hall, 1963), 147–59. On the representation of Cicero, see also Richard Dutton, *Ben Jonson: To the First Folio* (Cambridge, Cambridge University Press, 1983), 124–25.

48. Worden, "Politics in *Catiline,*" 170.

49. Goldberg, *James I,* 196.

50. Barton, *Ben Jonson, Dramatist,* 162.

51. Skinner, *Liberty before Liberalism,* 50–51.

52. Ibid., 51. He refers to John Milton's *Eikonokastes,* ed. F. R. Fogle and J. M. Patrick, vol. 5 of idem, *Complete Prose Works,* ed. Merritt Hughes (New Haven: Yale University Press, 1953–82), 458.

Afterword

1. Cicero, *Orations,* 3:4.11. Latin original: "Silent leges inter arma."

2. Nasser Hussain, *The Jurisprudence of Emergency: Colonialism and the Rule of Law* (Ann Arbor: University of Michigan Press, 2003).

Works Cited

"An Account of the Earl of Essex's Execution (1601)." BL Mss. Add. 4155.

Achienstein, Sharon. *Milton and the Revolutionary Reader*. Princeton, N.J.: Princeton University Press, 1994.

Adams, Robert P. "Despotism, Censorship and Mirrors of Power Politics in Late Elizabethan Times." *Sixteenth Century Journal* 10.3 (fall 1979): 5–16.

Adelman, Janet. *Suffocating Mothers: Fantasies of Maternal Origin in Shakespeare's Plays, Hamlet to the Tempest*. New York: Routledge, 1992.

Agamben, Giorgio. *Homo Sacer: Sovereign Power and Bare Life*. Trans. Daniel Heller-Roazen. Stanford: Stanford University Press, 1998.

Albright, Evelyn May. "Shakespeare's *Richard II* and the Essex Conspiracy." *PMLA* 42 (1927): 686–720.

Allen, Cardinal William. *A True, Sincere and Modest Defence of English Catholics* (1584). Ed. R. M. Kingdon. Ithaca, N.Y.: Cornell University Press, 1965.

Allen, J. W. *History of Political Thought in the Sixteenth Century*. London: Methuen, 1928.

Anon. [attributed to Philippe Duplessis Mornay]. *Vindiciae, contra tyrannos; or, concerning the legitimate power of a prince over the people, and of the people over a prince* (1579). Ed. and trans. George Garnett. Cambridge: Cambridge University Press, 1994.

"The Araignment and Execution of the late Traytors." London: Jeffrey Chorlton, 1606.

Archer, John Michael. *Sovereignty and Intelligence: Spying and Court Culture in the English Renaissance*. Stanford: Stanford University Press, 1993.

"The Arraignment and Execution of the Earl of Essex (1601)." Huntington Mss. 46714.

Austin, J. L. *How to Do Things with Words*. Oxford: Clarendon, 1962.

Ayres, Philip J., ed. Introduction to *Sejanus His Fall* by Ben Jonson. Manchester, U.K.: Manchester University Press, 1990.

——. "The Nature of Jonson's Roman History." *English Literary Renaissance* 16.1 (1986): 166–81.

Bacon, Francis. *The Essays.* Ed. John Pitcher. London: Penguin, 1985.

——. *The Letters and Life of Francis Bacon.* Ed. James Spedding. 7 vols. London: Longmans, Green, Reader, and Dyer, 1861–74.

——. *The Works of Francis Bacon.* Ed. James Spedding, Robert Leslie Ellis, and Douglas Denon Heath. 14 vols. London: Longmans, Green, Reader, and Dyer, 1857–74.

Bald, R. C. *John Donne: A Life.* Oxford: Clarendon, 1986 [1970].

Bale, John. "Faithful Admonition of a Certain True Pastor." 1554.

Barlow, William. "The Sermon preached at Paules Crosse, the tenth day of November, being the next Sunday after the Discovery of this late Horrible Treason." London: Mathew Law, 1606.

Barrell, John. *Imagining the King's Death: Figurative Treason, Fantasies of Regicide, 1793–1796.* Oxford: Oxford University Press, 2000.

Barroll, Leeds. "A New History for Shakespeare and His Time." *Shakespeare Quarterly* 39 (1988): 441–64.

Barron, Caroline. "The Deposition of Richard II." In *Politics and Crisis in Fourteenth-Century England.* Ed. John Taylor and Wendy Childs. London: Alan Sutton, 1990.

Barton, Anne. *Ben Jonson, Dramatist.* Cambridge: Cambridge University Press, 1984.

Beacon, Thomas. *The Sicke Mans Salve.* London: John Daye, 1582.

Beaty, Nancy Lee. *The Craft of Dying: A Study in the Literary Tradition of the Ars Moriendi in England.* New Haven: Yale University Press, 1970.

Bellamy, John. *The Law of Treason in England in the Later Middle Ages.* Cambridge: Cambridge University Press, 1970.

——. *The Tudor Law of Treason.* London: Routledge, Kegan and Paul, 1979.

Bellarmine, Cardinal Robert. "To the Very Reverend Mr. George Blackwell, Arch-priest of the English." In *Triplici Nodo, Triplici Ceneus, or An Apologie for the Oath of Allegiance.* London: Robert Barker, 1607.

Benjamin, Edwin B. "Sir John Hayward and Tacitus." *Review of English Studies,* n.s., 8 (1957): 275–76.

Benoit, Jack Gohn. "*Richard II:* Shakespeare's Legal Brief on the Royal Prerogative and the Succession to the Throne." *Georgetown Law Journal* 70 (1982): 943–73.

Berger, Harry, Jr. "*Ars Moriendi* in Progress, or John of Gaunt and the Practice of Strategic Dying." *Yale Journal of Criticism: Interpretation in the Humanities* 1.1 (1987): 39–67.

——. "The Early Scenes of *Macbeth:* Preface to a New Interpretation." *English Literary History* 47 (1980): 1–31.

——. *Imaginary Audition: Shakespeare on Stage and Page.* Berkeley: University of California Press, 1989.

——. "Richard II: An Exercise in Imaginary Audition." *ELH* 55.4 (winter 1988): 755–96.

——. "Text against Performance in Shakespeare: The Example of *Macbeth.*" In *Power of Forms in the English Renaissance,* ed. Stephen Greenblatt, 49–79. Norman, Okla.: Pilgrim Books, 1982.

Bergeron, David. "The Deposition Scene in *Richard II.*" *Renaissance Papers* (1974): 31–37.

Blackwell, George. "Mr. George Blackwel . . . his Answers." London: Robert Barker, 1607.

——. "Master Blackwels Letter to the Romish Catholikes in England." In *A Large Examination taken at Lambeth.* London: Robert Barker, 1607.

——. "The Examination of George Blackwell, January 20, 1607 [1608]." London: Robert Barker, 1607.

Bodin, Jean. *Methodus ad facilem historiarum cognitionem. Oeuvres philosophiques de Jean Bodin.* Ed. Pierre Mesnard. Paris, 1951.

——. *Method for the Easy Comprehension of History.* Trans. Beatrice Reynolds. New York: Columbia University Press, 1945.

——. *On Sovereignty: Four Chapters from the Six Books of the Commonwealth.* Ed. and trans. Julian H. Franklin. Cambridge: Cambridge University Press, 1992.

Book of Samuel. The Authorized King James Version. Pocket Canon ser. Edinburgh: Canongate, 1999.

Bourcier, Elisabeth, ed. *The Diary of Sir Simonds D'Ewes, 1622–24: Journal d'un Étudiant londonien sous le Régne de Jacques 1er.* Paris: Didier, 1974.

Bracton, Henry. *On the Laws and Customs of England* [*De legibus et consuetudinibus angliae*]. Ed. George E. Woodbine. Trans. Samuel E. Thorne. Cambridge, Mass.: Belknap Press of Harvard University Press, 1968.

Bradford, Alan T. "Stuart Absolutism and the 'Utility' of Tacitus." *Huntington Library Quarterly* 46.2 (spring 1983): 127–55.

Braunmiller, A. R. "King John and Historiography." *ELH* 55.2 (1988): 309–32.

Brown, Meg Lota. *Donne and the Politics of Conscience in Early Modern England.* Lieden: E. J. Brill, 1995.

Bruce, J., ed. *Annals of the first four years of the reign of Queen Elizabeth.* London: Publications of the Camden Society VII, 1840.

Bryant, Joseph Allen, Jr. "*Catiline* and the Nature of Jonson's Tragic Fable." In *Ben Jonson: A Collection of Critical Essays,* ed. Jonas A. Barish, 147–59. Upper Saddle River, N.J.: Prentice Hall, 1963.

Buchanan, George. *De jure regni apud Scotos; or, A dialogue, concerning the due priviledge of government in the kingdom of Scotland.* 1579.

Burgess, Glen. *Absolute Monarchy and the Stuart Constitution.* New Haven: Yale University Press, 1996.

——. *The Politics of the Ancient Constitution.* University Park: Pennsylvania State University Press, 1992.

Burns, J. H. "Scholasticism: Survival and Revival." In *The Cambridge History of Political Thought, 1450–1700,* ed. J. H. Burns, with the assistance of Mark Goldie, 132–55. Cambridge: Cambridge University Press, 1991.

Burns, J. H., with the assistance of Mark Goldie, eds. *The Cambridge History of Political Thought, 1450–1700.* Cambridge: Cambridge University Press, 1991.

Burt, Richard, ed. *The Administration of Aesthetics: Censorship, Political Criticism, and the Public Sphere.* Minneapolis: University of Minnesota Press, 1994.

———. *Licensed by Authority: Ben Jonson and the Discourses of Censorship*. Ithaca, N.Y.: Cornell University Press, 1993.

Calendar of Letters and Papers, Foreign and Domestic, Henry VIII. Ed. S. Brewer, J. Gairdner, and R. H. Brodie. London: Her Majesty's Stationary Office, 1862–1932.

Calendar of State Papers, Domestic series, of the reign of Elizabeth. Ed. R. Lemon and M. A. E. Lemon. London: Her Majesty's Stationary Office, 1865–70.

Calendar of State Papers, relating to Venice. Ed. Horatio F. Brown. London: Her Majesty's Stationary Office, 1900.

Calhoun, Craig, ed. *Habermas and the Public Sphere*. Cambridge, Mass.: MIT Press, 1992.

Camden, William. *The History of the Most Renowned and Victorious Princess Elizabeth, Late Queen of England*. 4th ed. London, 1688.

Caraman, Philip. *Henry Garnet 1555–1606 and the Gunpowder Plot*. London: Longmans, 1964.

Carey, John. *John Donne: Life, Mind and Art*. London: Faber and Faber, 1990.

Cavanagh, Dermot. *Language and Politics in the Sixteenth-Century History Play*. New York: Palgrave / Macmillan, 2003.

———. "The Language of Treason in *Richard II*." In *Shakespeare Studies* 27, ed. Leeds Barroll. London: Associated University Presses, 1999.

[Cecil, Robert]. "An Answere to Certaine Scandalous Papers, scattered abroad under colour of a Catholicke Admonition." London: Robert Barker, 1606.

Chapman, George. *Seven Bookes of the Iliades of Homer*. London: John Windet, 1598.

Cicero. *De Officiis*. Trans. Walter Miller. Loeb Classical Library. Cambridge, Mass.: Harvard University Press, 1913.

———. *Orations*. Trans. C. Macdonald. Loeb Classical Library. Cambridge, Mass.: Harvard University Press, 2001 [1977].

———. *Orations*. Trans. C. D. Yonge. Vol. 3. London: Bell and Daldy, 1872.

———. *On the Laws*. Trans. C. D. Yonge. Bohn's Classical Library. London: Bell and Daldy, 1868.

Clancy, Thomas H. *Papist Pamphleteers: The Allen-Persons Party and the Political Thought of the Counter-Reformation in England, 1572–1615*. Chicago: Loyola University Press, 1964.

Clare, Janet. *Art Made Tongue-Tied by Authority: Elizabethan and Jacobean Dramatic Censorship*. 2nd ed. Manchester, U.K.: Manchester University Press, 1999.

———. "The Censorship of the Deposition Scene in *Richard II*." *Review of English Studies*, n.s., 41 (February 1990): 89–94.

Clegg, Cyndia Susan, ed. *A Peaceable and prosperous regiment of blessed Queen Elizabeth: A facsimile from Holinshed's Chronicles (1587)*. San Marino, Calif.: Huntington Library Press, 2005.

———. "Archival Poetics and the Politics of Literature: Essex and Hayward Revisited." *Studies in the Literary Imagination* 32.1 (spring 1999): 115–32.

——. "Censorship and the Problems with History in Shakespeare's England." In *A Companion to Shakespeare's Works*. Volume 2, *The Histories,* ed. Richard Dutton and Jean E. Howard, 48–69. London: Blackwell, 2003.

——. *Press Censorship in Elizabethan England.* Cambridge: Cambridge University Press, 1997.

——. "*Richard II* and Elizabethan Press Censorship." *Shakespeare Quarterly* 48 (1997): 432–48.

Cobbett's Complete Collection of State Trials and Proceedings for High Treason and Other Crimes and Misdemeanors from the Earliest Period to the Present Time. Ed. John Cobbett and William Howell. 21 vols. Vol. 1 (1163–1600), Vol. 2 (1603–27), and Vol. 3 (1627–40). London: T. C. Hansard, 1809.

Coddon, Karin S. "'Suche Strange Desygns': Madness, Subjectivity, and Treason in *Hamlet* and Elizabethan Culture." In *Case Studies in Contemporary Literature: Hamlet,* ed. Susanne L. Wofford, 380–402. Boston: Bedford Books of St. Martin's Press, 1994.

——. "'Unreal Mockery': Unreason and the Problem of Spectacle in *Macbeth.*" *ELH* 56 (1989): 485–501.

"The Copy of a Letter to Mr. Antony Bacon concerning reports of the Earl of Essex's Execution." BL Mss. Add. 40838.

Coursen, H. R. *The Leasing Out of England: Shakespeare's Second Henriad.* Washington, D.C.: University Press of America, 1982.

Coward, Rosalind, and John Ellis. *Language and Materialism.* New York: Routledge, 1977.

Cowell, F. R. *Cicero and the Roman Republic.* London: Penguin Books, 1948.

Cowell, John. *The Interpreter: or book containing the signification of words.* Cambridge, 1607.

Cunningham, Karen. *Imaginary Betrayals: Subjectivity and the Discourses of Treason in Early Modern England.* Philadelphia: University of Pennsylvania Press, 2002.

Daly, James. "The Idea of Absolute Monarchy." *Historical Journal* 21.2 (1978): 227–50.

De Luna, Barbara N. *Jonson's Romish Plot: A Study of "Catiline" and Its Historical Context.* Oxford: Clarendon, 1967.

Dean, Leonard F. "Sir Francis Bacon's Theory of Civil History-Writing." *ELH* 8.3 (1941): 161–83.

[Devereux, Robert, the second Earl of Essex]. "A.B. to the Reader." In *The Ende of Nero and Beginning of Galba, and Fower Bookes of the Histories of Cornelius Tacitus.* Trans. Henry Savile. 2nd ed. London: Arn. Hatfield, 1598.

——. "Copy of a letter written by the Earl of Essex to the Earl of Southampton, March 1600." BL Add. 40838.

——. "Letter from the Earl of Essex to the Earl of Rutland." Undated. BL Mss. RP 6340 (iv).

Devereux, Walter Bouchier. *Lives and Letters of the Devereux, Earls of Essex, 1540–1646.* Vol. 1. London: John Murray, 1853.

Dickens, A. G. *The English Reformation.* 2nd ed. University Park: Pennsylvania State University Press, 1989 [1964].

Dictionary of Anonymous and Pseudonymous Publications in the English Language. Ed. John Horden, Samuel Halkett, and John Laing. 3rd ed. New York: Longman, 1980.

"A Discourse of the Maner of the Discovery of this late intended treason." London: Robert Barker, 1605.

Dolan, Frances E. *Dangerous Familiars: Representations of Domestic Crime in England, 1550–1700.* Ithaca, N.Y.: Cornell University Press, 1994.

———. "'Gentlemen, I Have One Thing More to Say': Women on Scaffolds in England, 1563–1680." *Modern Philology* 92.2 (November 1994): 157–79.

———. *Whores of Babylon: Catholicism, Gender, and Seventeenth-Century Print Culture.* Ithaca, N.Y.: Cornell University Press, 1999.

Doleman, R. [Robert Persons]. *A Conference about the Next Succession to the Crown of England* (1594).

Donne, John. *Life and Letters of John Donne.* Ed. Edmund Gosse. London: William Heinemann, 1899.

———. *Pseudo-Martyr, wherein out of Certain Propositions and Gradations, this Conclusion is evicted, that those which are of the Romane Religion in this Kingdome may and ought to take the Oath of Allegiance.* London, 1610. Ed. Anthony Raspa. Montreal: McGill-Queen's University Press, 1993.

———. *The Complete English Poems of John Donne.* Ed. C. A. Patrides. London: Everyman, 1985.

Dowling, Margaret. "Sir John Hayward's Troubles over His *Life of Henry IV.*" *The Library,* 4th ser., 9 (1931): 212–24.

Du Cann, C. G. L. *English Treason Trials.* London: Frederick Muller, 1964.

Du Moulin, Pierre. Minister in the Church of Paris. "The Accomplishment of the Prophecies; or, the Third Booke in defense of the Catholicke faith . . . Against the allegations of R. Bellarmine, F. N. Coëffeteau and other Doctors of the Romish Church." Translated from the French by J. Heath, Fellow of New College, Oxford University. Oxford: Joseph Barnes, 1613.

Dubrow, Heather. *Shakespeare and Domestic Loss.* Cambridge: Cambridge University Press, 1999.

Durst, Paul. *Intended Treason: What Really Happened in the Gunpowder Plot.* London: W. H. Allen, 1970.

Dutton, Richard. *Ben Jonson: To the First Folio.* Cambridge: Cambridge University Press, 1983.

———. *Licensing, Censorship, and Authority in Early Modern England: Buggeswords.* London: Palgrave / Macmillan, 2001.

———. "Buggeswords: Samuel Harsnett and the Licensing, Suppression and Afterlife of Dr. John Hayward's *The First Part of the Life and Reign of King Henry IV.*" *Criticism* 35.3 (summer 1993): 305–39.

Dykstal, Timothy. *The Luxury of Skepticism: Politics, Philosophy, and Dialogue in the English Public Sphere, 1660–1740.* Charlottesville: University Press of Virginia, 2001.

Elizabeth I. *Autograph Compositions and Foreign Language Originals.* Ed. Janel Mueller and Leah S. Marcus. Chicago: University of Chicago Press, 2003.

——. *Collected Works.* Ed. Leah S. Marcus, Janel Mueller, and Mary Beth Rose. Chicago: University of Chicago Press, 2000.

Elton, G. R. *Policy and Police: The Enforcement of the Reformation in the Age of Thomas Cromwell.* Cambridge: Cambridge University Press, 1972.

——. *Reform and Reformation: England, 1509–1558.* Cambridge, Mass.: Harvard University Press, 1977.

Engle, Lars. *Shakespearean Pragmatism: Market of His Time.* Chicago: University of Chicago Press, 1993.

"An Exposition of Certain Difficult and obscure words and terms of the Lawes of this Realme." London, 1592.

Faulkner, Thomas. *An Historical and Topographical Description of Chelsea and Its Environs.* Vol. 2 of 2 vols. Chelsea: T. Faulkner, 1829.

Figgis, J. Neville. *The Theory of the Divine Right of Kings.* Cambridge: Cambridge University Press, 1896.

Forker, Charles R. "'Edward II' and Its Shakespearean Relatives." In *Shakespeare's English Histories: A Quest for Form and Genre,* ed. John W. Velz. Binghamton, N.Y.: Medieval and Renaissance Texts and Studies, 1996.

——, ed. *King Richard II* by William Shakespeare. The Arden Shakespeare. London: Thompson Learning, 2002.

Fortescue, John. *A Learned Commendation of the Politique Lawes of Englande [De Laudibus Legum Angliae].* Trans. Robert Mulcaster. London: Richarde Tottell, 1573.

——. *On the Laws and Governance of England.* Ed. Shelley Lockwood. Cambridge: Cambridge University Press, 1997.

Foucault, Michel. *Discipline and Punish: The Birth of the Prison.* Trans. Alan Sheridan. New York: Pantheon, 1995 [1978].

——. *The History of Sexuality.* Vol. 1, *An Introduction.* Trans. Robert Hurley. New York: Random House, 1980.

Franklin, Julian H. "Sovereignty and the Mixed Constitution: Bodin and His Critics." In *The Cambridge History of Political Thought, 1450–1700,* ed. J. H. Burns, with the assistance of Mark Goldie, 298–328. Cambridge: Cambridge University Press, 1991.

Fraser, Antonia. *The Gunpowder Plot: Terror and Faith in 1605.* London: Mandarin, 1997.

G. M. [Gervaise Markham]. "Honour in His Perfection." London, 1624.

Gallagher, Lowell. *Medusa's Gaze: Casuistry and Conscience in the Renaissance.* Stanford: Stanford University Press, 1991.

Garber, Marjorie. *Shakespeare's Ghost Writers: Literature as Uncanny Causality.* Reprint. New York: Methuen, 1987.

Garnet, Henry. *A Treatise of Equivocation.* Ed. David Jardine. London: Longman, Brown, Green, and Longmans, 1851.

Gentili, Alberico. *De Jure Belli commentatio prima.* London: John Wolfe, 1588.

Gerard, John. *Narrative of the Gunpowder Plot.* Ed. John Morris London: Longmans and Green, 1871.

Gillespie, James L., ed. *The Age of Richard II.* New York: St. Martin's, 1997.

Goldberg, Jonathan. *James I and the Politics of Literature: Jonson, Shakespeare, Donne, and Their Contemporaries.* Stanford: Stanford University Press, 1989 [1983].

——. "*Macbeth* and Source." In *Shakespeare Reproduced: The Text in History and Ideology,* ed. Jean E. Howard and Marion F. O'Connor, 242–64. London: Methuen, 1987.

Goldberg, S. L. "Sir John Hayward, 'Politic' Historian." *Review of English Studies,* n.s., 6.23 (1955): 233–44.

Green, Richard Firth. *A Crisis of Truth: Literature and Law in Richardian England.* Philadelphia: University of Pennsylvania Press, 2002.

Greenberg, Janelle Renfrow. *Radical Face of the Ancient Constitution: St. Edward's 'Laws' in Early Modern Political Thought.* Cambridge: Cambridge University Press, 2001.

Greenblatt, Stephen. "Shakespeare Bewitched." In *New Historical Literary Study: Essays on Reproducing Texts, Representing History,* ed. Jeffrey N. Cox and Larry J. Reynolds. Princeton, N.J.: Princeton University Press, 1993.

Greer, C. A. "The Deposition Scene of *Richard II.*" *Notes and Queries* (November 1952): 492–93.

——. "More about the Deposition Scene of *Richard II.*" *Notes and Queries* (February 1953): 49–50.

Greg, W. W. "Samuel Harsnett and Hayward's *Henry IV.*" *The Library,* 5th ser., 9.1 (March 1956): 1–10.

Grenewey, Richard, trans. *The Annales of Cornelius Tacitus.* London, 1598.

Guy, John. "The 'Imperial Crown' and the Liberty of the Subject: The English Constitution from Magna Carta to the Bill of Rights." In *Court, Country and Culture: Essays on Early Modern British History in Honor of Perez Zagorin,* ed. B. Kunze and D. Brautigam. Rochester, N.Y.: University of Rochester Press, 1992.

——, ed. *The Reign of Elizabeth.* Cambridge: Cambridge University Press, 1995.

——. *Tudor England.* Oxford: Oxford University Press, 1988.

Habermas, Jürgen. *The Structural Transformation of the Public Sphere: An Inquiry into a Category of Bourgeois Society.* Trans. Thomas Burger, with the assistance of Frederick Lawrence. London: Polity, 1989.

Halask, Alexandra. *The Marketplace of Print: Pamphlets and the Public Sphere in Early Modern England.* Cambridge: Cambridge University Press, 1999.

Hale, Sir Matthew. *Pleas of the Crown; or, A Methodical Summary of the Principal Matters Relating to That Subject.* London, 1678.

Hall, Edward. *Chronicle Containing the Histories of England (1548–1550).* London: J. Johnson, 1809.

Hamilton, Donna B. "The State of the Law in *Richard II.*" *Shakespeare Quarterly* 34 (1983): 5–17.

Hammer, Paul E. J. "The Earl of Essex, Fulke Greville, and the Employment of Scholars." *Studies in Philology* 91 (1994): 167–80.

——. "Patronage at Court, Faction and the Earl of Essex." In *The Reign of Elizabeth*, ed. John Guy, 65–86. Cambridge: Cambridge University Press, 1995.

——. *The Polarisation of Elizabethan Politics: The Political Career of Robert Devereux, 2nd Earl of Essex, 1585–1597.* Cambridge: Cambridge University Press, 1999.

——. "Upstaging the Queen: The Earl of Essex, Francis Bacon, and the Accession Day Celebrations of 1595." In *The Politics of the Stuart Court Masque,* ed. David Bevington and Peter Holbrook, 41–66. Cambridge: Cambridge University Press, 1998.

——. "The Uses of Scholarship: The Secretariat of Robert Devereux, Second Earl of Essex, c. 1585–1601." *English Historical Review* (February 1994): 26–51.

Harleian Miscellany. Ed. William Oldys. Vol. 3. London, 1808–13.

Harris, Duncan. "Tombs, Guidebooks and Shakespearean Drama: Death in the Renaissance." *Mosaic* 15.1 (1982): 23.

Haynes, Alan. *The Gunpowder Plot: Faith in Rebellion.* Dover: Alan Sutton, 1994.

Hayward, John. "An Answer to a Conference concerning Succession." London, 1603. Facsimile edition: *The English Experience.* Vol. 741. Amsterdam: Walter Jonson, 1975.

——. *The First and Second Parts of the Life and Raigne of King Henrie IIII.* Ed. J. J. Manning. London: Royal Historical Society, 1991.

——. *The Lives of the III Normans, Kings of England.* London, 1613.

Heffner, R. "Shakespeare, Hayward and Essex." *PMLA* 45 (1930): 754–80.

Helgerson, Richard. *Forms of Nationhood: The Elizabethan Writing of England.* Chicago: University of Chicago Press, 1992.

Heninger, S. K., Jr. "The Sun-King Analogy in *Richard II.*" *Shakespeare Quarterly* 11 (1960): 324.

Henshall, Nicholas. *The Myth of Absolutism: Change and Continuity in Early Modern European Monarchy.* London: Longman, 1992.

Highley, Christopher. *Shakespeare, Spenser, and the Crisis in Ireland.* Cambridge: Cambridge University Press, 1997.

Hirst, Derek. *Authority and Conflict: England, 1603–1658.* Cambridge, Mass.: Harvard University Press, 1986.

"A History of the Gunpowder Treason, collected from Approved Authors as well Popish as Protestant." London: Richard Chiswel, 1678.

Hobbes, Thomas. *Leviathan.* Oxford: Oxford University Press, 1996.

Holderness, Graham. "'A Woman's War': A Feminist Reading of *Richard II.*" In *Shakespeare Left and Right,* ed. Ivo Kamps, 167–83. New York: Routledge, 1991.

Holinshed, Raphael. *Chronicles on England, Scotland and Ireland.* London, 1587.

——. *A Peaceable and prosperous regiment of blessed Queen Elizabeth: A facsimile from Holinshed's Chronicles (1587).* Ed. Cyndia Susan Clegg. San Marino, Calif.: Huntington Library Press, 2005.

Holmes, P. J. *Resistance and Compromise: The Political Thought of the Elizabethan Catholics.* Cambridge: Cambridge University Press, 1982.

Hoppe, Harry R. "John Wolfe, Printer and Publisher, 1579–1601." *The Library,* 4th ser., 14 (1933): 241–89.

Howard, Jean E. *The Stage and Social Struggle in Early Modern England.* London: Routledge, 1994.

Huntley, Frank L. "*Macbeth* and the Background of Jesuitical Equivocation." *PMLA* 79 (1964): 390–400.

Hussain, Nasser. *The Jurisprudence of Emergency: Colonialism and the Rule of Law.* Ann Arbor: University of Michigan Press, 2003.

Jacobean Journal. Ed. G. B. Harrison. London: George Routledge, 1941.

James VI and I. *His Majesties speach in this last session of Parliament, as neere his very words as could be gathered at the instant. Together with a discourse of the maner of the discovery of this late intended Treason, joyned with the Examination of some of the prisoners.* London: Robert Barker, 1605.

——. *The King Majesties Speach (March 21, 1609).* London: Robert Barker, 1609.

——. *The Political Works of James I.* Ed. C. H. McIlwain. New York: Russell and Russell, 1965.

——. *Political Writings.* Ed. Johann P. Sommerville. Cambridge Texts in the History of Political Thought. Cambridge: Cambridge University Press, 1994.

James, Mervyn. *Society, Politics and Culture: Studies in Early Modern England.* Cambridge: Cambridge University Press, 1986.

Jardine, David. *A Narrative of the Gunpowder Plot.* London: John Murray, 1857.

Jardine, Lisa, and Alan Stewart. *Hostage to Fortune: The Troubled Life of Francis Bacon.* London: Victor Gollancz, 1998.

Jonson, Ben. *Ben Jonson: Works.* Ed. C. H. Hereford and Percy Simpson. 11 vols. Oxford: Clarendon, 1925–52.

——. *Catiline.* Ed. W. F. Bolton and Jane F. Gardner. Regents Renaissance Drama series. London: Edward Arnold, 1972.

——. *The Complete Poems.* Ed. George Parfitt. London: Penguin Books, 1996 [1975].

——. *Sejanus: His Fall.* Manchester, U.K.: Manchester University Press, 1990.

Jordan, Constance. *Shakespeare's Monarchies: Ruler and Subject in the Romances.* Ithaca, N.Y.: Cornell University Press, 1997.

Journals of the House of Commons. Vol. 1 (November 8, 1547–March 2, 1628). Repr. by order of the House of Commons, 1803.

Journals of the House of Lords. Vol. 2 (1578–1614). London: Her Majesty's Stationary Office, n.d.

Justinian. *Institutes.* Trans. and intro. Peter Kirks and Grant McLeod. Latin text edited by Paul Krueger. Ithaca, N.Y.: Cornell University Press, 1987.

Kahn, Coppélia. *Man's Estate: Masculine Identity in Shakespeare.* Berkeley: University of California Press, 1981.

Kahn, Victoria. "Hamlet or Hecuba: Carl Schmitt's Decision." *Representations* 83 (summer 2003): 67–96.

Kahn, Victoria, and Lorna Hutson, eds. *Rhetoric and Law in Early Modern Europe*. New Haven: Yale University Press, 2001.

Kantorowicz, Ernst H. *The King's Two Bodies: A Study in Mediaeval Political Theology*. Princeton, N.J.: Princeton University Press, 1957.

Kastan, David Scott. *Shakespeare after Theory*. London: Routledge, 1999.

——. *Shakespeare and the Shapes of Time*. London: Macmillan, 1982.

Kay, W. David. *Ben Jonson: A Literary Life*. London: Macmillan, 1995.

Kernan, Alvin. *Shakespeare, the King's Playwright: Theater in the Stuart Court, 1603–1613*. New Haven: Yale University Press, 1995.

Kingdon, Robert M. "Calvinism and Resistance Theory, 1550–1580." In *The Cambridge History of Political Thought, 1450–1700*, ed. J. H. Burns, with the assistance of Mark Goldie, 193–218. Cambridge: Cambridge University Press, 1991.

Kinney, Arthur F. "Essex and Shakespeare versus Hayward." *Shakespeare Quarterly* 44. 4 (1993): 464–66.

——. "Scottish History, the Union of the Crowns, and the Issue of Right Rule: The Case of Shakespeare's *Macbeth*." In *Renaissance Culture in Context*, ed. Jean R. Brink and William F. Gentrup. Aldershot: Scolar, 1993.

Kocher, Paul H. "Francis Bacon and the Science of Jurisprudence." *Journal of the History of Ideas* 18 (1957): 3–26. Reprinted in *Essential Articles for the Study of Francis Bacon*, ed. Brian Vickers, 167–94. London: Sidgwick and Jackson, 1968.

Lake, Peter, with Michael Questier. *The Anti-Christ's Lewd Hat: Protestants, Papists and Players in Post-Reformation England*. New Haven: Yale University Press, 2002.

Lambard, William. *Archion; or, Commentary upon the High Courts of Justice in England*. London, 1635 [1591].

Landes, Joan B. "The Public and the Private Sphere: A Feminist Reconsideration." In *Feminists Read Habermas: Gendering the Subject of Discourse*, ed. Johanna Meehan, 91–116. New York: Routledge, 1995.

Laqueur, Thomas W. "Crowns, Carnival and the State in English Executions, 1604–1868." In *The First Modern Society: Essays in English History in Honour of Lawrence Stone*, ed. A. L. Beier, David Cannadine, and James M. Rosenheim, 305–55. Cambridge: Cambridge University Press, 1989.

Larkin, James F., and Paul L. Hughes, eds. *Stuart Royal Proclamations*. 2 vols. Oxford: Clarendon, 1973–80.

Leigh, William. "Great Britaines, great deliverance, from the great danger of the popish powder." London, 1606.

Les Reportes del Cases in Camera Stellata, 1593–1609. From the original manuscript of John Hawarde, ed. William Paley Baildon. Privately printed, 1894.

Levack, Brian P. *The Civil Lawyers in England, 1603–1641: A Political Study*. Oxford: Clarendon, 1973.

——. "Law and Ideology: The Civil Law and Theories of Absolutism in Elizabethan and Jacobean England." In *The Historical Renaissance*, ed. Heather Dubrow and Richard Strier, 220–41. Chicago: University of Chicago Press, 1988.

Levine, Nina. "Extending Credit in the Henry IV Plays." *Shakespeare Quarterly* 51.4 (winter 2000): 403–31.

Levy, F. J. "Francis Bacon and the Style of Politics." In *Renaissance Historicism: Selections from ELR*, ed. Arthur F. Kinney and Dan S. Collins. Amherst: University of Massachusetts Press, 1987.

———. "Hayward, Daniel, and the Beginnings of Politic History in England." *Huntington Library Quarterly* (winter 1987): 1–37.

———. *Tudor Historical Thought.* San Marino, Calif.: Huntington Library, 1967.

Lezra, Jacques. *Unspeakable Subjects: The Genealogy of the Event in Early Modern Europe.* Stanford: Stanford University Press, 1997.

Liebler, Naomi Conn. "The Mockery King of Snow: *Richard II* and the Sacrifice of Ritual." In *True Rites and Maimed Rites: Ritual and Anti-Ritual in Shakespeare and His Age*, ed. Linda Woodbridge and Edward Berry, 220–39. Urbana: University of Illinois Press, 1992.

Lockyer, Roger. *The Early Stuarts: A Political History of England, 1603–42.* London: Longman, 1989.

Lodge, E. C., and G. A. Thornton. *English Constitutional Documents, 1307–1485.* Cambridge: Cambridge University Press, 1935.

Loomie, Albert Joseph. *Guy Fawkes in Spain: The "Spanish Treason" in Spanish Documents.* London: Bulletin of the Institute of Historical Research. Special Supplement No. 9, November 1971.

Luce, Dorey, T. J. Woodman, and A. J. Woodman, eds. *Tacitus and the Tacitean Tradition.* Princeton, N.J.: Princeton University Press, 1993.

Lukacher, Ned. *Daemonic Figures: Shakespeare and the Question of Conscience.* Ithaca, N.Y.: Cornell University Press, 1994.

Lyte, H. C. Maxwell. *A History of Eton College, 1440–1875.* London, 1877.

MacCaffrey, Wallace. *Elizabeth I.* London: Edward Arnold, 1993.

———. *Elizabeth I: War and Politics, 1588–1603.* Princeton, N.J.: Princeton University Press, 1992.

MacDonald, Ronald R. "Uneasy Lies: Language and History in Shakespeare's Lancastrian Tetralogy." *Shakespeare Quarterly* 35 (1984): 22–39.

MacKenzie, Clayton G. "Paradise and Paradise Lost in *Richard II*." *Shakespeare Quarterly* 37 (1986): 318–39.

Mallin, Eric S. *Inscribing the Time: Shakespeare and the End of Elizabethan England.* Berkeley: University of California Press, 1995.

Manning, J. J., ed. *John Hayward: The First and Second Parts of the Life and Raigne of King Henrie IIII.* London: Royal Historical Society, 1991.

Marotti, Arthur. *John Donne, Coterie Poet.* Madison: University of Wisconsin Press, 1986.

Marshburn, Joseph H., and Alan R. Velie. *Blood and Knavery: A Collection of English Renaissance Pamphlets and Ballads of Crime and Sin.* Rutherford, N.J.: Fairleigh Dickinson University Press, 1973.

Maus, Katharine Eisaman. *Ben Jonson and the Roman Frame of Mind.* Princeton, N.J.: Princeton University Press, 1984.

———. "Introduction to *Henry V*." *The Norton Shakespeare.* Ed. Stephen Greenblatt, Walter Cohen, Jean E. Howard, and Katharine Eisaman Maus. New York: W. W. Norton, 1997.

———. *Inwardness and Theater in the English Renaissance.* Chicago: University of Chicago Press, 1995.

McCoy, Richard C. "'A Dangerous Image': The Earl of Essex and Elizabethan Chivalry." *Journal of Medieval and Renaissance Studies* 13.2 (1983): 313–29.

McIlwain, C. H. *Constitutionalism Ancient and Modern.* Ithaca, N.Y.: Cornell University Press, 1940.

———, ed. *The Political Works of James I.* New York: Russell and Russell, 1965.

Mellor, Ronald. *Tacitus.* New York: Routledge, 1993.

Mendle, Michael. "Parliamentary Sovereignty: A Very English Absolutism." In *Political Discourse in Early Modern Britain,* ed. Nicholas Phillipson and Quentin Skinner, 97–119. Cambridge: Cambridge University Press, 1993.

Meyer, Richard. *Outlaw Representations: Censorship and Homosexuality in Twentieth-Century American Art.* Oxford: Oxford University Press, 2002.

Miller, J. Hillis. *Speech Acts in Literature.* Stanford: Stanford University Press, 2001.

Miller, Peter N. *Defining the Common Good: Empire, Religion, and Philosophy in Eighteenth-Century Britain.* Cambridge: Cambridge University Press, 1994.

Milton, John. *Complete Prose Works.* Ed. Merritt Hughes. New Haven: Yale University Press, 1953–82.

Milward, Peter. *Religious Controversies of the Elizabethan Age: A Survey of Printed Sources.* Lincoln: University of Nebraska Press, 1977.

The Mirror for Magistrates. Ed. Lily B. Campbell. Cambridge: Cambridge University Press, 1938.

Mitchell, T. N. *Cicero: The Ascending Years.* New Haven: Yale University Press, 1979.

———. *Cicero: The Senior Statesman.* New Haven: Yale University Press, 1991.

Muir, Kenneth. "Image and Symbol in *Macbeth.*" *Shakespeare Survey* 19 (1966): 45–54.

———, ed. *Macbeth* by William Shakespeare. The Arden Shakespeare. London: Methuen, 1984 [1964].

Mullaney, Stephen. "Lying Like Truth: Riddle, Representation, and Treason in Renaissance England." *ELH* 47 (1980): 32–47. Repr. in *Shakespeare's Late Tragedies,* ed. Susanne L. Wofford, 61–73. Upper Saddle River, N.J.: Prentice Hall, 1996.

———. *The Place of the Stage: License, Play and Power in Renaissance England.* Ann Arbor: University of Michigan Press, 1995 [1988].

N. D. [Father Robert Persons]. "A Temperate Ward-word, to the turbulant and seditious Watch-Word of Sir Francis Hastings knight, who indevoreth to slaunder the whole Catholique cause." Imprinted with licence, 1599.

Nicholls, Mark. *Investigating Gunpowder Plot.* Manchester, U.K.: Manchester University Press, 1991.

Nichols, John. *The Progresses and Public Processions of Queen Elizabeth.* Vol. 3. London: Nichols, 1823 [1783].

Nora, Pierre. "The Return of the Event." In *Histories: French Constructions of the Past,* ed. Jacques Revel and Lynn Hunt, trans. Arthur Goldhammer. New York: New Press, 1996.

Norbrook, David. "'A Liberal Tongue': Language and Rebellion in *Richard II.*" In *Shakespeare's Universe: Renaissance Ideas and Conventions: Essays in Honor of W. R. Elton,* ed. John M. Mucciolo, 37–51. Brookfield, Vt.: Scolar, 1996.

———. "*Macbeth* and the Politics of Historiography." In *Politics of Discourse: The Literature and History of Seventeenth-Century England,* ed. Kevin Sharpe and Steven N. Zwicker, 78–116. Berkeley: University of California Press, 1987.

———. "The Monarchy of Wit and the Republic of Letters: Donne's Politics." In *Soliciting Interpretation: Literary Theory and Seventeenth-Century English Poetry,* ed. Elizabeth D. Harvey and Katharine Eisaman Maus, 3–36. Chicago: University of Chicago Press, 1990.

———. *Writing the English Republic: Poetry, Rhetoric and Politics, 1627–1660.* Cambridge: Cambridge University Press, 1999.

Oakley, Francis. "Jacobean Political Theology: The Absolute and Ordinary Powers of the King." *Journal of the History of Ideas* 29.3 (1968): 323–46.

O'Conner, Sister Mary Catharine. *The Art of Dying Well: The Development of the Ars Moriendi.* New York: Columbia University Press, 1942.

Orgel, Stephen. "Making Greatness Familiar." In *The Power of Forms in the English Renaissance,* ed. Stephen Greenblatt. Norman, Okla.: Pilgrim Books, 1982.

Omerod. "The Picture of a Papist, or a relation of the damnable heresies, detestable qualities, and diabolicall practices of sundry hereticks in former ages, and of the papists in this age." London: Nathaniel Fosbrooke, 1606.

Orr, D. Alan. *Treason and the State: Law, Politics and Ideology in the English Civil War.* Cambridge: Cambridge University Press, 2002.

Oxford Classical Dictionary. Ed. Simon Hornblower and Antony Spawforth. 3rd ed. Oxford: Oxford University Press, 1999.

Parkinson, C. Northcote. *Gunpowder, Treason and Plot.* New York: St. Martin's, 1976.

Parliamentary Debates 1610. Ed. Samuel Rawson Gardiner. London: Camden Society, 1862.

The Parliamentary History of England from the Earliest Period to the Year 1803. Vol. 1 (1066–1626). London, 1806.

Patterson, Annabel. *Censorship and Interpretation: The Conditions of Writing and Reading in Early Modern Europe.* Madison: University of Wisconsin, 1984.

———. "Quod Oportet Versus Quod Convenit: John Donne, Kingsman?" In *Critical Essays on John Donne,* ed. Arthur Marotti. New York: G. K. Hall, 1994. 141–79.

———. *Reading Holinshed's Chronicles.* Chicago: University of Chicago Press, 1994.

———. "'Roman Cast Similitude:' Ben Jonson and the English Use of Roman History." In *Rome in the Renaissance,* ed. Paul A. Ramsey, 381–94. Binghamton, N.Y.: Medieval and Renaissance Texts and Studies, 1982.

Paul, Henry. *The Royal Play of Macbeth.* New York: Macmillan, 1950.

Peck, Linda Levy. *The Mental World of the Jacobean Court.* Cambridge: Cambridge University Press, 1991.

Peltonen, Markku. *Classical Humanism and Republicanism in English Political Thought, 1570–1640.* Cambridge: Cambridge University Press, 1995.

Pepys, Samuel. *The Diary of Samuel Pepys.* Ed. Robert Latham and William Matthews. Vol. 9 (1668–69). London, 1970–83.

[Persons, Robert]. *A Conference about the Next Succession to the Crown of England.* 1594.

——. "A Discussion of the Answer of M. William Barlow to the book entitled 'Judgement of a Catholic Englishman living in banishment for his Religion.'" 1612.

——. "A Letter by Father Robert Persons on the oath of allegiance." BL Mss. Add. 14030.

——. "A Letter to Father Henry Garnet." BL Mss. Add. 14 / 140.

Pocock, J. G. A. *The Ancient Constitution and the Feudal Law: A Study of English Historical Thought in the Seventeenth Century.* Cambridge: Cambridge University Press, 1957.

Ponet, John. "A Short Treatise of Politic Power." 1556.

Privy Council Registers. Public Record Office.

Puttenham, George. *The Arte of English Poesie.* London, 1589.

Pye, Christopher. *The Regal Phantasm: Shakespeare and the Politics of Spectacle.* New York: Routledge, 1990.

Questier, M. C. *Conversion, Politics and Religion in England, 1580–1625.* Cambridge: Cambridge University Press, 1996.

——. "Loyalty, Religion and State Power in Early Modern England: English Romanism and the Jacobean Oath of Allegiance." *Historical Journal* 40 (June 1996): 311–29.

Rackin, Phyllis. *Stages of History: Shakespeare's English Chronicles.* Ithaca, N.Y.: Cornell University Press, 1990.

Raspa, Anthony, ed. *John Donne: Pseudo-Martyr.* Montreal: McGill-Queen's University Press, 1993.

——. "Time, History and Typology in John Donne's *Pseudo-Martyr.*" *Renaissance and Reformation* 11.1 (1987): 175–83.

Rastell, John. "A Collection in English, of the Statutes now in force, continued from the beginning of the Magna Charta . . . until the end of the session of Parliament holden in the 23rd yeere of the Reigne of our gratious Queen Elizabeth." London: Christopher Barker, printer to the Queenes Majestie, 1583.

Raymond, Joad. *The Invention of the Newspaper: English Newsbooks, 1641–49.* Oxford: Oxford University Press, 1996.

——, ed. *News, Newspapers, and Society in Early Modern Britain.* Portland, Ore.: Frank Cass, 1999.

——. *Pamphlets and Pamphleteering in Early Modern Britain.* Cambridge: Cambridge University Press, 2003.

Rezneck, Samuel. "Constructive Treason by Words in the Fifteenth Century." *American Historical Review* 33.3 (April 1928): 544–52.

———. "The Trial of Treason in Tudor England." In *Essays in History and Political Theory in Honour of C. H. McIlwain*. Ed. Carl Frederick Wittke. 258–88. Cambridge, Mass.: Harvard University Press, 1936.

Richardson, Lisa. "Sir John Hayward and Early Stuart Historiography." Ph.D. dissertation, University of Cambridge, 1999.

Riggs, David. *Ben Jonson: A Life.* Cambridge, Mass.: Harvard University Press, 1989.

Rosenberg, Marvin. *The Masks of Macbeth.* Berkeley: University of California Press, 1978.

Ryan, Clarence J. "The Jacobean Oath of Allegiance and English Lay Catholics." *Catholic Historical Review* 28.2 (1942): 159–83.

Sallust. *The Conspiracy of Catiline.* Trans. Thomas Heywood. London: Constable, 1924.

Salmon, J. H. M. "Catholic Resistance Theory, Ultramonanism and the Royalist Response, 1580–1620." In *Cambridge History of Political Thought, 1450–1700,* ed. J. H. Burns, with the assistance of Mark Goldie, 219–53. Cambridge: Cambridge University Press, 1991.

Sanders, Julie. *Ben Jonson's Theatrical Republics.* London: Macmillan, 1998.

Sanders, Wilbur. *The Dramatist and the Received Idea.* Cambridge: Cambridge University Press, 1968.

Saul, Nigel. *Richard II.* New Haven: Yale University Press, 1997.

Savile, Henry. "Sir H. Savile Advice to the Earl of Rutland." BL Egerton Mss. 2262 (f4r).

———. The Ende of Nero and the Beginning of Galba, and *Fower Bookes of the Histories of Cornelius Tacitus.* London, 1591.

Schellhase, Kenneth C. *Tacitus and Renaissance Political Thought.* Chicago: Chicago University Press, 1976.

Schramm, Percy Ernst. *A History of the English Coronation.* Trans. Leopold G. Wickham Legg. Oxford: Clarendon, 1937.

Scott, Edward John Long, ed. *Letter-booke of Gabriel Harvey.* London: Camden Society, 1884.

Scott, William O. "Landholding, Leasing, and Inheritance in *Richard II.*" *Studies in English Literature, 1500–1900* 42.2 (2002): 275–92.

Searle, John R. *Expression and Meaning: Studies in the Theory of Speech Acts.* Cambridge: Cambridge University Press, 1979.

———. *Speech Acts: An Essay in the Philosophy of Language.* Cambridge: Cambridge University Press, 1969.

Shakespeare, William. *The Norton Shakespeare.* Ed. Stephen Greenblatt, Walter Cohen, Jean E. Howard, and Katharine Eisaman Maus. New York: W. W. Norton, 1997.

———. *Macbeth.* The Arden Shakespeare. Ed. Kenneth Muir. London: Methuen, 1984 [1964].

———. *Richard II.* The Arden Shakespeare. Ed. Charles R. Forker. London: Thomson Learning, 2002.

Sharpe, J. A. "Last Dying Speeches: Religion, Ideology, and Public Execution in Seventeenth-Century England." *Past and Present* 107 (1985): 144–67.

Sharpe, Kevin. "The King's Writ: Authors and Royal Authority in Early Modern England." In *Culture and Politics in Early Stuart England,* ed. Kevin Sharpe and Peter Lake, 117–38. Stanford: Stanford University Press, 1993.

——. *Reading Revolutions: The Politics of Reading in Early Modern England.* New Haven: Yale University Press, 2000.

Shewring, Margaret. *King Richard II.* Manchester: Manchester University Press, 1996.

Shuger, Debora Kuller. *Habits of Thought in the English Renaissance: Religion, Politics, and the Dominant Culture.* Berkeley: University of California Press, 1990.

Sidney, Philip. "The Defence of Poesy." In *Sir Philip Sidney: Selected Prose and Poetry,* ed. Robert Kimbrough, 102–58. Madison: University of Wisconsin Press, 1983.

Siemon, James R. "'Word Itself against the Word': Close Reading after Voloshinov." In *Shakespeare Reread: The Texts in New Contexts,* ed. Russ McDonald, 226–58. Ithaca, N.Y.: Cornell University Press, 1993.

Silverman, Lisa. *Tortured Subjects: Pain, Truth and the Body in Early Modern France.* Chicago: University of Chicago Press, 2001.

Simpson, Evelyn M., ed. *John Donne: Selected Prose.* Oxford: Clarendon, 1967.

——. *A Study of the Prose Works of John Donne.* 2nd ed. Oxford: Clarendon, 1948.

Sinfield, Alan. *Faultlines: Cultural Materialism and the Politics of Dissident Reading.* Berkeley: University of California Press, 1992.

Skinner, Quentin. *The Foundations of Modern Political Thought.* Vol. 1, *The Renaissance.* Vol. 2, *The Age of Reformation.* Cambridge: Cambridge University Press, 1978.

——. *Liberty before Liberalism.* Cambridge: Cambridge University Press, 1998.

Skura, Meredith. "Marlowe's *Edward II*: Penetrating Language in Shakespeare's *Richard II*." In *Shakespeare Survey,* vol. 50, ed. Stanley Wells, 41–56. Cambridge: Cambridge University Press, 1997.

Slights, William W. E. *Ben Jonson and the Art of Secrecy.* Ontario: University of Toronto Press, 1994.

Smith, Lacey Baldwin. "English Treason Trials and Confessions in the Sixteenth Century." *Journal of the History of Ideas* 15 (1954): 471–98.

——. *Treason in Tudor England: Politics and Paranoia.* Princeton, N.J.: Princeton University Press, 1986.

Smith, Nigel. *Literature and Revolution in England, 1640–1660.* New Haven: Yale University Press, 1994.

Smith, Sir Thomas. *De Republica Anglorum.* London, 1583.

Smuts, Malcolm. "Court-Centered Politics and the Uses of Roman Historians, c. 1590–1630." In *Culture and Politics in Early Stuart England,* ed. Kevin Sharpe and Peter Lake, 21–43. Stanford: Stanford University Press, 1993.

Sommerville, Johann P. "Absolutism and Royalism." In *The Cambridge History of Political Thought, 1450–1700,* ed. J. H. Burns, with the assistance of Mark Goldie, 347–73. Cambridge: Cambridge University Press, 1991.

———. "Jacobean Political Thought and the Controversy over the Oath of Allegiance." Ph.D. dissertation, University of Cambridge, 1981.

———. "James I and the Divine Right of Kings: English Politics and Continental Theory." In *The Mental World of the Jacobean Court*, ed. Linda Levy Peck, 55–70. Cambridge: Cambridge University Press, 1991.

———, ed. *King James VI and I: Political Writings*. Cambridge Texts in the History of Political Thought. Cambridge: Cambridge University Press, 1994.

———. *Politics and Ideology in England, 1603–1640*. New York: Longman, 1986.

———. *Royalists and Patriots: Politics and Ideology in England, 1603–1640*. London: Longman, 1999.

Speed, N. *The History of Great Britaine under the conquests of ye Romans, Saxons, Danes and Normans*. Vol. 2. London, 1611.

Spierenburg, Peter. *The Spectacle of Suffering*. Cambridge: Cambridge University Press, 1984.

Stallybrass, Peter. "*Macbeth* and Witchcraft." In *Focus on Macbeth*, ed. John Russell Brown, 189–209. London: Routledge, 1982.

State Papers, Domestic, Elizabeth I. Public Record Office.

State Papers, Domestic, James I. Public Record Office.

Statutes of the Realm. Vols. 1–4. London: G. Eyre and A. Strahan, 1810–19.

Steffen, Lisa. *Defining a British State: Treason and National Identity, 1608–1820*. Basingstoke, U.K.: Palgrave, 2001.

Strier, Richard. "John Donne and the Politics of Devotion." In *Religion, Literature, and Politics in Post-Reformation England, 1540–1688*, ed. Donna B. Hamilton and Richard Strier, 93–114. Cambridge: Cambridge University Press, 1996.

———. "Radical Donne: 'Satire III.'" *ELH* 60.2 (1993): 283–322.

Sutcliffe, Matthew. "An Answer to a certain calumnious letter published by John Throckmorton." London, 1594.

———. "A Brief Reply to a certain odious and scandalous libel." London, 1600.

———. "A New Challenge made to N.D." London, 1600.

Tacitus. *Annales*. Trans. Richard Grenewey. London, 1598.

———. *Histories I–III*. Loeb Classical Library. Trans. Clifford H. Moore. Cambridge, Mass.: Harvard University Press, 1996.

———. *Histories IV–V, Annals I–III*. Loeb Classical Library. Trans. Clifford H. Moore and John Jackson. Cambridge, Mass.: Harvard University Press, 1992.

Tennenhouse, Leonard. *Power on Display: The Politics of Shakespeare's Genres*. New York: Methuen, 1986.

Thomas, Donald, ed. *State Trials: Treason and Libel*. Vol. 1. London: Routledge and Kegan Paul, 1972.

Thornley, Isobel D. "Treason by Words in the Fifteenth Century." *English Historical Review* 32.128 (October 1917): 556–61.

Trevor, Douglas. "John Donne's *Pseudo-Martyr* and the Oath of Allegiance Controversy." *Reformation* 5 (2000): 103–37.

"A True and Perfect Relation of the Whole Proceedings against the late most barbarous Traitors." London: Robert Barker, 1606.

"A True Declaration of the Happy Conversion, Contrition and Christian Preparation of Francis Robinson, Gentleman, who for Counterfeiting the Great Seale of England was Drawen, Hang'd and Quartered at Charing Crosse, on Friday Last, being the Thirteenth Day of November, 1618." London, 1618.

Tuck, Richard. *Philosophy and Government, 1572–1651.* Cambridge: Cambridge University Press, 1993.

Tutino, Stefania. "Notes on Machiavelli and Ignatius Loyola in John Donne's *Ignatius His Conclave* and *Pseudo-Martyr.*" *English Historical Review* (November 2004): 1–14.

Unton, Henry. *Correspondance of Sir Henry Unton.* Ed. Joseph Stevenson. London, 1847.

Ure, Peter. *King Richard II* by William Shakespeare. The Arden Shakespeare. Ed. Peter Ure. London: Methuen, 1984 [1956]).

Walker, Roy. *The Time Is Free: A Study of Macbeth.* London: Andrew Dakers, 1949.

Walton, Isaac. *Lives of Doctor John Donne, Henry Wotton, Richard Hooker, and George Herbert.* London, 1670.

Watson, Robert N. *Shakespeare and the Hazards of Ambition.* Cambridge, Mass.: Harvard University Press, 1984.

Weston, Corinne Comstock, and Janelle Renfrow Greenberg. *Subjects and Sovereigns: The Grand Controversy over Legal Sovereignty in Stuart England.* Cambridge: Cambridge University Press, 1981.

Wilkinson, Bertie. *Constitutional History of Medieval England, 1216–1399.* 3 vols. Vol. 2, *Politics and the Constitution, 1307–1399.* Vol. 3, *The Development of the Constitution, 1216–1399.* London: Longmans, Green, 1952.

Williams, Penry. *The Later Tudors: England, 1547–1603.* Oxford: Clarendon, 1995.

Williams, Roger. *A Brief Discourse of War.* London: Thomas Orwin, 1590.

Wills, Gary. *Witches and Jesuits: Shakespeare's Macbeth.* Oxford: Oxford University Press, 1995.

Wilson, Luke. *Theaters of Intention: Drama and the Law in Early Modern England.* Stanford: Stanford University Press, 2000.

Wofford, Susanne L. "The Body Unseamed: Shakespeare's Late Tragedies." In *Shakespeare's Late Tragedies,* ed. Susanne L. Wofford. Upper Saddle River, N.J.: Prentice Hall, 1996.

——, ed. *Shakespeare's Late Tragedies.* Upper Saddle River, N.J.: Prentice Hall, 1996.

Woolf, D. R. *The Idea of History in Early Stuart England.* Toronto: University of Toronto Press, 1990.

Wooton, David. *Divine Right and Democracy: An Anthology of Political Writing in Stuart England.* London: Penguin Books, 1986.

Worden, Blair. "Ben Jonson among the Historians." In *Culture and Politics in Early Stuart England,* ed. Kevin Sharpe and Peter Lake, 67–89. Stanford: Stanford University Press, 1993.

——. "Politics in *Catiline:* Jonson and His Sources." In *Re-Presenting Ben Jon-*

son: Text, History, Performance, ed. Martin Butler, 152–73. London: Macmillan, 1999.

——. *Republicanism, Liberty and Commercial Society, 1649–1776,* ed. David Wootton, 45–196. Stanford: Stanford University Press, 1994.

——. "Which Play Was Performed at the Globe Theatre on 7 February 1601?" *London Review of Books* 25.13 (July 10, 2003): 22–24.

Zaret, David. *Origins of Democratic Culture: Printing, Petitions and the Public Sphere in Early Modern England.* Princeton, N.J.: Princeton University Press, 2000.

——. "Religion, Science, and Printing in the Public Spheres in Seventeenth-Century England." In *Habermas and the Public Sphere,* ed. Craig Calhoun, 212–35. Cambridge, Mass.: MIT Press, 1992.

Index

Persons or characters from works discussed in the text are identified in the index followed by the name of that work in parentheses. For example: Bolingbroke, Henry (*Richard II*)

223

Cethegus (*Catiline*), 146, 147, 153
Chapman, George, 36
chivalry, Essex and, 37, 175n39
Christian of Denmark (king), 84
Cicero: discretionary power and rule of
law, 144–45, 161–62; exile of, 145, 162;
exposure of Catiline, 139; and s.c.u.
(*senatus consultum ultimum*), 141, 145,
151; "the laws are silent in war," 144,
145, 161–63, 200n38
Cicero (*Catiline*): and Robert Cecil, 139;
conscience and, 150–51; election of,
150; on fabrication of crime, 149–50;
hypocrisy of, 153; as idealized figure,
137, 149; invoking discretionary
power, 140–41, 151–57, 158, 200n38;
and the s.c.u., 154–55
civil law: Bacon and, 49; common law
vs., 44–45; Hayward and, 26, 40–41,
43–45, 47–49. *See also* common law
Clegg, Cyndia Susan, 16, 24, 35, 48–49,
173n22, 180n6
Coddon, Karin S., 94–95
Coeffeteau, Nicolas, 110
Coke, Sir Edward: on absolute power in
case of war, 141–42; on authenticity of
repentance, 91; on the Gunpowder
Plot letter, 3; on Hayward's choice of
story, 27, 33–34
common good: contractual sovereignty
and, 58; Jonson's *Catiline* and, 151,
155, 158–59; shifting definitions of,
164; tyranny in defense of, 158–59
common law: civil law contrasted to, 45;
interdependence of monarchy with, 59,
65, 141, 143, 163, 183n37, 199n19; royal
prerogative as supplement to, 142;
treason by words and precedent in,
168n28. *See also* rule of law
*Conference about the Next Succession to the
Crown of England* (Persons), 31–32, 34,
53, 61
confession: Catholic, 88; scaffold
speeches and, 88, 90
conscience: casuists and, 126; imaginative fiction supporting conception of,
4–5; James and oath of allegiance,
118; Jonson's *Catiline* and, 150–51,
156–57, 158; as province of the divine,
127; sovereignty of, 112, 126–33, 134–
36, 157, 197n89
consensus, ideology of, 121–22
constitutionalism: deposition of Richard

II and, 55–58; and discretionary
power of sovereign, 141–45, 156,
199n19, 200n38; oath of allegiance
and, 110. *See also* rule of law
constructive treason, 6–7, 167n19,
167n20, 167n23
contractual sovereignty: Hobbes on,
166n10; Persons on, 31–33, 57–58; in
Richard II, 67–69, 73–74
Coursen, Henry, 68
Crassus (*Catiline*), 149–50, 151
Crew, Thomas, 143–44
Cromwell, Lord, 80
Cromwell, Thomas, 168n26
Cuffe, Henry, 19, 91–92
Cunningham, Karen, 3, 7
Curius (*Catiline*), 146–47, 152–53

Daly, James, 143
Daniel, Samuel, 184n1
David (biblical king), 112–13, 193n23
Davis, Jacques (Cardinal du Perron),
111, 119, 193n23
Dean, Leonard F., 34
decisionist sovereignty, 166n10
Declaration of 1308, 55, 67
Defense of Poesy (Sidney), 26, 85, 131
Defining a British State (Steffen), 13
De Jure Belli (Gentili), 36
De Legibus (Bracton), 144, 199n19
De Officiis (Cicero), 144
De Republica Anglorum (Smith), 141
Devereaux, Robert. *See* Essex, Earl of
Digby, Sir Everard, 90, 92, 188n42
Digest (Justinian), 41
Disce Mori (Sutton), 90
Discorsi (Machiavelli), 16
discretionary power and the rule of law:
Bacon on, 143–44, 145; Cicero on,
140–41, 144–45, 151–57, 158, 161–62,
200n38; constitutionalism and, 141–
45, 156, 199n19, 200n38; crises with no
foreseeable end and, 162–64; impositions and, 143; James and, 142–44;
Jonson's *Catiline* and, 137, 140–41,
144, 151–57, 158, 199n19, 200n38;
oath of allegiance and, 142, 199n26;
Richard II and, 55–56; rights and, 137;
tyranny and, 140, 155–57, 158–59;
wartime and, 141–42, 143–45, 161–64
dissent. *See* literary texts; moderation;
obedience; public sphere; resistance
and resistance theory

divine grace, Donne and, 131
divine right of kings: ascendance of, Elizabethan, 32; sacred kingship and, 114; Shakespeare's *Macbeth* and, 84, 96, 101–4, 186n24; Shakespeare's *Richard II* and, 60, 68, 69–71, 114, 181n25, 184n41. *See also* absolutism; divine right of kings, James and; sovereignty
divine right of kings, James and: discovery of Gunpowder Plot as evidence of, 108–9, 113; doctrine of nonresistance and, 99, 113–14; Donne and obedience to, 125–26, 134; Donne's sovereignty of conscience modifying, 112; European audience and, 109–10; oath of allegiance and, 112–14, 193n23; papacy as subject to, 119, 120; and recusancy legislation, 82; scripture and, 119
doctrine of nonresistance, 99, 113–14
Dolan, Frances, 2, 88–89, 165n3, 188n37
Donalbain (*Macbeth*), 100
Donne, John: on Barlow, 133–34; *Biathanatos*, 196n73; as converted Protestant, 122, 123, 127–28; *Essays in Divinity*, 133, 197n89; interest in the oath of allegiance controversy, 123–24; as moderate, 17, 135–36, 157–59; and oath of allegiance, 110; on suicide, 124, 196n73; "The Sun Rising," 130. See also *Pseudo-Martyr*
Drake, Sir William, 198n18
Drummond, William, 137–38
Dubrow, Heather, 182n30
Duncan, King (*Macbeth*): and Cawdor's treachery, 94, 95–96, 97, 98, 102; corpse of, as Medusa figure, 187n30; inadequacies of, as monarch, 95–97, 98, 103; Macbeth's killing of, 96, 97, 101; succession of, systems of inheritance for, 99
Dutton, Anthony, 184n9
dying words. *See* scaffold speeches

early modern public sphere. *See* public sphere
Eastward Ho (Jonson), 138
Edward II, 2, 33
Edward III, treason statute of (1352), 5–9, 8–9, 10, 167n17, 167n19, 167n20, 167n23
Edward III (*Macbeth*), 101–3
Edward VI, 8–9, 168n30
Elizabeth I: on civil lawyers, 44;

clemency toward Essex Rebellion participants, 79–80; confession (Catholic) abolished by, 88; and Essex, 34, 37, 51; on Hayward as author of *Henry IV*, 44; and Hayward as treasonous, 49, 50; Hayward's *Henry IV* as allegory and, 34, 51, 179n79; Parry plot and, 189n55; Tacitus, interest in, 38–39
Elton, G. R., 10, 168n28
Engle, Lars, 68
"Epistle Apologeticall" (Hayward), 40
Essays in Divinity (Donne), 133, 197n89
Essex, Earl of: burning of papers of, 50, 77–78; chivalry of, 37, 175n39; as dedicatee and associate of Hayward, 24–25, 28–29, 34–40; as dedicatee and associate of military and history works, generally, 34, 36, 37–39, 52, 77–78; first Thane of Cawdor compared to, 189n51; interest in comparative models of sovereignty, 39, 177n52; and James, loyalty to, 80–81; Jonson's *Catiline* and, 139; legacy of, James and, 80; as Protestant loyalist, 13–14, 169n41; public sympathy for, 79; scaffold speech of, 79; Shakespeare as praising, 36–37; and Spain, 80–81, 169n41; Tacitism, association with, 36, 38–39, 40, 50, 176n41, 177n52. *See also* Essex Rebellion
Essex Rebellion (1601), 13–14; as analogical history, 51; Catholics and, 14–15, 81; Elizabeth's clemency toward participants of, 79–80; performance associated with, 24, 29, 52, 54–55, 77, 171n2, 173n22; produced by the queen's suspicions, 51; scaffold speeches, 91–92; as textual event, 11, 12–13, 83
Exeter, Marquis of, 10
Exton (*Richard II*), 69
extralegal power. *See* discretionary power and the rule of law

Fawkes, Guy, 14, 83, 165n4
Figgis, J. Neville, 55–56, 192n10
The First Part of the Life and Raigne of King Henrie IIII. See *Henry IV* (Hayward)
Fisher, Bishop, 8, 192n6
Fisher, Robert, 8
Fish, Stanley, 72
Fitzherbert, Thomas, 110, 133
Forker, Charles R., 59–60

Hickford, Robert, 7
Highley, Christopher, 60–61
Hirst, Derek, 81, 83, 108–9, 144
Histories (Tacitus: Savile, trans.), 38–40, 177n46, 177n52
Hobbes, Thomas, 166n10
Holinshed, Raphael, 56, 57, 64, 97, 173n15, 191n68
An Homily on Obedience, 54
Howard, Katherine, 7

The Iliad (Chapman, trans.), 36
Imaginary Betrayals (Cunningham), 7
imagination, as term in treason law, 6–7
imaginative fiction. *See* literary texts
impositions, 143
impotency of kings, 64–65, 66–67, 183n34, 183n38
intention, 6–7, 167n23
interpretation and interpretive contraction: dissent and, 162; Essex Rebellion and, 25, 50–51, 77–78; Gunpowder Plot and, 83; public sphere and, 19–21

James I: Catiline, reference to, 139; discovery of Gunpowder Plot, 1, 97–98; and doctrine of nonresistance, 99, 113–14; Essex legacy and, 80; Essex's loyalty to, 80–81; impositions by, 143; Jonson's loyalty to, 138, 140; moderation of rule claimed by, 109–10, 111, 135, 157; and order theory of kingship, 192n13; pragmatic sovereignty of, 107, 110; *A Premonition to all most mighty Monarches*, 112, 118–19, 120, 124; and publication of *Pseudo-Martyr*, 123–24; and recusancy legislation, Elizabethan, 81–83, 185n16, 185n21; recusancy legislation, expansion of, 107–8, 120, 138, 142–43, 191n2; *A Remonstrance for the Right of Kings*, 114, 119; and Scotland, union with, 143; and Spain, 83, 109; succession of, 192n10; *Trew Law of Free Monarchies*, 99; *Triplici Nodo*, 112, 118, 119, 124, 125. *See also* divine right of kings, James and; oath of allegiance
Jardine, David, 185n12
Jonson, Ben: as converted Catholic, 137–39, 140; *Eastward Ho*, 138; and Gunpowder plotters, 138, 139; interrogations and imprisonment of, 138;

loyalty to state, 138, 140; moderation of, 17, 157–59; on poor reception of *Catiline*, 146; *Sejanus*, 138, 184n1, 198n18, 200n42. *See also Catiline*
Jonson's Romish Plot (de Luna), 139
Jordan, Constance, 11–12
Justinianic code, 45, 49, 55, 59, 65, 181n22

Kahn, Victoria, 4, 166n10, 167n11
Kastan, David Scott, 86–87, 99, 190n65
Kay, W. David, 139
Kent (*King Lear*), 75
Kernan, Alvin, 186n24
Keyes, Robert, 188n37
King Lear (Shakespeare), 54, 75
The King's Book, 98, 190n61
Kinney, Arthur, 24

Lake, Peter, 17, 18, 88, 89, 121
Lambarde, William, 141
Landes, Joan B., 20
Laqueur, Thomas, 88, 89
law: legal jargon, 64, 182n30; as protecting and encroaching upon rights, 162–64. *See also* civil law; common law; discretionary power and the rule of law; oath of allegiance; recusancy legislation; rule of law; treason law
Leech, Humphrey, 110
legal jargon, 64, 182n30
Leigh, William, 140
Lentulus (*Catiline*), 146–47, 153
Levack, Brian P., 41, 44, 45
Levy, F. J., 24
Liebler, Naomi Conn, 60
literary texts: and formation of the public sphere, 18–19, 20, 159; interplay of event and, 4–5, 11–12, 15; moderation of, 17–18; questions of representation and, 164
Lockyer, Roger, 110
Longinus (*Catiline*), 148
Lopez Plot, 14
loyalty. *See* allegiance; obedience
Luna, Barbara de, 139

Macbeth (*Macbeth*): and Cawdor as foreshadowing of, 94–95, 105–6; claim to throne by, 99; death of, 84, 105–6; disclosure of murders by, 101; Duncan's indebtedness to, 97; Malcolm's deception of, 101–2; as male Medusa, 86; as

126, 127, 133, 134, 135, 196n71; sympathy for Catholics in, 122–23, 127–28,
131; temporal vs. spiritual authority
and, 124–25, 128–29, 133, 134–36
public sphere: articulation of rights and,
159; Habermas's model of, 18–20, 111;
literary community helping to produce, 18–19, 20, 159; oath of allegiance and development of, 111–12;
treason charges as stimulating formation of, 19–21
Puttenham, George, 85, 187n29
Pye, Christopher, 71

Questier, Michael, 88, 89, 109, 111

Rackin, Phyllis, 56–57
Raspa, Anthony, 134
recusancy legislation: expanded by
James, 107–8, 120, 138, 142–43, 191n2;
retained by James, 81–83, 185n16,
185n21. *See also* Catholicism; oath of
allegiance
Rehnquist, William H., 161–62
A Remonstrance for the Right of Kings
(James I), 114, 119
republicanism masking absolutism,
155–56
resistance and resistance theory:
Donne's sovereignty of conscience
and, 135–36; Hayward's rhetoric
echoing, 29–34, 41, 43, 47; James condemning, 109, 192n10; James's doctrine of nonresistance forbidding, 99,
113–14; moderation and, 159; of Persons (*see* Persons, Robert); tradition of,
17. *See also* absolutism; moderation;
pamphlets; resistance, Shakespeare's
anatomy of
resistance, Shakespeare's anatomy of:
active obedience (courageous speech),
61–64, 65–66, 67, 72, 74, 75–76; active
resistance of Bolingbroke, 61, 66, 67–
69, 70, 71–72, 75; dangers and limitations of, 54–55; as inevitable, 72; justified resistance, 53; passive obedience
of York, 74–77; shift of focus in
Richard II and, 68–69
Rezneck, Samuel, 10
Richard II: constitutionalism and deposition of, 55–58; fears of treason justified by murder of, 2; Persons on
tyranny of, 31–32, 33, 57–58; power

consolidation through treason
charges, 169n38; sacred kingship and,
114; sovereign prerogative and, 55–
56. *See also Henry IV* (Hayward);
Richard II (Shakespeare)
Richard II (Hayward, *Henry IV*), 34, 46–
48
Richard II (Shakespeare), 52–77; comedic
interlude in, 72–74; contractual sovereignty and, 67–69, 73–74; date of, 53,
180n4; deposition scene of, 56, 180n6;
duality of tyranny/resistance in, 53,
68–69; and Essex Rebellion perfor-
mance/association, 52, 54–55, 77,
171n2; Hayward's *Henry IV* and, 53,
173n22; interpretive contraction and,
77–78; law-centered sovereignty in,
53, 56, 59, 65, 75, 82, 183n–37; legal
jargon and, 64, 182n30; Persons in relation to, 52–53, 54, 58, 59, 61, 64; state
production of treason in, 53, 64–65,
71, 182n33. *See also* resistance, Shakespeare's anatomy of; *individual characters*
Richard II (*Richard II*): audience sympathy for, 60, 76; definition of treason
and, 58–59; and divine right kingship,
60, 68, 69–71, 114, 181n25, 184n41; impotence of, 65, 66–67, 183n34, 183n38;
as martyr, 59–60; production of treason by, 53, 64–65, 71, 182n33; as traitor, 53, 70–71; tyranny of, 53, 59–61,
65, 75, 181n19
Richardson, Lisa, 39–40
Riggs, David, 138, 139
rights of subjects: conception of, supported by imaginative fiction, 4–5; to
conscience, 122, 135–36, 159; expansion of state at expense of, 22, 162–64;
to law, 122, 137, 159. *See also* public
sphere; sovereignty
Robinson, Francis, 89
Roman law, 45
Rome, ancient, Catiline treason. See
Catiline (Jonson); Cicero
Ross (*Richard II*), 62, 64, 67–68
Rosse (*Macbeth*), 93, 97
royalists: Hayward as, 24, 26, 43–48,
173n12; as term, 173n12. *See also* allegiance; sovereignty
The Royal Play of Macbeth (Paul), 84
royal prerogative. *See* discretionary
power and the rule of law

Ruckwood, Ambrose, 90, 91
rule of law: charges of treason provoking defense of, 12; deposition of Richard II and, 53, 55–58, 59, 65, 75, 183n37; James I and, 82, 192n10; precedent for deposition, 55; as protecting and encroaching upon rights, 162–64; right to, 122, 137. *See also* civil law; common law; constitutionalism; discretionary power and the rule of law; oath of allegiance; recusancy legislation; treason law
Rutland, Earl of, 80

sacred kingship, 32, 114. *See also* divine right of kings
Salisbury, Earl of. *See* Cecil, Robert
Sallust, 139, 148–49, 151, 154, 157
Salve for a Sicke Man (Perkins), 90
Sanders, Julie, 140
Sanders, Wilbur, 86–87
Sandies, Lord, 80
Sanga (*Catiline*), 153
Savile, Sir Henry, 12, 38–39, 40, 176n42, 177n46, 177n52
scaffold speeches: audience suspicion of authenticity of, 86, 90–91, 92, 93, 95; as confessional, 88, 90; economic pressure in, 89–90; of Essex, 79; fabrication of, 91–93, 97; of first Thane of Cawdor (*Macbeth*), 84–86, 87, 94–95, 102, 103, 105; formula for, 85–86, 88–93, 105; formula for, breaking of, 88–89, 188n37, 188n42; of Father Henry Garnet, 87–88; Macbeth's dying words contrasted to formulaic, 105–6; pamphleteers and, 91–93, 97; spiritual pressure in, 90, 188n42
Schellhase, Kenneth C., 176n41
Schmitt, Carl, 166n10, 167n11
Scott, William O., 64
Sejanus (Jonson), 138, 184n1, 198n18, 200n42
Sempronia (*Catiline*), 149
Shakespeare, William: Essex praised by, 36–37; *Hamlet*, 85; Holinshed and, 97, 191n68; *King Lear*, 54, 75; moderation of characters in, 17; multi-textual approach of, 53–54. See also *Macbeth*; resistance, Shakespeare's anatomy of; *Richard II*
Sharpe, J. A., 88, 186n28
Sharpe, Kevin, 198n18

Shewring, Margaret, 52
Shuger, Debora, 129
Sicke Manne's Salve (Beacon), 90
Sidney, Sir Philip, 26, 85, 103–4, 131
Simpson, Evelyn, 123
Sinfield, Alan, 87
Six Livres de la Republique (Bodin), 16, 42–43
Skinner, Quentin, 134, 156
Smith, Lacey Baldwin, 10, 88, 186n28
Smith, Nigel, 18
Smith, Thomas, 16, 32, 141, 143
Somerset, Lord Protector, 8, 168n30
Sommerville, J. P., 16, 109, 111, 119, 173n12
sovereignty: absolutism (*see* absolutism); activism of subjects on topics of, 16–17; allegiance to state vs. person of the king, 55, 57; civil lawyers and inquiries into nature of, 40–41, 43–45; of conscience, 112, 126–33, 134–36, 157, 197n89; contractual nature of (*see* contractual sovereignty); decisionist, 166n10; divine right (*see* divine right of kings); impotent, 64–65, 66–67, 183n34, 183n38; literary texts and alternate theories of, 16–18; mixed, 32; pragmatic (*see* pragmatic sovereignty); sacred kingship, 32, 114; Shakespeare's *Macbeth* and models of, 12, 84, 86–87, 96, 99, 101–4, 137, 186n24; treason as crisis of, 5, 12, 13. *See also* discretionary power and the rule of law; rights of subjects; succession
Spain: Essex and, 80–81, 169n41; Gunpowder Plot and relations with, 15, 80–81, 83, 184nn9–10, 185n21; James I and, 83, 109
speech regulation. *See* treason by words
Speed, John, 184n10
Stallybrass, Peter, 87
Star Chamber, 82
state: expansion of, at expense of subjects' rights, 22, 162–64; invention of evidence by, 153, 155; as producing treason, 4, 25, 51, 53, 64–65, 71, 182n33. *See also* discretionary power and the rule of law; interpretation and interpretive contraction; rule of law; sovereignty
Steffen, Lisa, 13, 167n13
Stowe, John, 57